Knowledge

&

I0450224

Belief

Illustrated:

Their Natures & Relationship in Ancient Greek Thought.

G. G. Bolich, Ph.D.

EVS PRESS

EVS Press
Spokane, Washington (printed in Raleigh, North Carolina)
©**2019 G. G. Bolich**

Cover by Susan Bachmeier (bachscrafts@yahoo.com)

For

Justin,

who stretches toward knowledge.

Publisher Cataloging-in-Publication Data

Knowledge and belief illustrated: Their natures & relationship in ancient Greek thought
Bolich, G. G. (1953-)
First paperback edition.
ISBN 13: 978-0-359-83924-7
1. Knowledge, Theory of 2. Belief and doubt
I. Title
BD143.B65 2019
121.B689—dc23

Printed in the United States of America

1st edition

Contents

Introduction

Aristotle writes, "All people by nature stretch themselves toward knowledge."[1] That conviction guides this book. This volume is intended for those who in their stretching toward knowledge do not mind taking the time to exercise their minds perhaps a bit more strenuously than they are generally accustomed to do. It takes time, patience, and dedicated effort to pursue to completion the task ahead. In this introduction I shall try to indicate what can be expected in the pages of this volume—the program of exercise, as it were.

First to be noted is that this volume is an abridged edition of an earlier work whose title varies only in the addition of the word "Illustrated." That addition is to highlight that this work focuses on a visual aspect already present in the original—illustrations meant to simplify and visually present important ideas. In this smaller edition all of the illustrations from the original appear, but the accompanying text has been significantly reduced.

The original work aims to reach as broad an audience as possible, including both interested novices and expert scholars. This work ignores the latter and hopes to help the former. Here scholarly details such as most of the references to secondary literature and most reproductions of the original text are left aside (with what does occur placed in the footnotes). Translated portions from the ancient authors and summary explanations are fitted around the illustrations. In addition to a reduction in length, some rewriting has been done. The intended goal is a reasonably short, simple, and satisfactory introduction to the subject.

Overview & Structure of the Book

Step one, here in the introduction, is to introduce our topic, indicate the challenges it poses and our manner of tackling them, and generally trying to provide a first orientation to our task. So let us begin with a basic question: *What is knowledge?* For the moment let us simply posit that knowledge is the achievement of true and sufficient information, with understanding—in other words, it is possessing the information we need fully enough and correctly enough to provide reasonable certainty in understanding something or making and acting on some decision. Clearly that is highly desirable.

---

[1] Aristotle, *Metaphysics*, 980a21. The word translated "knowledge" is εἰδέναι (*eidenai*, fr. οἶδα (*oida*). If nothing else, people seek to know themselves. As Marcus Aurelius, *Meditations*, II.8 remarks, "Truthfully, a person is not easily tormented by not seeing what goes on in another person's *psyche*, but anyone who does not follow the motions of his own *psyche* will inevitably be miserable."

What do we do, though, when certainty eludes us? What happens when doubt creeps in? Or worse, comes flooding in, threatening to cripple us with paralyzing anxiety? Doubt is answered in such cases by belief, which exists to function like knowledge where the latter is absent or uncertain.

Both knowledge and belief are important. Those who think about such things easily see this. Nevertheless, *why* they matter is not often considered, but merely assumed. The relation between them—where one leaves off and the other begins, or whether they are ever one and the same—is the crucial interest of this book, which in many respects serves as a basic introduction to *epistemology* (the study of how we know) by looking back to the ancient Greeks.

We must carefully consider what we mean by each term; we must describe both knowledge and belief. This task is addressed very obviously in chapters 1 and 2. But that hardly ends the matter. Chapters 3-7, discussing the views of Protagoras, Socrates, Plato, Isocrates, and Aristotle all wrestle with the fundamental question of, "*What* is knowledge?" And in so doing, each wrestles also with the nature of belief and how it relates to knowledge. A shift occurs in chapters 8-10, as our historical survey turns to Stoicism, Epicureanism, and Skepticism. The question of what knowledge is recedes in importance as different philosophic schools debate, "Is knowledge *possible*?" Thereafter, we close our study in the final chapters by comparing and contrasting these thinkers in relation to knowledge and belief, and by considering what these ancient Greeks may have to say to us today in figuring out our own epistemology. (After reading the first two chapters, one may either proceed in a straightforward manner through the whole book or skip ahead to the final chapters (11-15), which relate to the first two and tie the book together, and read the middle chapters last.)

Reading Philosophy

My intended audience is the person who sees in him- or herself one reaching toward knowledge and willing to work to achieve progress in that process. Toward that end philosophers can be of great value. For more than two millennia many of the greatest minds in human history have sought to explain the natures of both knowledge and of belief—and the relation between them. I am interested in readers who want to join their conversation. Still, philosophical thinking offers some challenges. This is not a particularly 'easy read,' though it is one that can be accomplished by those with patience.

In order to help ease the difficulties ensuing from the imposing task in front of us I have attempted to provide a number of aids. First, I have aimed at staying focused on the matters relevant to our task: the nature of knowledge and of belief, and the relation between them. I have tried to explain the use of technical terms as simply as possible. I have intentionally repeated the pairings of technical words with their English equivalents. I have supplied a good number of illustrations both to show basic ideas in relation to one another and also show how the thinking of various figures develops. More detailed information is kept in the footnotes.

Special Note: Translating & Making Use of Sources

Granted, the thinking of philosophers to most of us seems dense under the best of conditions, and a technical use of terms is to some degree unavoidable because philosophers tend to insist on careful and exact definitions. So, in what follows while trying to cut through the thickets and make matters plain, I still offer attention to definitions and note special terms. I also rely on that old trick of teachers and preachers alike—repetition. It is unrealistic to expect to always get terms or ideas on the first bounce, so some practice bouncing a matter a few times in slightly different presentations is meant to help catch it well.

As an aspect of this repetition—and one way to build learning—I use a gradual introduction of key terms and then their repetition to show their continued importance and any changes. Because these terms are English renderings of Greek words, I have favored building a Greek vocabulary by repeated use of transliterated terms. To assist in remembering such key words a chart at the end of this volume presents the more important ones. In the same way, I gradually increase exposure to more difficult matters building on what has preceded.

The translations are my own and aimed at showing how our thinkers interact with one another. Ancient Greek varies from modern English in a number of important respects. We are today accustomed to relying on what our eyes see. The peoples of the ancient world were far more attuned to *hearing* their authors' books. Ancient authors constructed their works with the ear in mind as well as the eye. Inflection—changes in how a word is formed—makes possible some things in writing that simply cannot be replicated well in English. An effort, for example, to translate Greek into English word-for-word, in strict order of appearance, results in ridiculous and often unrecognizable English that cannot convey the Greek sensibility. To translate ancient Greek into modern English calls for a guiding principle: convey the basic sense dynamically, that is, as it might plausibly read had it been written originally in English. Of course, this is a fiction and it means that all translation is also an act of interpretation.

That last point is what often frustrates those who are not readers of the original language. One often hears such a complaint, for example, among those who read the Bible but are unable to read the ancient Hebrew or Greek. How can any translator be trusted? I suggest that some degree of caution is warranted but that paranoid doubt may be easily avoided by some common sense actions. First and best is the recommendation to learn the original languages! I grant this course, for any number of reasons, is impractical for most people. So, instead, make use of what tools one may have to better understand the nature of the language and key terms for the subject at hand. Let me recommend—strongly—the value of consulting more than one translation when reading ancient authors. Although I read ancient languages like the Greek and Latin ones translated herein, I make it a habit to compare my renderings with those of other translators. By combining a familiarity with an author's thinking, and a reasonable sense of what key words mean and how they are used, alongside the way such things are conveyed by several translators, all facilitated by expert commentary and serious scholarly study, any person can feel confident in achieving a solid enough grasp for a well-acquired understanding.

One need not be able to read ancient Greek, or Latin, to follow things here because I have tried to supply the essentials in the main body of text. There, for example, one will find key terms transliterated (i.e., written in English letters to reproduce the sound of them) immediately behind the English word used to translate them. In quotations I have retained the inflected form of the original word. This will help the novice begin to learn to recognize key terms in the various inflected forms in which they might occur. I have utilized a gradual process of immersion in the language of the ancients so that less intrusion of original words occurs at the start and then, bit-by-bit, more and more exposure. All this is intended to assist anyone who wants to master as fully as possible—short of learning the language itself!—the things useful to getting at the ideas. The original language texts are indicated in the bibliography. I also offer occasional notes in the main body of text explaining *why* I have translated something a particular way. But the footnotes bear the burden of conveying details, such as what key words are being translated. This, again, occurs more early on, and less later on when I presume a degree of familiarity has been achieved.

To assist those with no prior knowledge of Greek I have provided both the original Greek form of key words, what they are derived from, their transliteration (i.e., as mentioned above, how it looks in English when the Greek is sounded out), and any special notes to help better understand them. Though it is scholarly convention to use abbreviations for classical sources, I have instead each time supplied the full title. Those unacquainted with the literature are thus spared any frustration of having to pause to look up what an abbreviation means. The person who wants to learn more may do so, but one who chooses not to do so can still adequately follow the thread of what is being presented.

As mentioned earlier, I also rely on a generous use of visual aids. These are best used in conjunction with the written text, but even apart from that they should serve as quick and convenient glimpses of basic but important matters. Always—always!—everything presented here, from the choices of authors and texts, to translations, and all my summaries and comments, should be seen as intended to facilitate an ongoing stretching toward knowledge that is not content to end here or to accept my words as final on any subject.

I mention all of this up front because I do not want anyone feeling intimidated simply because this book talks about and uses some foreign terms. Most of us who speak English as our primary tongue already know a substantial portion of our language's vocabulary has roots in older languages like Greek and Latin. To get at our English words "knowledge" and "belief" requires examining the concepts each embraces and the various older words from other languages that have contributed to our modern senses for each word. No one has to master Greek to acquire a better understanding of knowledge and belief, but one does have to acquire a bit of exposure to Greek to *better* understand each.

1

The Puzzle of Knowledge

"All people by nature stretch themselves toward knowledge." So said Aristotle, and I concur. *All* of us possess an inherent drive to *know*. I use the word 'drive' advisedly; it is more than desire. We are impelled to stretch toward knowledge, and not merely because of its demonstrably desirable products. I mean that such stretching is biologically driven. Aristotle is quite right in declaring this stretching is "by nature." To be human is to seek to know.

Why? The answer, at least on one level, is easy enough to deduce: by knowledge we keep ourselves from endless, needless, wasteful repetition experimentally searching for what we need in any given situation. Knowledge possesses a certain durability and constancy, retained in memory, deepened by experience and learning, ready for new applications. In short, it is practical and, indeed, necessary for the achievement of complex tasks and for advancement in various arts, skills, and the social constructions of politics and ethics.

But is that all there is to its value—its utility? I think not. We stretch toward knowledge often because of our curiosity. We like understanding, and not merely how a thing works, but why it is. A substantial part of stretching toward knowledge is the human desire to apprehend reality *as it is*, rather than merely *as it appears to be*. Now to be sure we can conclude that reality is exactly as it presents itself to us in our experience. Yet enough experiences accumulate to challenge such an easy presumption. At some point, in a moment of reflection, we experience doubt. Our minds wonder if reality might be different than our experience, that appearances might distort some real but invisible essence. We quest, then, to peek behind the curtain to see, if we can, what is there.

Defining "Knowledge"

We cannot put a puzzle together without gathering the pieces and having some idea of what the end picture might look like. Let us specify the following bits as key puzzle pieces, with some representing the interior heart of the puzzle and others the borders that hem in and qualify the center. First the heart pieces:

➢ Information
➢ Reality
➢ Judgment

Now the border pieces, characterized as the elements that delimit and qualify the heart pieces:

- ➢ Certainty
- ➢ Clarity
- ➢ Recognition
- ➢ Sufficiency

With the pieces on the board we are ready to consider a definition, but let us be careful how we define knowledge. After all, we can propose definitions that would make it impossible for belief to ever be knowledge, or contrarily, we might define one or both in such a manner as to make it inevitable that sometimes they should be the same.

My aim is to start with the senses for each word found in English dictionaries. Some dictionaries go a step further and offer etymological information, which helps uncover a word's history and roots, and that also is helpful. But because words inevitably live in usage and not in dictionary definitions, we shall most of all depend on how these words have been used as great minds have wrestled with whether belief and knowledge can ever be the same. Don't get me wrong. I am not saying that we shall start with the dictionary but then abandon it for the cleverness of theorists. Rather, I am reminding us that dictionary definitions follow from how people actually use words. The words belief and knowledge were not first written in a dictionary and then used by people, but defined in dictionaries based on how people were using them.

Unfortunately, if one takes the time to review different dictionaries, we find that this common noun shows considerable vigor, sporting a number of senses that are described by using a surprising range of words. This discovery underscores the notion that knowledge has what people refer to as "shades of meaning" depending on specific contexts. Without belaboring the matter, let us look to the history of the English word. It has what can be termed fairly an uncertain origin and its etymological history is partly a matter of speculation. It seems to be a noun that depends on the verb form ("to know"), because the basic or root sense is "after knowing." *We say we know something when we judge we recognize that we have clear and sufficient information so that a full and firm grasp of it is attained, i.e., we achieve enough certainty about the object of the information to understand it.* This suggests knowledge is a kind of familiarity, recognition, or acknowledgment that accompanies and follows hard on the heels of this process of "knowing."

We often use the word knowledge to refer to a sum of information or some particular information that is certain and true, or as an understanding whether general or specific. In fact, this indicates a split in emphasis found among epistemologists across history as they talk about knowledge. There are those who place so much emphasis on the idea of *certainty* that knowledge is virtually made synonymous with it. There are others who instead focus on *understanding* so that knowledge appears to be about that instead. We will be wise, then, to keep in mind this divergence (which our definition above has carefully skirted).

Since we will be engaging with ancient Greek philosophers—many of whom engaged strenuously in defining terms—we might hope for some help from that quarter. Perhaps Greek offers a more straightforward course by a single term clearly defined, understood, and used. It takes only a moment to disabuse ourselves of this notion. Let us go back to Aristotle's short assertion that all human beings stretch toward knowledge.

Consider what Classics scholar Rosemary Wright says about its key word:

> The word Aristotle uses here for knowing is *eidenai*, which has a root connection with the verb for 'seeing': a knowing *that*, grasped by the rational mind. This contrasts with *epistēmē*, a knowing *how*, connected with scientific understanding, and also *gnōmē* or *gnōsis*, recognition from acquaintance, *noēsis*, intellectual activity, and *phronēsis*, practical wisdom. These terms often overlap, and, in their multiplicity, we find that the Greeks continually raised questions about knowledge and the different kinds of knowing.[2]

There are many things I'd like to say about her comments, but let me just point out one or two. Most important to us here is that she identifies several different Greek words related to this matter of knowing and knowledge. If we were to liken a concept to a vehicle within which are words acting like parts, each of these different parts has its own history and character contributing to the overall nature of the vehicle and its functioning. Although we will be focused more on the word *epistēmē*, we will encounter all of these other words—and more. There is in defining knowledge both an effort to capture a holistic sense and an effort to ascertain individual aspects. Thus, there is not infrequently an effort like that in our quote to distinguish different kinds of knowledge (e.g., knowing *that* from knowing *how*), ranging the concept of knowledge along a continuum from lower to higher: mundane knowledge to sublime knowledge.

But there is another comment I think important to make. Wright's remarks on these different words should not be treated like a dictionary entry. The exact meaning of words is dependent on context and while we can describe any given word in some general sense—as in saying that it carries a basic idea we might capture in a few words—the truth is that words, like people, are complex things. When Wright, for instance, speaks of *epistēmē* as 'a knowing *how*,' it must be remembered she immediately adds, 'connected with scientific understanding.' I would place the emphasis more on the latter part than the former, for in a figure like Aristotle *epistēmē* is a body of knowledge derived from an epistemological process. It isn't as much in contrast with *eidenai* as one might imagine, because the stretching Aristotle has in mind wants most of all to achieve *epistēmē* even if we for the most part must settle with an *eidenai* that keeps stretching. In other words, to use her English phrasing, our knowing *that* ultimately aims at achieving the deeper understanding of knowing *how*. I know *that* my car dependably

---

[2] Wright, *Introducing Greek Philosophy*, 132.

gets me to the store, but how much better off I am when I also know *how* it does so, because if it breaks down I'm in a position to make a more effective response. This distinction helps remind us why knowledge matters.

Now let us return to our elements, which can be pictured in relationship to one another like this portrait of a puzzle:

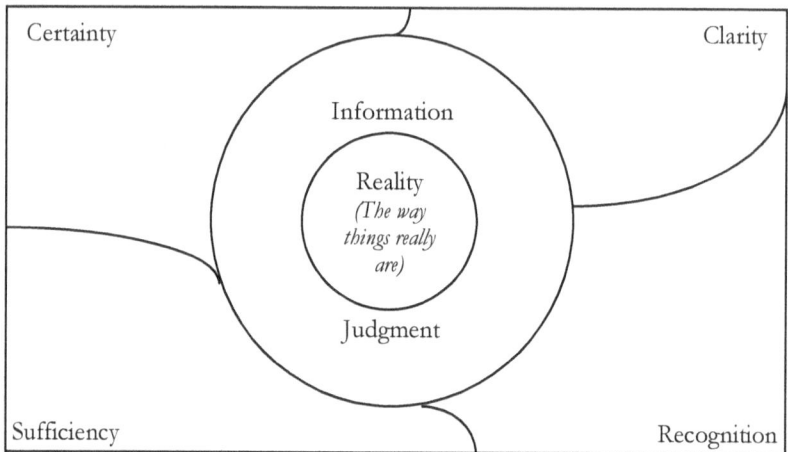

The object of the information is desired to be known *as it is* and not just *as it appears* (unless the two are the same). That is pictured above as "reality." It is the heart of the body of information—what the information is about. Judgment occurs with respect to information, assenting to it as true or dissenting from it as false. Such judgment is related to ascertaining and affirming what is real.

The four elements of certainty, clarity, recognition and sufficiency delimit, color, and qualify the character of the information we call knowledge. In short, they are generally conceived of as required pieces, however variously understood. The information must be clear enough to be grasped, arouse a sense of recognition or familiarity, be of an adequate completeness, and demonstrate certainty, whether relative or absolute. In the last part of our volume we shall return to all these pieces—heart pieces and border pieces—and examine how our Greek thinkers have addressed them.

One important last note is needed. If we all stretch toward knowledge, what role, if any, does belief play? I imagine that most of us when we consider "belief" think that it is much the same as knowledge. It is information about reality, related to truth, and possessing qualities like clarity, recognition, and sufficiency. The element of certainty appears to be the one where debate most surfaces. For if we grant the same certainty to belief, and keep everything else the same, then all belief is knowledge. But in ordinary practice and sophisticated theology alike, belief is *confident* but not certain (in the epistemic sense; it can be psychologically). However, lest we get ahead of ourselves, let us now turn to belief and see if we can do with it what we have attempted to do here for knowledge.

2

The Problem of Belief

As with knowledge, for belief we again find a range of senses and a history of conceptual development through usage—a history that is deeply rooted in Greek philosophy.[3] In brief, the noun "belief," related to the verb "believe," rests originally in the approval of a person, thing, or idea as valuable, important, meaningful, and trustworthy. It seems originally to have been especially used in a personal, relational sense. Thus to "believe" a person was to esteem them as dear—'beloved'—and trustworthy so that actual trust was vouchsafed to them. We can make, if we wish, a very good argument that genuine belief is always actionable belief; we believe when we act, and the act is one of trust. Believing is the process of which belief is the product. But that does not make belief something either passive or fixed. Belief and believing are constantly interacting so that the process is always capable of modifying an existing belief, discarding it, or initiating a new one. All talk of belief at least implicitly includes believing.

Perhaps we can identify the core of belief, as having these elements:

➢ Trust
➢ Assertion
➢ Judgment

And around this center are other defining qualities that accompany and color it:

➢ Confidence
➢ Persuasion
➢ Reliance
➢ Malleability

A "belief" is an actionable approval (assertion)—an actual placing of trust in a person, thing, or idea because it is judged trustworthy, meaningful, and important (even if only relatively so). A belief is a fundamental value judgment, one reflecting a personal investment based on what we regard with high esteem. Belief generates confidence based not on a certainty of information so much as a commitment of

---

[3] For anyone interested in a much more thorough examination of the word, its history and meaning, I refer you to my volume *Honest Belief, Credible Faith*. That volume also offers a more extensive review of the word "knowledge."

trust founded on the judgment that what is being trusted is trustworthy. Love and hope, not certainty of information or statement, generate belief.

Can these seven characteristics used to define belief be matched to knowledge? They cannot all be identical or we would simply be saying that knowledge is belief and erasing all distinction between them. At the same time, if there is no resemblance whatsoever, nor any relevance for the aspects of knowledge to belief, then the suggestion that belief might in some cases be knowledge is *prima facie* absurd. The truth must be somewhere in-between. For now, though, let us picture how these elements relate to one another.

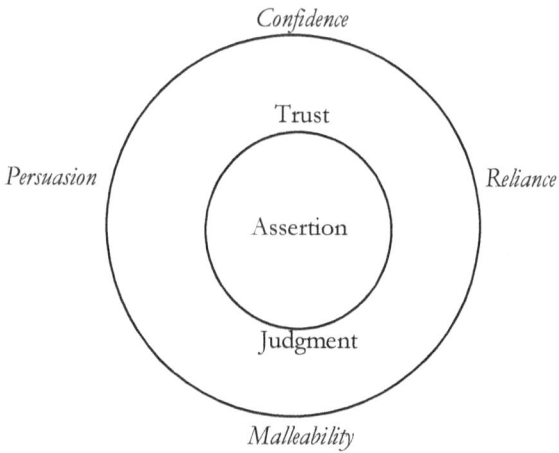

Defining "Belief"

As with knowledge, a number of Greek words have helped influence our developing idea of belief. Two stand out. The one we will be most concerned with is δόξα (*doxa*). Though a familiar word to philosophers, because our English word "belief" has become especially associated with religious ideas and joined to the concept of "faith" it is less familiar to most people than the other chief Greek term, πίστις (*pistis*), a key word in the Christian New Testament. Between them these two words and the ideas associated with them have greatly shaped our views on belief. Here it is proposed that these two words together inform a sense of belief's core elements.

To the extent that our English words reflect Greek concepts as developed in philosophical discourse we can say that our English "belief" and "believing" both entail a core sense of "taking up a position," which of course entails forming and asserting some judgment. This is quite like the English root of approval because something or someone is judged trustworthy, meaningful, and important. The coloration of the English words' roots adds the element of trust and/or trustworthiness, which sometimes emerges as especially prominent, but at other times recedes into the background. That is why, for example, when the element of trust is highlighted the word "faith" tends to replace the word "belief," because our sense of faith has come to emphasize that quality. On the other hand, when the aspect of trust is deemphasized, and especially when the belief itself is seen as weak, the English word "opinion" is often preferred. Beliefs can be stated propositionally and often are set forward as assertions of knowledge. Whether this practice is warranted matters to us.

Also like knowledge, the word belief has different senses and has through actual usage evolved so that it today can be used in a statement like, "My belief is it will rain today," just as it can be used in a statement such as "My belief is that God loves me." Both expressions reflect assertions of judgment and each leads to some act of trust (e.g., if I believe it is going to rain I am more likely to grab an umbrella). These two examples lead to a basic consideration for us. Just as was said about knowledge, that we are interested principally in propositional assertions, so also with belief. In this book we will focus on *statements*, though such statements aim to say something true about human experience and/or reality. Belief statements express a level of trust and a degree of confidence. Both of those elements are central instead of a certainty of information or a certainty of statement. If knowledge can be expressed in propositional assertions based on certainty of information and truthfulness, belief can be expressed in propositional assertions based on trust and confidence. These offer two paths to propositional assertions, which are statements (propositions) making claims (assertions). Obviously, then, assertion is a keystone characteristic. Our primary interest is in assertion in the form of statements or propositions. However, as I have discussed elsewhere,[4] assertion can be *assent* or it can be *action*. An assertion can be intellectual, emotional, volitional, or behavioral in manifestation. What unites all of these forms is the essence: a vested declaration, constructive in nature, with trust as its object.

Trust, including trustworthiness, is the object of belief, its *raison d' être*. This core element has been decisively influenced by the Greek word *pistis*. This interesting word takes a secondary place in discussions about knowledge, but pride of place in discussions about belief, especially in the context of religious faith. As we saw above, the original sense of our English word was a *subjective approval* of a person, thing, or idea, and in a particular way—as valuable, important, meaningful, and trustworthy. Belief, in other words, is at its core personal, even when shared with others. Trust always entails relationship. As such, trust also always involves a decision—to trust or to be worthy of trust—and that then leads us to the third core element.

If the element of trust owes most to the influence of *pistis*, then that of judgment is most indebted to the influence of *doxa*. Judgment itself is the taking up of a position in a decisive way, as 'for' or 'against'—a view with a point of view that takes a stance. Implicit in the idea of assertion is the notion of judging (or forming a judgment), and so "belief" can and should be thought of as fundamentally a judgment, and "believing" the process of judging, or forming a

---

4 Bolich, *Honest Belief, Credible Faith*, 750-52.

11

judgment (a belief as a position adopted about someone or something with respect to trustworthiness). It is, broadly, the taking up of a position, but not neutrally. Belief always 'takes a side' as it were.

The defining qualities of belief arrayed around this core are confidence, persuasion, reliance, and malleability. They are traditionally viewed as essential, and yet not of the very essence of belief but, instead, associated features. Perhaps the chief of these is confidence, which must both be present enough to vouchsafe trust and which is generally bolstered by an assertive act. Second, belief typically follows from persuasion and then engages in it toward self and others. This particular element is influenced both by *doxa* and by *pistis*. The idea in *doxa* of taking up a position almost invariably means being persuaded and then seeking to persuade others. The word *pistis* is closely related to a pair of Greek words—a noun and a verb—meaning "persuasion" and "to persuade." Thus from both sides the sense of persuasion as an aspect of belief has been long and strongly developed. Reliance expresses another key relational aspect; belief is a kind of *dependence* on another person or thing—including ideas. Closely related to trust, it varies mostly in that reliance expresses a sense of need. Reliance can easily be seen as a consequence of persuasion, but it also can be a motivation to be persuaded or to persuade others. Finally, malleability reflects the fact that belief is adaptive and variable. Unlike knowledge, which *must* be true, belief can be either true or false—and perhaps even change from one to the other when circumstances alter—even though belief always proclaims itself true.

In this volume a number of different and influential positions put forward by some of the greatest minds of Western civilization about the nature of knowledge, and of belief, and of the relation between them will be examined. Perhaps one or another of these will seem to offer the best answer. Or perhaps one or another will spark some new idea and offer an even better answer. In each of these answers there is a keen interest in understanding what knowledge and belief are and then on the basis of such an understanding expressing what relation might exist between them. That means each answer proposes to tell us what belief and knowledge are.

Shall we proceed with examining some of history's most influential ideas?

.

3

Protagoras' Provocation

In the 5ᵗʰ century before the Common Era, in Greece, lived a man named Protagoras of Abdera (c. 481-c. 411 B.C.E.). He made a living as a sort of travelling intellectual, who was eagerly sought after as a teacher of how to speak persuasively, live well, and develop good character. Protagoras was a professional Sophist—"pursuer of wisdom"—and in his time the label enjoyed more approval than it has come to have in our own. We today think of these early Sophists as philosophers of the period just before thinkers like Plato and Aristotle would create the great philosophies at the foundation of Western civilization.

Protagoras was not the first philosopher, nor is he the most famous one, even of the early Greeks. His position seems to have been formed in response to Parmenides of Elea, who contemplated the nature of reality—an activity today known as metaphysics. Protagoras' response, though, was not to develop a rival metaphysics but rather to articulate an epistemological response—a view of knowing that challenged Parmenides' thinking. Later philosophers like Plato and Aristotle found Protagoras' teaching so vexing they bent their considerable intellectual powers to contesting it. Yet neither of them, nor anyone else, has so compellingly refuted Protagoras as to extinguish the influence of his position.

Relativism

A particular perspective and an especially provocative idea is attached to Protagoras. Today we label his perspective as *relativism*, most famously expressed in declaring that "Man is the measure of all things."[5] Relativism, at least in its more extreme form, denies any absolute, universal truth (save for the absolute universal truth of relativism itself). This means that *knowledge and truth are always context dependent*; what is true and known varies from situation to situation and from person to person. It operates like this illustrative example shows:

(A late Spring day, with cloudy skies.) 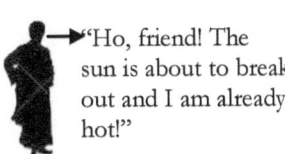 "Ho, friend! The sun is about to break out and I am already hot!"   "No, friend, it is about to rain, and I am chilled to the bone!"

---

[5] The saying is preserved in Plato's *Theatetus* (152a), as voiced by Socrates, who represents it as what Protagoras actually said.

13

Like many others, Protagoras had been bothered by a contention of Parmenides of Elea (early 5th century B.C.E.). Parmenides claims that in our normal conversation, based on how things appear to us, we speak about changes we perceive. Hot things become cool, small things become large, hard things become soft, and so forth. But to Parmenides this is a casual and altogether slippery way of thinking because it implies that a "thing" can both *be* and *not be*—for example, "be hot" and "not be hot" (cool). This he reckons is the same as claiming it both *is* and *is not*—or simultaneously existing and real, yet not existing and unreal! Parmenides ties his thinking to the proposition of a single 'Being' as a unified, persistent and unchanging reality, and thus thoroughly discounts the role of the human senses, which continually register changes.

At the opposite end of the spectrum from Parmenides is Heraclitus of Ephesus (early 5th century B.C.E.), famous for making change the very center of reality—the one constant of the universe. Where for Parmenides a thing *is* and it is nonsensical to say it *is not*—(a thing and its opposite cannot both be true)—for Heraclitus there is a unity of opposites within the universal flux of constantly changing things. These two perspectives make for a lively debate:

 "A thing either *is* or it *is not*. It cannot be both, nor can it be one thing and then another!"

"You cannot step into the same river twice. A thing *is not* and then *is* and then *is not* again!"[6]

Parmenides   Heraclitus

Protagoras staked out his own position at the same end of the metaphysical spectrum as Heraclitus, but he is not principally a metaphysician.

Protagoras' Reasoning

Protagoras' relativism goes something like this: we live in a world whose reality is communicated to us in our sense perceptions, but as these vary from person to person, with no way to judge further as to their truthfulness, we must accept all perceptions and individual judgments as valid for the person who has them. No one has the right to claim their perception is 'more true' than mine, nor their truth 'truer' than mine. He has no desire for speculations about some reality behind the reality we perceive. It is enough for him to deal with the world as we have it moment-to-moment. His view is easily illustrated.

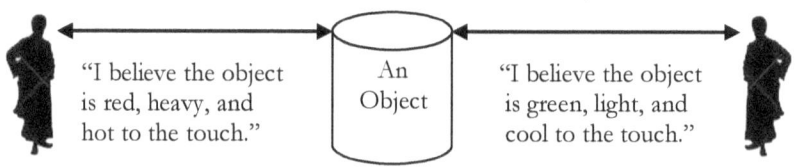

"I believe the object is red, heavy, and hot to the touch."   An Object   "I believe the object is green, light, and cool to the touch."

---

[6] This idea of Heraclitus is found in fragments preserved by many ancient authors, including Plato, *Cratylus*, 402a.

What is real—and what a person acts upon—is what the person experiences. The person on the left (above) is unlikely to touch a heavy, hot object. The other person, however, may perceive it as something easy to lift and take home.

Now this particular example may raise an obvious objection. One might say, "The object is either red or green, either heavy or light, either hot or cool. Just because someone perceives it one way and not another does not make the object *be* as that person believes!" But such an objection presumes something that Protagoras avoids. He sidesteps the issue of what an object actually *is* in order to highlight the importance and experiential impact of an object as it *appears to be*. The latter, he argues, is what governs thinking and action and is all we really need be concerned about; it is reality enough. His position looks like this:

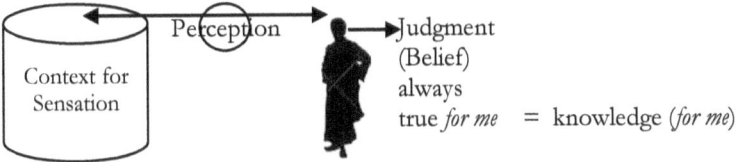

In any given context my perception generates a *belief* that is both true and certain for me and so is what I *know*.

"Man Is the Measure of All Things."

Protagoras' most famous saying is, "Man is the measure of all things." There is some uncertainty as to exactly what Protagoras meant by the word "measure" (*metron*). But we can start by noting that all we have quoted so far is a portion of a larger statement. It reads in full: "Man is the measure of all things—of those things that are, about their existence; of things that are not, about their nonexistence."[7]

In the late 2nd century of the Common Era, the philosopher Sextus Empiricus (c. 160-c. 210 C.E.) offered his explanation of this saying.

> And Protagoras likewise says, "Man is the measure of all things—of those things that are, about their existence; of things that are not, about their nonexistence." By 'measure' (*metron*) he means 'criterion' (*kritērion*), and by 'things' he means 'perceived objects,' so he is actually saying, 'Man is the criterion of all perceived objects, of those things that are, about their existence; of things that are not, about their nonexistence.' As a result, he concerns himself only with appearances (*phainomena*) to each individual person, by which he makes all things relative.[8]

---

7 Plato, *Theatetus*, 152a.

8 Sextus Empiricus, *Outlines of Pyrrhonism* (*Pyrrhōneioi hypotypōseis*), I.32.216-217. [The citation is to book [I], chapter [32], and sections in the Greek [216-217]. The phrase "perceived objects' translates πραγμάτων (*pragmatōn*), which can mean simply 'things' in general. See also I.32.218-219, where Sextus expands on Protagoras' view, which includes grounding all appearances in matter

A "criterion" (κριτήριον, *kritērion*) is a standard upon which decisions are based. If Sextus Empiricus is right, Protagoras intends us to think that everything is measured with human beings as the yardstick. All of reality is measured with human beings in mind, and every judgment of reality is a human one. This, explains Sextus Empiricus, is how relativity is born: every human being measures what appears to her or him, and every measurement is against what the individual experiences as a human being. Human beings and their perceptual experiences are the measuring stick of reality, at least insofar as it can be known.

Now we need to remember in Protagoras' saying nothing is said about *how* human beings are the measure of all things except that it applies to both what exists and what does not exist. The saying is enigmatic—or obscure, or befuddling, depending on one's mood at the time when reading it. Plato in his dialog *Theaetetus* casts it in light of perception. It seems reasonable enough a claim, since the work was well known when Plato was writing and had he made some outrageous claim it would surely have been seen as such.

Of course, human experience of reality is not merely as a *passive* sense perceiver. We do much more than stand in the pasture and smell the flowers. Reality is both physical and social. We are communal beings, interacting with each other through our senses but also reflecting on what appears to us and constructing judgments about it. These values and our decisions guide us. We form complex ideas about Nature and Society, and these are rooted in actual sense experience. What *seems* to be *is*, as it is all we have to go on.

If Protagoras' epistemology is set in a metaphysical context it looks like this:

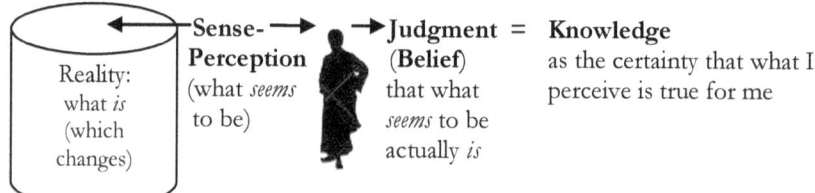

This understanding that knowledge is sense-perception is explored by Plato's Socrates in one of the greatest works written exploring the puzzle of knowing.

Theaetetus' 1ˢᵗ Definition: "Knowledge Is Perception."

Plato, in his dialog named *Theaetetus*, examines Protagoras' position. In the portion we are interested in Socrates is carrying on a discussion with Theaetetus concerning the nature of knowledge. They are not interested in knowledge primarily in the sense of some body or *product* of accumulated information, but knowledge as a *process*—"knowing." How do we know? Answering that question guides us to understanding what knowledge is.

(real objects) and that all perception is context-dependent. "Appearances" (*phainomena*) are "that which appears"; we shall see much more on this term later.

After some time discussing the general subject, Socrates gets Theaetetus to state plainly what he thinks knowledge is. Theaetetus says, "I suppose for myself, then, that if a person has knowledge, that means having a perception of what is known, and so I would presently explain it as 'knowledge (*epistēmē*) is sense-perception (*aisthēsis*)."[9]

There is more than one Greek word that can be translated into English as "knowledge." Here the word used is ἐπιστήμη (*epistēmē*)—the very word from which we get our term "epistemology," the study of how we know and what knowledge is. The word translated "sense-perception" (or simply "perception") is αἴσθησις (*aisthēsis*), and refers to what our senses perceive. These are two special words in the history of philosophy and we shall meet them again and again.

At this very point Plato has Socrates offer the remark quoted earlier: "Man is the measure of all things—of those things that are, about their existence; of things that are not, about their nonexistence." Socrates' interpretation of Protagoras' teaching is then set forward: "In effect, then, does he not say that any particular thing *is* as it *appears* to me, and just so any given thing is as it appears to you, as well, because 'man' applies to both of us?"[10] Socrates then uses an example; he remarks that when the wind blows one of them might feel slightly chilled while the other feels quite cold. Socrates follows up on this point by distinguishing between the question of any objective assessment of the wind itself and the matter of individual perception. He asks whether they should agree with Protagoras that the latter matter is the important one, and Theaetetus tells Socrates this seems to him a reasonable position.[11]

Socrates then links things together: "So, then, an appearance (*phantasia*) and a sense-perception (*aisthēsis*) are the same. . . ."[12] Here we have another word that emerges in Greek philosophy as critically important: *phantasia*. Plato appears to have coined the term, which becomes a key one in subsequent epistemological discussions. He employs the word sparingly—just seven times across the dialogs, and only twice here in the *Theaetetus*.[13] One of those other occasions where he uses it is especially instructive.

In his dialog *Sophist*, a sequel to the *Theaetetus*, a Foreigner from Elea who has been a student of Parmenides, has with Theaetetus the following exchange:

> FOREIGNER: Now, then, isn't this clear?—'thought' (*dianoia*) and 'belief' (*doxa*) and 'appearance' (*phantasia*); can not these occur as either false (*pseude*) or true (*alēthē*) in our rational soul (*psychais*)?
>
> THEAETETUS: How?
>
> FOREIGNER: I can help you see this if you first permit me to distinguish each of these from the others.
>
> THEAETETUS: Enlighten me.

---

[9] Plato, *Theaetetus*, 151e.
[10] Plato, *Theaetetus*, 152a. I have used italics to highlight the tension implicit in the wording.
[11] Plato, *Theaetetus*, 152b.
[12] Plato, *Theaetetus*, 152c.
[13] *Theaetetus*, 152c and 161e; *Republic*, II.382e; and *Sophist*, 260c, 260e, 263d, and 264a.

FOREIGNER: Okay. Aren't 'thought' (*dianoia*) and speech (*logos*) identical, except that the former is within the rational soul (*psychēs*) as a dialog with itself but without sound?

THEAETETUS: That is entirely correct.

FOREIGNER: On the other hand, the stream of sound through the mouth is speech (*logos*)?

THEAETETUS: True.

FOREIGNER: And in speech (*logois*) we know there to be. . . .

THEAETETUS: To be what?

FOREIGNER: Affirmation, and also denial.

THEAETETUS: I know that!

FOREIGNER: May we suppose, then, that whenever in the rational soul (*psyché*) such a thought (*dianoian* [i.e., of affirmation or denial]) occurs silently it should be called 'belief' (*doxēs*)?

THEAETETUS: How could we not?

FOREIGNER: But what if this happens, not by itself, but through sense-perception (*aisthēseōs*)—then when such happens is it not right to say it is an 'appearance' (*phantasian*)?

THEAETETUS: No one can disagree.

FOREIGNER: Therefore, since speech (*logos*) can be either true (*alēthēs*) or false (*pseudes*), and it looks to be that thought (*dianoia*) is the rational soul (*psychēs*) dialoging with itself, and belief (*doxa*) to be the result of thought (*dianoias*), and when we say "it appears" (*phainetai*) we refer to the comingling of sense-perception (*aisthēseōs*) and belief (*doxé*), then it follows that as all of these are like speech, some of them at times must be false (*pseudé*).

THEAETETUS: How could it not be so?[14]

Let us picture the matter like this:

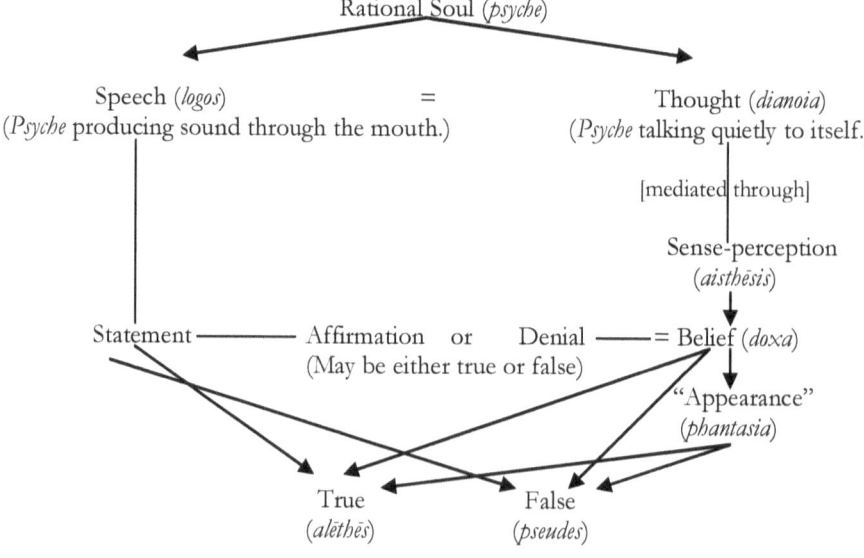

[14] Plato, *Sophist*, 263d-264b.

In this manner the Foreigner from Elea thinks he has proven to Theaetetus the existence of some false beliefs. Now on this last term—belief (*doxa*)—we shall have much more to say very shortly. Let us here note simply that the sense of "belief" in this context is one of taking up a position by forming a judgment—an affirmation or denial.

Knowledge Is Belief

Although narrowing the range of the word "appears" to just sense-perception works for Plato's argument on the lips of Socrates, in fairness to Protagoras we should note the term has a wider scope. Perception in the sense of how things appear involves not just sense-perception but also the act of valuing, decision-making, and a sensibility about what is "true."

For now let us picture the links Socrates has drawn, which Theaetetus confirms as a reasonable enough view of Protagoras' position:

Knowledge = perception (= 'appearing to be' to an individual)

Let's dissect these links a little further. Protagoras' epistemology is one rooted in what people would call 'common sense.' It resonates with ordinary experience and ordinary conversation, and so it would be popular with people as a sensible notion of what knowledge is. He starts right where human experience begins: sensations perceived by our physical bodies and interpreted by our minds. We take it for granted that we know things to *be*, and how they *are*, based on how they appear to us. It is a simple, appealing picture:

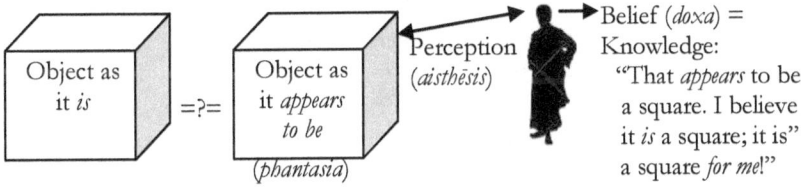

Protagoras simply isn't concerned with solving the metaphysical component of whether appearances match the actuality of things since what matters in everyday living is the practical problem of, 'What do I do about the world as I experience it?' Human beings depend on perception to understand reality, to know things, and it is human judgment that determines for each person what is real or not in accord with that individual's perception.

Doxa

So where does "belief" enter in? Nothing in Protagoras' famous saying declares that knowledge is belief. Yet it probably isn't hard to see that the line of reasoning being developed implies an important role for belief. We tend today to think of knowledge as something objective—absolute and universal. We either know a thing, or we do not, and if we do, our information is certain and true in a way that anyone who takes the time to test can likewise discover. But if knowledge instead is subjective, a matter of individual perception and personal judgment, then this relativizing of knowledge means "knowing" is the same as what we commonly refer to when we use the word "believing."

This implicit link is eventually made explicit by Socrates. When Protagoras' friend Theodorus enters into the dialog a new term is introduced into the mix. This new term is, as it were, the 'missing link' we need. The Greek word is δόξα (*doxa*), and is variously translated as "belief" or "opinion."[15] In the history of Western philosophy this noun has become exceptionally important in epistemology because understanding what knowledge (*epistēmē*) is means figuring out its relation to *doxa*. The basic sense is "taking up a position." We may picture it this way, as four closely bundled elements:

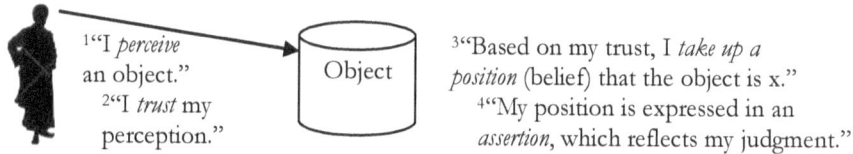

1"I *perceive* an object."
2"I *trust* my perception."

Object

3"Based on my trust, I *take up a position* (belief) that the object is x."
4"My position is expressed in an *assertion*, which reflects my judgment."

The coloring of the English word "belief" is that the position is taken up in an affirmation expressing trust. The word "opinion" offers the same basic idea, though perhaps without the same strong sense of trust.

The taking up of a position, of course, reflects a judgment, and so words like "supposition," or "conjecture," or "judgment" also are used sometimes. In the illustrations provided earlier the element of a judgment in belief has been highlighted since it reflects the idea that if what we perceive is what *appears* to us to be the case, such an "appearance" reflects personal cognitive involvement as we form a belief, that is, as we take up a position that judges the nature of what is being perceived. This is what Socrates has in mind when he remarks that he understands Protagoras to mean that for each of us what we know as being true and real is exactly and only what that thing appears to be to each of us.

However one construes the matter, the basic question remains the same: is the taking up of a position the same as "knowledge"? Because the context in which this question is asked is most usually of individuals the position-taking is personal, and so our word "belief" is a common and reasonable choice. Given Western civilization's development under the influence of Christian thinking, the word "belief" has become very important. Further, because it is so often claimed that "belief" is, under at least some conditions "knowledge," it seems especially appropriate to use this term for our discussion.

---

[15] The noun *doxa* (δόξα) derives from the verb *dokeō* (δοκέω), "to suppose," or "to hold an opinion." This makes it cousin to the verb *dechomai* (δέχομαι), "to take hold of" or "to take up," which less literally can mean to hold an idea, i.e., a belief or an opinion. Another verb, *doxazō* (δοξάζω; infinitive form, *doxazein* (δοξάζειν)), "to hold an opinion," or "to suppose," derives from *doxa*. All told, this family has a number of ways to express a basic concept related to acts of thinking where a position is taken whether based on knowledge or not.

In addressing Protagoras' friend Theodorus, Socrates returns to Protagoras' famous saying. Once more he offers his interpretation, but notice how this time Socrates explicitly adds in the idea of *believing* and *belief* as part of his understanding of what Protagoras teaches:

> For if what each person believes (*doxazē*) results from his or her perception and so will be true for him or her, and if no one is better than anyone else in deciding such, and if also no one is in position to pass judgment on someone else's belief (*doxan*) as true or false, and—as has been repeatedly said—each person is to have his or her own beliefs (*doxasei*) unique to him- or herself, and in all cases such are right and true . . . .[16]

The word "believes" (*doxazō*) is the verb counterpart to the noun *doxa*. We can see that the translation above looks like a classic 'If . . . then' formulation, only the 'then' portion is missing. I've left off how this section ends, because while Socrates is summarizing Protagoras' position he is doing so in order to make a point against it—and that point shall have to wait until our next chapter.

Socrates has no doubt that what Protagoras has done is create a formulation that we can depict in this manner:

Knowledge = perception (= 'appearing to be' to an individual) = belief (doxa)

The relativism of Protagoras' perspective makes it inevitable that perception is the same as individual judgments of what is true or false.

Knowledge as Perception as Belief: An Illustration

How does this look in the world of human experience? Let us consider an anecdote offered by the 2nd century writer Plutarch, who in writing his biographical account of Pericles provides an instance of a conversation that Pericles' son reports his father having had with Protagoras.

> For instance, one who competed in the Pentathlon accidentally struck Epitimus the Pharsalian with a javelin and killed him. Pericles used up an entire day with Protagoras debating whether it was the javelin, the one who cast it, or the administrator of the games, who—strictly speaking—should be held accountable for what had happened. [17]

The situation readily lends itself to a variety of plausible beliefs. If we see the goal as knowledge of the cause of the accident, this knowledge can only be according to one's perceptual point of reference. Lawyers involved in civil legislation on behalf of the victim's family would not be interested in the javelin itself, except as to whether it was defective or not. They are trying to find who to hold responsible, whether the manufacturer of the javelin, the negligence of the one who threw it, or the carelessness of the administrators of the games. On the other hand, each of these parties who might be accused also have a vested inter-

---

[16] Plato, *Theaetetus,* 161d. Forms of our key Greek words in this passage are: "believes" (δοξάζω, *doxazō*); "perception" (αἰσθήσεως, *aisthēseōs*); "belief" (δόξαν, *doxan);* and "beliefs" (δοξάσει, *doxasei*).
[17] Plutarch, *Lives: Pericles*, 36.3.

est—in perceiving fault as resting with someone else! Perception, then, is not just a matter of sense-perception, but involves values and judgments that reflect a personal frame of reference—*belief*.

The taking up of a position in belief derives from information judged *relevant* and *adequate* from the pool of all possible information on the matter. Each person, relative to her or his situation, draws upon a different portion of the pool of information in deciding what is relevant and adequate, i.e., what is needed to be known. It looks like this (using the above anecdote to construct a few of many possible perspectives):

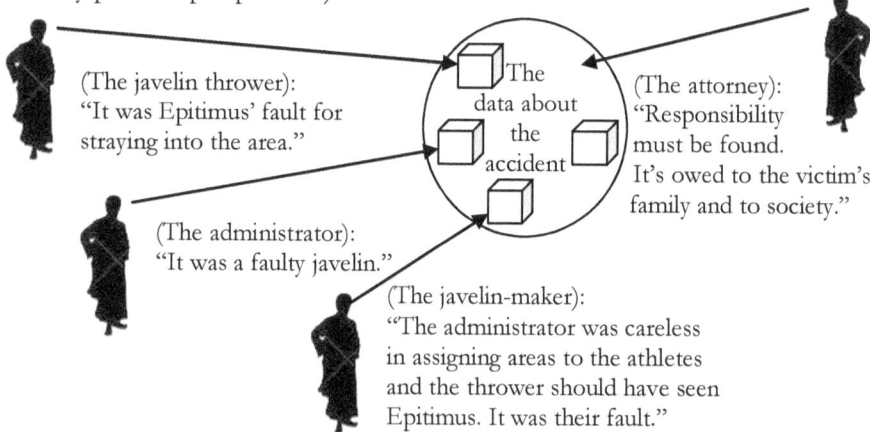

(The javelin thrower): "It was Epitimus' fault for straying into the area."

The data about the accident

(The attorney): "Responsibility must be found. It's owed to the victim's family and to society."

(The administrator): "It was a faulty javelin."

(The javelin-maker): "The administrator was careless in assigning areas to the athletes and the thrower should have seen Epitimus. It was their fault."

Protagoras thinks he is being entirely practical and realistic in adopting relativism because it seems very much to be the way the social world of human beings works. Each person perceives from all the information available what they believe to be relevant and adequate—and they then call this knowledge.

Beliefs and Consequences

It seems clear that knowledge-as-belief—because individuals act on their beliefs and society has a stake in them—has practical implications at more than one level. There are *consequences* to the varying beliefs of individuals in any given setting—and as the beliefs change so do the consequences. It looks like this:

"Because it was a faulty javelin, there must be changes made in javelin production and in the instructions for proper use."

"Because there was negligence at the games, there must be changes in policy and law about how such games are conducted."

Changing beliefs in the direction of healthier consequences is a good—a moral—thing.

Knowledge—*belief*—affects human interest. But is it the interest and well-being of the individual or of the group? Protagoras would argue that it is both. Sure, individuals can be so self-involved and selfish that they consciously pay little if any mind to others, but that is why wise teachers are needed. They can persuade people that it is in their best interests to concern themselves with the welfare of others as well as their own.

Perception & Persuasion: Belief Changes

Because human beings are the measure of all things they are the creators and judges of everything. They can, and do, change things. An important way in which they do so, a way that affects others, is through persuasion. So we must turn to Protagoras' faith in the art of persuasion.[18] From a practical standpoint, mastering the art of rhetoric—the ability to speak persuasively—is valuable since it presents the speaker's reality in a way that may influence others. Each person's perception may be equally valid, but *not all perceptions are equal in their consequences.*[19] Some perceptions are less desirable because they are unhealthy. They promote unhappiness, dissatisfaction, or discord. If the person can be persuaded to perceive differently, then he or she might move toward health.

This idea needs to be connected with another one: *the perceiver changes.* We are not exactly the same from moment to moment. As we change so do our perceptions.[20] Take merely the matter of simple sense-perception of an object. Change the position of the person perceiving it—say, moving closer or further away, or moving around the object—and the perception changes. In Protagoras' terms, the knowledge of it changes because the way it appears to us to be known changes. No single perception (knowledge) of an object is *truer* than another, but a particular knowledge (perception) might be *better.*

Such ideas are raised in the *Theaetetus.* At a certain point in the discussion, after some serious questioning of Protagoras' position by Socrates, it is decided that it is only fair that a defense such as Protagoras would offer be presented on his behalf. Protagoras himself being absent, Socrates undertakes this effort. A part of that defense reads as follows (Socrates speaking as Protagoras):

> For I indeed do say that the truth is as I have written: each one of us is a measure of the things which actually exist and those that do not. However, there is an incalculable difference between one person and another in this same matter, that to one a thing is and appears to be, and to another it is different. With respect to this situation, I am far from denying that wisdom and a wise person exist, because the one I call 'wise' is someone who can elicit changes in us so that what appears to one as bad—and is bad for that one—is made to appear good and is then good to that person.
>
> Now don't pick at the way I've put this matter, but let me offer an illustration to explain it more plainly. Be reminded of what we were discussing before: to someone who is sick food appears bitter in taste and so it is, while to one who is healthy the food is and appears differently. Neither of these persons should be made out as wiser—that is impossible—nor should we

---

[18] See Plato, *Protagoras,* 320c-328d for a presentation of Protagoras belief that virtue can be taught, but that such teaching does not guarantee virtue. Some incline toward it by nature, and some teachers of virtue are more skilled than others. He argues this is the 'accepted' view.

[19] The remarks here are mostly based on the reasoning found in *Theaetetus,* 166c-167d.

[20] See Sextus Empiricus, *Outlines of Pyrrhonism,* I.32.218-219.

accuse the ill person of being stupid in belief, or claim the healthy person is wise for holding a different belief. Yet a change is needed by the ill person to a more desirable state.

This is what education is about—change from a poorer condition to a better one. While a physician uses medicines for this purpose, a Sophist does it by reasoned persuasion. But don't misunderstand me: no one can claim that a person held a false belief that was afterwards changed to a true one; a person is unable to believe what to him is unreal, nor believe anything other than what he experiences, which to him is always true. Rather, the case is this: a person of a poorer state of mind believes in a corresponding manner; one possessing a better state of mind by virtue of an improved condition believes in a manner corresponding to that improvement. Some folk inaccurately say this means they come to hold 'truer' beliefs, but I do not call them 'truer' though I do think them better.[21]

Protagoras, as Socrates presents him, then again appeals to the example of the physician, and adds to it one about a person who cares for sick plants; in each instance the goal is to change the underlying condition toward health. In the healthy state the perceptions and beliefs of the improved condition flow naturally from it.

This matter is easily illustrated in three brief exchanges:

 [1]"I feel like I've been cheated! I bought this item 50% off at store A, but store B's price, with no discount, is less!"

[2]"I can see why you would be unhappy! But did you notice that the one you bought was made of better materials?"

Unhappy consumer

Helpful friend

 [3]"Now that I look at it again, I see your point. My item is really very finely made. I think I made a good purchase after all!"

The consumer's perceptions originally and later are true for her, but she feels much better after being persuaded by her friend. Her 'education' has brought her to a healthier belief, not a truer one.

From Protagoras' perspective, all perceptions have equal merit. They are all what a person "knows" at a given moment. But while at one level it may be true that all knowledge is equal—that none of us can judge what is true or false for another—at another level, because beliefs vary in consequences, we all have a vested interest in changing beliefs in the direction of becoming healthier. This conclusion is an important one because it moves the discussion out of a limited context of just individual perceptions, beliefs, and knowledge into a broader one where social judgments also matter. In other words, the notion of there being

---

[21] Plato, *Theaetetus*, 166d-167b.

'better' rather than 'truer' perceptions means our perceptions are not completely independent of others and society can have a say in them in order to move us collectively toward harmony.

The Importance of Good Judgment

Protagoras is dedicated to the precise and correct use of words.[22] He is purposeful in language because he views it as the way of developing character. When asked by Socrates (as Plato writes in his dialog entitled *Protagoras*) what the aim of his teaching is with his young students, Protagoras answers with a single purpose that reaches in two directions: the personal and the public. "The one lesson," Protagoras says, "is *good judgment*—both concerning his daily affairs managing his own house, and also the city so that in its management he may ably contribute by what he does and what he says."[23] It looks like this:

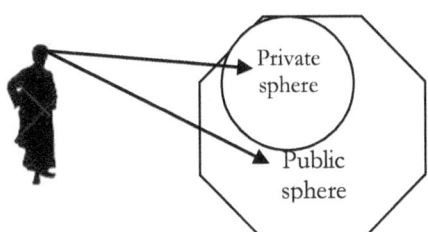

"I am obliged to exercise good judgment privately and publicly, and that means managing my affairs *reasonably* so as to make both my home and world a better place."

In managing personal and public affairs good judgment is not merely guessing about things, or hoping for lucky outcomes, but proceeding with reasonable discretion in accord with plausible, credible expectations given the circumstances at hand. It is, as a lawyer might say, doing what is reasonably expected by reasonable people.

It seems congenial to deduce that when he says, "Man is the measure of all things," he means knowledge and truth are human *decisions*—and ought to be responsible ones. These may follow from individual perceptions or reasoning, or reflect cultural judgments and values, but ultimately they are always determined—*made*—by human beings as they take up positions (i.e., express beliefs). Truth is subjective and knowledge is really just personal and/or social opinion.

Social institutions like government, education, and religion all tell us how we should see the world. For example, a society's government tells its citizens whether the world is one where divine right is given to kings, or all have a say. Schools do more than teach objective facts; they inculcate values that tell students how the world is supposed to be. Religion addresses fundamental issues

---

[22] In Greek, this is termed *orthopeia*. Protagoras' interest in this matter, according to some ancient sources, led him to compose one of the earliest grammars. From a practical standpoint, in training young men who would practice law, he was concerned to help them understand how to use words (rhetoric), but also how to understand them (such as in interpreting the intent of a speaker or author).

[23] Plato, *Protagoras*, 318e-319a. "Good judgment" is *euboulia*. It embraces prudence (or wisdom), good counsel, and sound judgment.

like the nature of reality, the place of human beings within it, and where ulti-mate meaning is to be sought and found. But all such things are decided by people, particularly those most skilled at persuading others.

These points are made by Protagoras, as represented by Socrates, in the *Theaetetus* in the portion immediately following his comment on education.

> Wise and good public speakers persuade States that what is good, rather than what is evil, is just. Whatever each State reckons as just and good is so to that State for so long as it is the customary practice. But the wise person op-poses evil by making appear to fellow citizens what is good and so they reckon it to be good and it is good.[24]

In this manner every State, which constructs its own reality, continually needs the wise persons who can persuade the State toward a better condition.

We may ask whether such confidence in humanity is justified. History is re-plete with instances of societies whose ideologies—like Nazism—encourage perceptions that lead to the benefit of a few at the expense of many. If all per-ceptions are equally justifiable, how can one argue that the democracy that Pro-tagoras was familiar with and favored is superior to a dictatorship? Remember, the Nazis were democratically elevated to power. Even if one grants that the differences in consequences among beliefs means we ought to favor beliefs whose consequences lead toward health, when power is concentrated in a few their belief that what is "healthy" is what is good for them, no matter the cost to others, leads to social constructions that justify themselves as "good" and "healthy" even though a majority of citizens experience otherwise.

On the other hand, the idea of promoting healthy consequences, coupled with the drive to do so for all people, might help correct social constructions that hurt many members in a given society. Yet it also has dangers of its own. Today in mental health counseling a theory of "cognitive therapy" is very popu-lar. It purports to combat depression, alleviate anxiety, and effectively address many psychological conditions that lead to distress in the individual and dys-function in relationships and the world. It does so by addressing the individual's thoughts, challenging them and encouraging change in them, which is then paired with behavioral changes. Much like the notion adhering to Protagoras' perspective this kind of change is in the direction of conforming to the way most people see things. It is a therapy of *adjustment* so that the individual can fit in better with the majority. But what if the majority is wrong? Is health promot-ed, for example, by a person who has been denied employment because of gen-der, race, or sexual orientation reframing the matter in their thinking so as to 'go along to get along'? Or is the majority mind diseased and the individual who rebels the healthy one? With Protagoras' perspective, the answers are uncertain.

---

[24] Plato, *Theaetetus*, 167c.

4

Socrates' Skepticism

Socrates (c. 470-399 B.C.E.), the teacher of Plato, is presented by the latter as having called into serious question not only the conclusions of Protagoras, but his very manner of reaching them. Protagoras relies on the power and practice of rhetoric, a way of setting out matters that many admire, but one that many others find tiresome and confusing. Socrates advocates a dialectical method. This style uses questions as it probes alternative positions, typically presented as a discussion between representatives of the parties holding different views. Plato's dialogs, including the *Theaetetus*, are examples of the dialectical method.

Let's return to the *Theaetetus* and Protagoras' idea that knowledge is perception. Socrates' interpretation of "Man as the measure of all things" is that Protagoras means a thing is as it appears to a given person; perception is how anything real appears to be to someone.[25] Over the course of this section of the dialog Socrates examines the nature of perception.[26] The epistemological point Socrates is trying to make seems to be that rather than perceiving what actually *is*, because things are always in process (in flux) all we perceive is what is *becoming*, and thus what *is*—the object of knowledge—remains hidden to perception. Perception is fine for explaining how things *appear* to us through our senses, but forever inadequate to get at things as they really are.

If we try to illustrate this perspective of Plato's it might look like this:

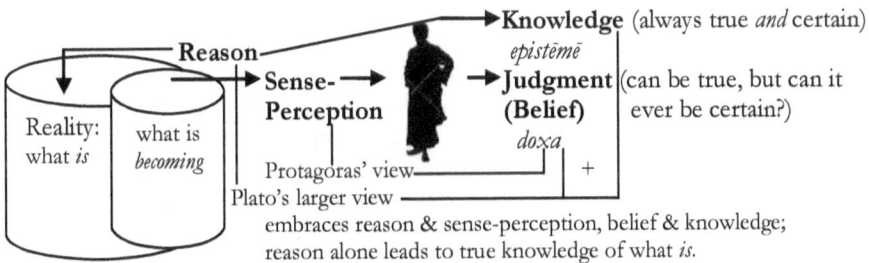

Put simply, Socrates does not think matters are as simple as Protagoras represents them.

---

[25] Plato, *Theaetetus*, 151d-152c.
[26] Plato, *Theaetetus*, 152c-157c.

Socrates' 1st Challenge: Who Is the Measure of All Things?

In Plato's dialectical process a foundation is built with a clear and full sense of some position, contention, or proposal. That means carefully defining key terms, tracing lines of argument, and in general seeking to fairly reveal as completely as feasible what is at hand. At this point in the *Theaetetus* the position of Protagoras and his provocative proposal have been thoughtfully set forth. Now Socrates' aim changes. Having *exposed* the thinking his goal becomes to *test* it.[27]

Socrates opens his testing of Protagoras' position by asking a seemingly innocent question about why Protagoras began his work *Truth* the way he did, with his famous saying. Why make 'man' the measure of all things? Further, it seems to Socrates that by his own logic Protagoras is caught:

> For if what each person believes results from his or her perception and so will be true for him or her, and if no one is better than anyone else in deciding such, and if also no one is in position to pass judgment on someone else's belief as true or false, and—as has been repeatedly said—each person is to have his or her own beliefs unique to him- or herself, and in all cases such are right and true, then how in the world, my friend, can Protagoras be so wise that he is judged to be a teacher worthy of being paid very well, while we are regarded as ignoramuses who must be schooled by him, even though each person is (supposedly) the measure of his or her own wisdom?!?[28]

The early portion of this remark we saw in chapter 1. At that time it was promised that Socrates' punch line would be later shown, and here it is. The criticism is basic, and simple, but telling enough. If, by his own logic, no perception—no knowledge or belief—is truer than another, then why waste money on a teacher whose belief/knowledge is no truer than mine? We saw, of course, that Protagoras rebuts this criticism with a distinction between 'right' or 'true' on the one hand, and 'better' on the other. From his standpoint, everyone can be right, and all beliefs true, but some beliefs—some knowledge—can still be 'better.'

But Socrates' point is being made in a broader context; it is not really so much a personal attack on Protagoras as a more basic question: why make *human* beings the measure of all things? Why not, instead, make a pig, or baboon, or any other thinking being the measure of all things? Socrates is thus not just raising the question of what makes Protagoras so special, but what makes human beings so special? In a sense, Socrates continues, Protagoras' position makes human beings as wise as any god![29] Theaetetus is troubled by this realization. Yet from Protagoras' perspective, says Socrates, the line of reasoning that Socrates has been advancing is so much empty speculation. Therefore they must start afresh in considering the question of knowledge.[30]

---

[27] Plato, *Theaetetus*, 160e-161b is the portion of the dialog marking this transition.

[28] Plato, *Theaetetus*, 161d-e. The portion from 161d was quoted in chapter 1.

[29] Plato, *Theaetetus*, 162c.

[30] Plato, *Theaetetus*, 162c-163a.

Socrates now turns to testing some implications of the 'knowledge is perception' position. He invites Theaetetus to consider the situation of encountering a foreign language that one does not understand. The letters of the language can be seen, and the sounds of it heard. Does this then mean the person "knows" the language? Theaetetus acknowledges that the form of the letters and their sounds can be "known," but he also acknowledges that this does not equal knowing what such things mean. We can picture the dilemma this way:

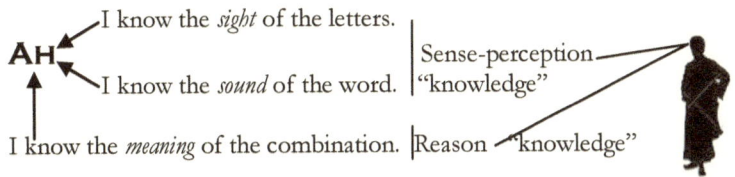

The "knowledge" the person has from sense-perception is not the same as the "knowledge" a person such as an interpreter or teacher may have of that language. Theaetetus readily sees the distinction: not everything termed "knowledge" is merely a matter of sense perception.

Next Socrates turns to a more important matter that raises doubts about equating knowledge with perception. He calls attention to *memory*. His chain of reasoning is uncomplicated as he uses a simple example: First, a person sees something; according to Protagoras the person thus gains knowledge of what has been seen. Second, a person remembers what was seen—even when her or his eyes are closed. But, third, this means the person has knowledge of what is not being perceived![31] It looks like this:

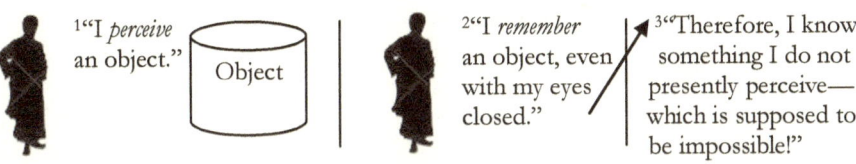

How, Socrates, wonders, is it possible to know what isn't seen if the equation "knowledge is perception" holds up? After all, the Protagorean logic would seem to say plainly, "If you don't see it, you don't know it." According to Socrates, by that logic the conclusion would have to be that anyone who comes to know a thing by perception when remembering it apart from perception cannot know it! Thus, the equation "knowledge is perception" leads to a fantastic and absurd conclusion, which proves it incorrect.[32]

Much like the example before it, concerning a foreign language, Socrates' argument can be criticized as unfair to Protagoras by limiting too much the

---

[31] Plato, *Theaetetus*, 163d-164a.
[32] Plato, *Theaetetus*, 164b.

sense of what is meant by perceiving. Socrates' point holds up only if the actual formula is "knowledge is *sense*-perception"—and immediate sense-perception at that. Both examples point to the reality of mental processes apart from sense-perception. In Socrates' view it looks like this:

8 a.m.: an immediate *sense-perception* of **A**= knowledge.

(one of many over time)

A

8:05 a.m.: **A** leaves.

10 a.m.: No sense-perception (sight) of **A**, but a *memory* of **A**. Therefore, something more than sense-perception must be involved.

If Protagoras is right, how is what happens at 10 a.m. to be explained, since it, too, is said to be "knowledge"? If knowledge can be retained after sense-perception, when it is absent, then there must be something else going on.

Socrates continues to press the point, even as he acknowledges that poor Protagoras is not himself available to defend his position. Socrates presents the case of someone who sees something with one eye open and one eye closed. Does such a person "know" the object which only one eye sees? Or is that object both known and unknown? He then quickly raises a number of other questions all aimed at the same basic goal of showing the weakness of identifying knowledge with mere sense-perception.[33]

At this point Socrates undertakes a defense of Protagoras (which we discussed in part in chapter 3). He begins by noting that Protagoras could point out that all Socrates has done with the topic of memory is demonstrate that perception includes it! Obviously the memory of a thing is not identical to the sense-perception of it so any criticism that memory perception cannot be knowledge is ridiculous. It is simply a different image in the mind that is being seen, and so both the image of sight and the image of memory are true.

As for the person with one eye open and other closed, why shy away from saying the object is both known and unknown? One can claim justifiably that the open eye "knows" the object and the other eye does not. Or, if one prefer, the point can be made that the perceiver changes—as is the case of all things in the universe—and so necessarily the matter of perception and knowledge is one of change, too.[34] Although Socrates does not himself make the point here, we might apply this to the initial example of encountering a foreign language. At first for the perceiver it is a matter of only knowing the visual form of letters and hearing the sounds. Later it might be the making sense of those letters and sounds. All of the perceptions from first to last are "true," but with the change in the perceiver's condition we can argue that the later situation of understanding what the foreign words mean is "better."

[33] Plato, *Theaetetus*, 164c-165e.
[34] Plato, *Theaetetus*, 165e (end)-168b.

Socrates now begins to probe more sharply certain matters related to Protagoras' notion of knowledge. He begins by recalling Protagoras' claim that "any particular thing *is* as it *appears* to me, and just so any given thing is as it appears to you."[35] But now the matter is phrased a little differently, and the new phrasing restates the Protagorean position so that it relates to the present context: "Does he not say, 'what *seems* the case to each person *is* to that person as he supposes it to be'?"[36] The *belief*, or opinion, component is highlighted. The equation thus becomes:

What *seems* true (to the person) = what *is* true (for the person)
(belief)   (knowledge)

This leads directly to Socrates' next remark: "Now then, Protagoras, are we not declaring the belief of a person—or rather everyone's belief—when we say that all people without exception regard themselves wiser in some respects than others, and others as wiser in different respects?"[37] Across a wide range of situations, people seek out those whose knowledge they deem better than their own on some particular matter. Thus people learn trades and gain education. Everyone agrees there is a difference between "wisdom" and "ignorance."[38]

Having begun with his proclamation of what he sees as a universal belief—that all people see themselves as wiser than others in some respects, but others as wiser than themselves in other respects—Socrates now reaches for another very wide belief based on the opinion that both wisdom and ignorance exist. He asks, "Are we not to say in all such cases that people believe wisdom to be true belief and ignorance false belief (*doxan*)?"[39]

This is what we can call a 'trap question.' Accepting it, as Protagoras' friend Theodorus does here, leads directly into the trap Socrates now springs. But before we examine that trap we should acknowledge at least two things. First, Protagoras had said that wisdom was true belief, and that there is a difference between wisdom and ignorance. It seems logical then to conclude that ignorance must be false opinion. However, Protagoras consistently advances the argument that all perceptions are true; all knowledge is true. If knowledge really is equal to belief, then all beliefs are true, too. How, then, can ignorance be termed false belief? Socrates wants Theodorus, and the others nearby like Theaetetus, to recognize that the widely held belief he has stated does not agree with Protagorean thinking. By Protagorean logic all beliefs are true and therefore there can be no ignorance such as people commonly believe.[40]

---

35 Plato, *Theaetetus*, 152a. The text is quoted more fully in the previous chapter.
36 Plato, *Theaetetus*, 170a.
37 Plato, *Theaetetus*, 170a.
38 Plato, *Theaetetus*, 170a-b.
39 Plato, *Theaetetus*, 170b.
40 Plato, *Theaetetus*, 170c-d.

Suppose, Socrates ventures, some people perceive Protagoras' teaching to be incorrect. Such a person's belief (*doxa*) is set against the belief (*doxa*) of any Protagorean. According to Protagoras, both beliefs are true. What is true for the Protagorean is false for those who disagree, while what is true for them is false for the Protagorean. But how can a matter be both true *and* false?[41]

Now the real bite of the trap is sprung. Socrates observes that Protagoras himself must, if logically consistent, grant that the beliefs of those who think him wrong are true. Their perceptions of his perspective are as true for them as his is for himself. But here is the problem: if Protagoras admits their belief is true, then isn't he also admitting his belief is false? On the other hand, those who disagree with him, because they do not see things through the prism of relativism, do not have the same logical necessity of admitting their own position wrong. What a dilemma! It all sorts out like this:

<u>Protagoras' Relativists</u>   <u>Everyone Else (Non-Relativists)</u>

 "I believe I am right."   "I believe you are wrong!"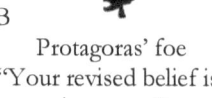

   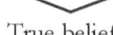

        True belief A   True belief B

Protagoras   Protagoras' foe
    "Hmm. Since belief B is true,   "Your revised belief is
    my original belief (A) must be false!"   is correct!"

Thus a curious situation arises: everyone can agree that Protagoras' position is wrong—including Protagoras when he admits his opponent's belief is true—even though Protagoras might believe his view is true![42] This line of argument undermines the relativistic teaching that 'Man is the measure of all things.'

If the Wiser Believe Better, then Aren't the Wiser the Better Measure?

Socrates now posits that Protagoras' position is strongest in linking the wise person to a situation such as health, where it is plain that a physician's belief is "better" than a lay person's belief. He also is interested in the matter of a State intending to establish beliefs that are true and advantageous for itself.[43] After an extended digression,[44] Socrates resumes the main line of discussion by first mentioning the matter of the State in its intent to adopt and promote beliefs that are *better*, in the sense of being judged helpful to itself (i.e., as helping its

---

[41] Plato, *Theaetetus*, 170d-171a.
[42] Plato, *Theaetetus*, 171a-d.
[43] Plato, *Theaetetus*, 171d-172b.
[44] Plato, *Theaetetus*, 172b-177c. Theodorus at the end of the digression remarks he prefers Socrates' digressions to the main discourse because they are easier to follow! The digression is not unrelated to the epistemological issues at hand, but it is nevertheless a digression and will be passed over here.

citizens).[45] But, Socrates points out, when a State enacts legislation—which constitutes the formal statement of its beliefs—it is always presumptive of the *future*. In other words, the belief expressed is about some future condition, not one at the present. In essence what a State is doing is predicting an outcome.[46]

The distinction Socrates is making can be pictured as follows:

Belief about something as *true*. | Belief is true for the person or group who judges it true. | Belief may be true or false because it has no present way to know. | Belief about something as *better*.

Belief about what is *true* is about the *present*. | Belief about what is *better* is about the *future*.

Socrates then asks a loaded question directly tied to the idea that human beings are the measure of all things. "With respect to things still to come," Socrates proceeds, "we shall say to him, 'Protagoras, does a person possess within the self the means for judging what will be such that whatever is predictively believed comes about just so?'"[47] It is a potent query.

Socrates then turns to the other matter where he has said Protagoras' case seems strongest—the matter of health and the varying perceptions (beliefs) of a layperson and a physician. It already has been set forth that the physician aims to bring the patient to a better condition—health rather than illness—and can be judged in matters of health to be wiser than the layperson who self-diagnoses. But now, with the future in view, Socrates rattles off a series of questions. Supposing a situation where a person believes a fever is coming on, but a physician believes otherwise, which belief produces the expected outcome? Can both of them be right?[48]

Now the dilemma for Protagoras is this: he maintains each person's belief is true for that person and that no person's belief is truer than another's. In any given present moment, both the patient's and the physician's perception of the patient's condition are equally true for each of them. But when we consider the future, where the patient's belief and the physician's oppose one another, *neither is directly perceiving anything*. The future 'fact' is still just a hypothetical.

Protagoras, remember, also maintains that there are "better" beliefs and that the physician's goal is to move the patient to a better condition so that the patient's belief is improved. Much as with the situation of a State enacting laws

[45] Plato, *Theaetetus*, 177d. The Greek word, ὠφέλιμα (*ōphelima*), from the root ὠφέλιμος (*ōphelimos*), can be rendered by words that suggest some form of helping or being helpful, such as "useful," or "advantageous," or "beneficial."
[46] Plato, *Theaetetus*, 177c-178a. Socrates says, "When we legislate, we frame our laws intending them to be beneficial (ὠφέλιμους, *ōphelimous*) in a time yet to come. . . ."
[47] Plato, *Theaetetus*, 178b-c.
[48] Plato, *Theaetetus*, 178b-c.

meant to advantage its citizens in the future, the physician's goal is what is advantageous in the future and all the doctor's expertise is bent toward that end. Although the future condition of the patient is unknown, since the beliefs of doctor and patient conflict, with the idea of what is most beneficial, helpful, or advantageous in mind, clearly the physician's belief is better. But it might still turn out to be wrong.

And that latter possibility is what Socrates is aiming at to make his point. Protagoras teaches that the wise person is the one who can persuade another to a condition wherein the latter's beliefs become better. This is the goal of the State and the aim of the physician. But this requires beliefs about the future. The State predicts its laws will be good, just, and beneficial; the physician predicts his diagnosis and treatment will be helpful. Yet, as Socrates already had gotten Theodorus to admit, the State makes mistakes.[49] Certainly the same can be said for medical doctors. What is "better" in the future is uncertain.

Socrates finishes this line of reasoning with its logical conclusion:

> So we can reasonably say to your teacher that he must necessarily concur that one person is wiser than another—and that the wiser person is truly "the measure"; an ignoramus such as myself is not in any way whatsoever compelled to become a "measure," despite what my earlier defense of Protagoras tried to argue, whether I so wished it or not.[50]

Theodorus finds both this line of argument and Socrates' previous one to be persuasive. Protagoras' notion that every belief of every person must be true appears to be undone.[51]

Theaetetus' 2nd Definition: "Knowledge Is True Belief."

By now Theaetetus has been persuaded that knowledge is *not* merely a matter of "perception." He grants that the mind is actively involved and that alongside perception *thinking* happens, an activity that can reflect upon sense impressions, but also can reflect on matters apart from such impressions (e.g., the concept of existence).[52]

So now Socrates and Theaetetus converse as follows:

> SOCRATES: Now when we began our discussion surely it was not for the purpose of uncovering what knowledge is *not*, but what it *is*. Still, we have made enough progress to not at all seek it in perception, but—whatever name you call it by—in that aspect of the *psyche* whenever it occupies itself with what *is*.
>
> THEAETETUS: But surely, Socrates, this is called by the name, it seems to me, "to take up a position" (δοξάζειν, *doxazein*, fr. *doxazo*).
>
> SOCRATES: You are correct, my friend. And so go back to the beginning, clearing away all that has preceded, and from this advanced vantage point see

[49] Plato, *Theaetetus*, 178a; also see 179a.
[50] Plato, *Theaetetus*, 179b.
[51] Plato, *Theaetetus*, 179b–c.
[52] See particularly Plato, *Theaetetus*, 186a–e.

whether you have a clearer view. Now tell me again what knowledge (*epistēmē*) is.

THEAETETUS: It cannot be every taking up of a position (δόξαν, *doxan*), Socrates, which is impossible because there exist falsely taken positions (*doxa*). I will risk saying that "knowledge (*epistēmē*) is 'a position taken' (*doxa*) that is true." Let that be my answer.[53]

Considering 'False' Belief: 3 Lines of Examination

The notion that "Knowledge is a belief that is true" raises the idea that some beliefs must be "false." Socrates begins with a frank admission that the matter of forming or holding a false belief is a difficult one for him to wrap his mind around. How can such a thing happen? In trying to answer that question he starts with a simple notion: *in every case, leaving aside the possibility of forgetting, a person either knows something or does not know it.* Theaetetus agrees these are the only possibilities. Socrates asks, "But then, surely when a person forms a belief, isn't what he or she is believing either something known or unknown?"[54]

Using the example of an individual recognizing other persons, Socrates and Theaetetus reason that the individual either knows another person, or does not. If, for instance, a third person knows neither Socrates nor Theaetetus, then can such a person *know* that Socrates is Theaetetus, or the other way around? Socrates wonders if it is possible to *believe* something (e.g., Socrates is Theaetetus) when one *knows* they do not know the thing. That would be the same as maintaining that the person knows the very thing she or he doesn't know! In the same manner, if the person already *knows* Socrates and Theaetetus, how then could that individual *believe* Socrates was Theaetetus, or vice versa?[55]

We may illustrate the above ideas this way:

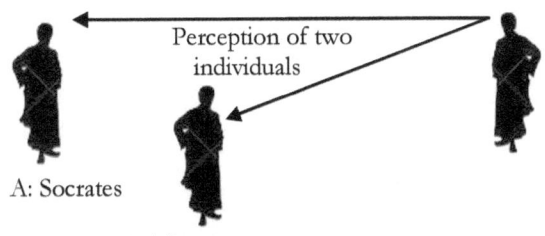

Perception of two individuals

A: Socrates

B: Theaetetus

"I believe B is Socrates."

This cannot be a mistaken belief because all belief is true, which means it is knowledge. But the person does not know either Socrates or Theaetetus. So how is such a belief possible?

Is this exposing a fatal weakness in Protagoras' position?

Wait, Socrates continues. Perhaps there is a different way of looking at it—one, in fact, quite along Protagorean lines. Maybe false belief merely means "be-

---

[53] Plato, *Theaetetus*, 187a-b. The *psyche* is the realm of human mind and personality; the term is often rendered "soul."

[54] Plato, *Theaetetus*, 187c-188b. The quote is from 188a. Socrates seems to assume that the certainty and sufficiency of knowledge means a thing is fully known or it is not really "known" at all. If so, then a mistaken belief indicates the person did not "know" the thing in the first place.

[55] Plato, *Theaetetus*, 188b-c.

lieving what *is not.*" If so, this means false belief concerns the matter of what is real (*is* or *is not*). Protagoras says human beings are the measure of what is, that it *is*, and of what *is not*, that it *is not*. Maybe the solution is in this '*is not*' aspect.

Yet that raises a question: can anyone believe what *is not?* Wouldn't this be like, suggests Socrates, a person seeing something and claiming nothing is seen? The same could be said with reference to hearing and touch, too. But more importantly, it can be said about believing itself; one believes *some*thing, not *noth*ing! To say one "believes what *is not*" is the same thing as saying that one does not believe at all. That means it is impossible to actually believe what *is not*—and that means "believing what *is not*" cannot be "false" belief.[56]

Since this line of inquiry is fruitless, Socrates takes a different look at the possibility of "false" belief being a matter of "mistaken" belief. Perhaps it results from mentally transposing one thing for another, such as one person for another.[57] Socrates asks Theaetetus whether he agrees that this is true, too, for what constitutes "thinking."[58] Theaetetus asks Socrates to clarify what he means by the term and Socrates answers:

> I call it the discourse which the *psyche* passes through with itself on any matter it is contemplating. Of course, I am presenting this to you as something I don't actually know. But this seems to me to be what is happening in thinking—the *psyche* talks to itself, questioning and answering itself, both affirming and denying. And when it has reached a decision, whether deliberately or all at once, when the time has come on a matter it affirms without doubt, and this we set down as "belief" (*doxan*). On this basis I say for myself that believing (*doxazein*) is asserting, and belief its assertion, not addressed to another or spoken aloud, but offered silently to itself.[59]

We may illustrate his reasoning like this:

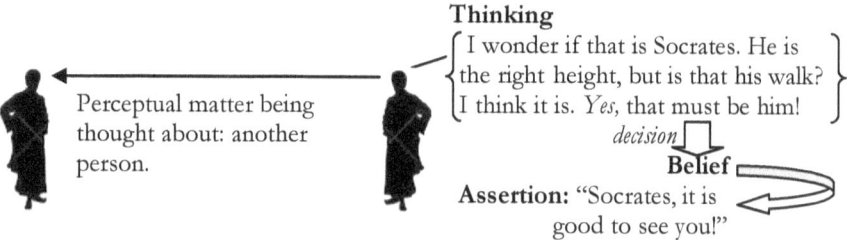

Thinking

I wonder if that is Socrates. He is the right height, but is that his walk? I think it is. *Yes*, that must be him!

decision

Belief

Perceptual matter being thought about: another person.

Assertion: "Socrates, it is good to see you!"

The individual thinks, debating internally, takes up a position (a judgment that is a belief), and then expresses it in an assertion.

---

[56] Plato, *Theaetetus*, 188c-189b.

[57] Plato, *Theaetetus*, 189b-200d.

[58] Plato, *Theaetetus*, 189d-e.

[59] Plato, *Theaetetus*, 189e-190a. My choices "asserting" and "assertion" would be more literally rendered as "speaking" and "spoken word." The variations among translators depends on not merely the immediate context but larger considerations of the sense intended for the words (the verb λέγειν, *legein*, and the noun λόγον, *logon*, respectively), which have a fairly broad range. Mine is a reasonable translation but hardly a definitive one. (Also see ch. 13 in this volume on assertion.)

A false belief would then be one where a person's thinking leads to taking up a position that one thing is another when it is not. But, questions Socrates, does this ever happen? Does a person, for example, having formed the belief that the numbers 1, 3, 5 are 'odd' numbers then ever form the mistaken belief that they are 'even' numbers like 2, 4, 6? Or once having formed a belief as to what an ox is, does one ever then decide to believe it is a horse?[60]

So Socrates refocuses the discussion on the element he had excluded—*memory*. He likens it to the impression made by a ring on wax (e.g., when a document is sealed). We compare sense-perceptions against memories of earlier perceptions. Perhaps false beliefs are indeed possible, rooted not in direct perceptions but rather in our *thinking* about them. Our perceptions can be true (e.g., "That fellow looks like Socrates."), and our memories also true (e.g., "I remember well what Socrates looks like."), but our joining them together may result in a false belief (e.g., "That fellow must be Socrates!") because we mismatch a perception and a memory.[61]

Socrates next compares two things independent of a sense-perception: the numbers 5 and 7. When a person thinks about them together a belief may arise that the resulting sum is 12. But some may instead believe the sum is 11—a false belief. To explain such an error Socrates proposes knowledge must be regarded not as something that one always *has* at hand, but rather like a garment that one *possesses* but may not be wearing. Memory is like an aviary where the stored bits of information are like birds flocking together or flying by themselves. A little at a time we add birds to our aviary. When some information is needed, a 'bird' must be caught. A false belief may come about when the wrong bird (11) is mistakenly caught. The true belief (12) is also there and so both true and false beliefs are possible. False beliefs are a matter of *mis*-thinking.[62]

Naturally, Socrates is bothered by how such a mistake could occur. Theaetetus suggests imagining the birds in the aviary to include not just bits of knowledge, but bits of ignorance, too. The error is in grabbing a bit of ignorance. It all looks like this:

Memories in the aviary of the mind

5+7=12 (true belief)

5+7=11 (false belief)

knowledge

ignorance

Catching a false belief

---

[60] Plato, *Theaetetus*, 190b-e.

[61] Plato, *Theaetetus*, 190e-195b. For example, Socrates points out (193b-d), he might glimpse both Theaetetus and Theodorus at a distance (sense-perception), but apply his memories of each to the wrong figure. Mismatches of perception and memory can easily result in false beliefs.

[62] Plato, *Theaetetus*, 195b-199c.

Socrates points out that in such a case the person will conclude the belief is actually a true one and not ignorance. He will presume he correctly grabbed a bit of knowledge. This kind of reasoning does not clear the waters but muddies them. One could then ask how one knows that one knows—or does not know—and so *ad infinitum* in a circle of questions that leads nowhere.[63] The end result is seeing that maybe thinking about "false" belief is the wrong road.

Socrates suggests Theaetetus try again. But Theaetetus is stuck. As he struggles, Socrates uses the difference between a teacher and a lawyer to illustrate the role of persuasion. Unlike a teacher who has time to patiently stitch together the facts so that a student has sufficient and correct information to make a judgment, a lawyer *convinces* rather than *proves* a case for which the jurors have inadequate firsthand information.[64] There is a difference between "belief" and "knowledge," even if the jury's belief turns out to be "true." The jurors simply cannot "know" in the same way that an eyewitness can, and so there must be some difference between knowledge and true belief. This discussion jogs Theaetetus' memory of what some fellow had said: "He said, 'Only with sufficient grounds can true belief be knowledge; belief absent adequate grounds stands outside knowledge.' Thus, a thing without adequate explanation is not 'knowable'—and he used that very term—while a thing that is sufficiently supported is knowable."[65] Thus there forms a new equation:

$$\text{Knowledge } (epist\bar{e}m\bar{e}) = \text{Belief } (doxa)\text{, when belief is:}$$
$$[1] \text{ true } (al\bar{e}th\bar{e}) \text{ and}$$
$$[2] \text{ warranted } (logou).$$

Thus, two conditions must be met by belief to be knowledge.

The addition of this new element—a warrant or reason (*logos*)—is crucial because it offers a way to distinguish knowledge from a lucky guess. Let us say that we believe a certain person we know has just received a job promotion. Let us also say that this belief is true; the person was this very day promoted. But without *logos* for the belief it could be a mere expression of a wish or a fortunate speculation. Knowledge has to be more than just holding a belief that by some fortuitous coincidence is true. Adding reasonable grounds for holding a belief transforms a "true belief" into "knowledge" by distinguishing it from a lucky guess.

---

[63] Plato, *Theaetetus*, 199c-200c.

[64] Plato, *Theaetetus*, 200d-201c.

[65] Plato, *Theaetetus*, 201c-d. To highlight the key Greek terms, here is the same translation with the key parts in quotes and Greek following: Only with 'sufficient grounds' (λόγου, logou) can 'true belief' (ἀληθῆ δόξαν, alēthē doxan) be 'knowledge' (ἐπιστήμην, epistēmēn); belief 'absent adequate grounds' (ἄλογον, alogon) stands outside 'knowledge' (ἐπιστήμης, epistēmēs). Thus, a thing without 'adequate explanation' (λόγος, logos) is not 'knowable' (ἐπιστητά, epistēta)—and he used that very term—while a thing that is 'sufficiently supported' (λόγος, logos) is 'knowable' (ἐπιστητά, epistēta). (The word *logos* does not appear this last time but is necessary in context.)

Socrates suggests focusing on what is meant by *logos*, the grounds for belief. He ventures that one of three possibilities must be meant by the term:

1. *Logos* = vocalizing in language a reflection of the thing believed.
2. *Logos* = answering a query by listing the parts making up a thing.
3. *Logos* = an account of how the thing differs from other things.

The first is the simplest: verbal expression as a kind of mirror of inner thought. In other words, perhaps *logos* should be understood as merely making a statement of what one believes. In this case the grounds for a belief are reduced to a plain declaration of the belief. But reducing *logos* to mere speech does not really add anything to the definition that knowledge is true belief because how else would such be shown anyway? Any true belief is going to be accompanied by some account.[66] This leaves us unable to differentiate between a person who really *knows* and one who just happens to give voice in the correct way.

The second possibility is stronger. Perhaps *logos* means an answer to a question about a belief concerning some 'thing' by analyzing that thing's component parts. *Logos* might be an explanation of what makes up a thing so that a belief that it is that thing is justified. Socrates offers the example of a wagon. Such a belief might explain that a wagon is comprised of a body, with an axle and wheels, a seat, and so forth. If the thing in question actually has all the elements of a wagon then the belief it is a wagon is a reasonable one. But does such an account add anything of value? Our *logos* for the belief that a thing is a wagon is a true belief, but does merely listing parts of something mean we truly *know* it? Socrates offers another example: a young child learning to write the letters of his or her name. All the elements—letter by letter, syllable by syllable—are put down, and in the proper order; the child's belief that this is her or his name is correct, but is it knowledge if all the child has done is copy his or her name?[67]

One other alternative remains—and it, Socrates says, is what most people think of as the proper sense for *logos*. It is an account of what in a thing makes it stand out from other things as itself and nothing other. He offers the example of the sun; the *logos* is that it is the brightest object in the sky.

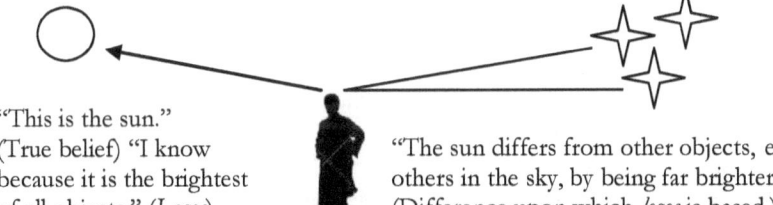

"This is the sun."
(True belief) "I know because it is the brightest of all objects." (*Logos*)

"The sun differs from other objects, even others in the sky, by being far brighter."
(Difference upon which *logos* is based.)

Knowledge = true belief + *logos* (based on distinctive difference)

---

66 Plato, *Theaetetus*, 206c-e. Theaetetus in 208c expresses this as putting an image into sounds.
67 Plato, *Theaetetus*, 206e-208b. At 208c Theaetetus labels this as pursuing the way to the whole through its parts.

Socrates argues that one might already have had the true belief that the sun is the brightest object in the sky, but with the additional recognition that this brightness is what makes it unique and is why it is called 'the sun' one has achieved real *knowledge*—at least according to what some folk claim. To probe this further, Socrates turns to another example: his knowledge of Theaetetus. What makes Theaetetus different from all others such that when Socrates sees him on the street he "knows" him to be Theaetetus and not, for instance, Theodorus? Such a difference is elusive; any particular suggestion (e.g., his distinctive nose, or prominent eyes) probably fits a number of other people, too. So somehow one must take all such possible differences and make each uniquely tied to Theaetetus. This means each individual feature must also be recognized as different from every other person who has a similar feature—*this* nose belongs to Theaetetus and no other, even though similar noses are found on others. It is easy to see how one can get caught up into an endless cycle of making distinctions in order to "know" something. Yet, Socrates says, all of such activity presupposes one already knows what makes Theaetetus unique and so the whole matter is a bit like a blind man advising someone to pick up something he or she is already holding! In essence, then, Theaetetus third definition is "knowledge is true belief *plus a knowledge of differentness*." How does that help? It is absurd to say, as this turns out to do, "Knowledge is true belief plus knowledge."[68]

So it turns out, Socrates contends, that the strongest sense of what *logos* might mean leads to a circular argument: to know a thing is to already know a thing. One cannot know a wagon, or Theaetetus, without already knowing what makes each different from other things. My awareness of these differences is already a part of my awareness of each thing so it can hardly be an 'addition' that supplements the notion of true belief. So what is to be done?

The dialog ends on a dissatisfying note for the reader hoping to gain a dependable definition of "knowledge." Socrates notes that he has merely served as a 'midwife,' helping Theaetetus give birth to certain ideas. Even if at present all that seems to have been birthed is 'empty wind,' still these notions may help him in any future thinking on the subject. Yet if his future thinking about knowledge also proves barren, at least the present experience may have tempered his manner so that he is gentler and more agreeable with his companions because he no longer supposes to know what in fact he does not know[69]—and that is not a bad place to end!

Still, as both his contemporaries and many since have found, Socrates' skill at questioning everything can be quite unsettling. He raises far more questions than he answers—and when his answers come they seem mostly to show how insufficient various ideas and positions are. Like the Skeptics who would come later, he excels at showing problems but not so much their solutions.

---

68 Plato, *Theaetetus,* 208b-210b.
69 Plato, *Theaetetus,* 210b-d.

5

Plato's Belief

In the previous chapter we saw Theaetetus offer his third and most famous definition for knowledge, that it is "true, *justified* belief."[70] This definition added the element of *logos*—the warrant, or reason, that justifies a belief. Yet Socrates raises concerns and the dialog ends with the question about the relation of belief and knowledge still unsettled. Plato's *Phaedo* also considers *logos*. His famous *theory of recollection* argues that all knowledge is *remembered*. The *psyche* acquires knowledge before birth. The introduction of the *psyche* into the world of sensations means a temporary disconnect with this knowledge. Living is a lifelong process of reclaiming knowledge through recollecting it—the process we call *learning*[71]—and specifically learning through dialectics: "when people are asked questions, if they are asked well enough, they answer fully from what they have—and they could not do so unless they possessed already both knowledge (*epistēmē*) and a correct *logos* (*orthos logos*)."[72] Socrates asks, "Can not a person who has knowledge give *logos* to what he knows?"[73] The picture presented is this:

Before birth . . . knowledge   *After birth . . .*   *learning*

The *psyche* has an unobstructed view of reality (the Eternal Forms) and thus *knows*.

The *psyche* has an obstructed view of reality because of sense-perception and thus forgets what it knows.

Dialectics, with its skillful questions, aids recollection.

Thus, dialectics restores. . .
Knowledge + *Logos*

Here *logos* is compatible with knowledge (*epistēmē*), but not necessarily a constituent part of it as the formula "knowledge = true, justified belief" proposes. Knowledge is set alongside *logos*, the latter having the sense of "reason," the ability and action of providing rational explanations and accounts. They seem

---

[70] Plato, *Theaetetus,* 201c-d.

[71] Plato, *Phaedo,* 72e-76a. Cf. Plato, *Meno,* 81-86.

[72] Plato, *Phaedo,* 72e-73b. The phrase "knowledge acquired through learning" translates the noun μάθησις (*mathēsis*). The word "learned" translates μεμαθηκέναι (*memathēkenai,* fr. *manthanō*); see the note below on *Gorgias,* 454c-d.

[73] Plato, *Phaedo,* 76a-b.

equal partners. What Socrates says suggests that knowledge—specifically that flowing from recollection—generates *logos*, an "explanation." But it is unclear if it does so intrinsically, because *logos* is an aspect of *epistēmē*, or because knowledge can, when asked to do so, provide *logos*.

Plato's Masterpiece

It might help us at this point to take a step back and try again to look at the 'big picture.' The birth of Greek philosophical thinking came in its first steps to explain the nature of Nature—to divulge the essence of the way reality *is*. But Plato understands that before reality can be explained we must understand how it is possible for us to know it. His masterpiece, the *Republic*, relates knowing specifically to knowing what is real; in other words, genuine knowledge is about reality—the way things actually *are* and not merely as they *seem to be*. In this context, "knowledge" (*epistēmē*) represents a certainty of one's information that quells doubt and gives rise to a justified confidence such that what one might say about reality can and will be recognized by other knowers as true.

Where, then, does belief (*doxa*) fit?

To answer that we must look at a portion of the *Republic*:

SOCRATES: Would we not be right in calling the thinking of this man, because he *knows*, "knowledge," while the other fellow's thought is mere "belief" (*doxan*), because he only *believes* what is the case?

GLAUCON: Absolutely.

SOCRATES: What if this second fellow argues with us, disputing our conclusion? Can we offer him some soothing solace, while gently persuading him, and without disclosing to him that his thinking is disordered?

GLAUCON: That would certainly be advisable.

SOCRATES: Come, then, and let us figure what we may say to him. Shall we start with the assurance that whatever he does know is most welcome and that we are pleased about his knowing it? But then we would also like to hear from him the answer to this: Does anyone who has knowledge, know *something* or *nothing*? Please, Glaucon, answer on his behalf.

GLAUCON: I shall answer, 'He knows something.'

SOCRATES: Is this something what *is* or *is not*?

GLAUCON: It must be something that *is* for how can something that *is not* be known?

SOCRATES: Are we confident of this conclusion, no matter how many ways we consider it, that what actually *is* can entirely be known, while what *is not* cannot be known?

GLAUCON: We may be sure of it.

SOCRATES: Very well. Now, if there is something somehow of a nature to be both *is* and *is not*, will it not then take a place between these two states of *is* and *is not*?

GLAUCON: Yes. It would be between them.

SOCRATES: So, just as "knowledge" (γνῶσις, *gnosis*) corresponds to what *is*, and "ignorance" (ἀγνωσία, *agnosia*) to what *is not*, then must there also be some state between knowledge and ignorance, one corresponding to the state between *is* and *is not*—if, in fact, such an intermediate state exists?

GLAUCON: Indeed.

SOCRATES: Can we say that "belief" (*doxan*) is something?

GLAUCON: Of course.

SOCRATES: Is "belief" a mental power the same as "knowledge" (ἐπιστήμης, *epistēmēs*), or different?

GLAUCON: Different.

SOCRATES: Then it follows that "belief" (*doxa*) and "knowledge" (*epistēmē*) each depend on different kinds of things and that this difference corresponds to a difference in the mental powers employed.

GLAUCON: Yes, that is the case. [74]

This exchange not only establishes a difference between knowledge and belief, but it now also appears there is a scale with a true 'bottom': ignorance.

The Contrast between "Knowledge" and "Belief"

Socrates, having established the profound difference between ignorance (*agnosia*) and knowledge (*gnosis* or *epistēmē*), introduces the possibility of belief (*doxa*) as existing as an intermediate state. Further probing discussion confirms that knowledge is human thinking's highest faculty, and distinct from belief, which in turn is distinct from ignorance. Belief is, in Socrates' words, "darker than knowledge, but lighter than ignorance"[75]—and situated between them. Yet a little later, Socrates likens the contrast between just knowledge and belief as like that between one who can see and one who is blind![76]

Building on Socrates' metaphor, we can picture the resulting scheme as a kind of parallelism (signified by //) imagined between epistemological states and metaphysical ones:

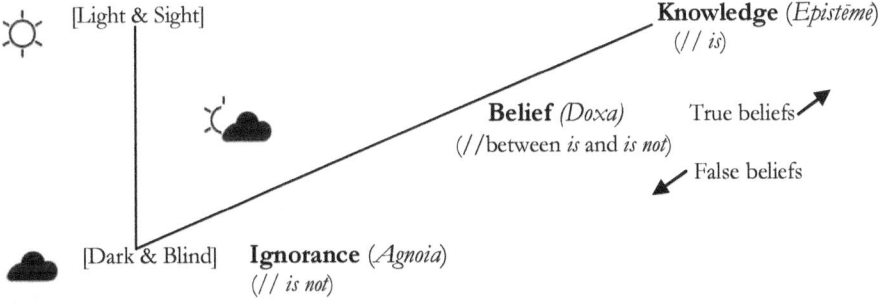

---

[74] Plato's *Republic*, V.476d-477b; cf. through 480a. Key words in Socrates' first remark: "thinking" (διάνοιαν, *dianoian*); "knows," (γιγνώσκοντος, *gignōskontos* (fr. γιγνώσκω, *gignōskō*)) [the second 'g' I silent]; "knowledge" (γνώμην, *gnōmēn*); "belief" (δόξαν, *doxan*); "believes" (δοξάζοντος, *doxazontos* (fr. δοξάζω, (*doxazō*)). The last word, "believes" has the sense of "supposes."

[75] Plato's *Republic*, V.478c-d. In this passage two words for "knowledge"—*epistēmē* and *gnosis*—are used synonymously. From Socrates on, the term *epistēmē* was preferred. The exact difference between *epistēmē* and *gnosis* has been debated.

[76] Plato's *Republic*, VI.484c.

When Socrates is asked for his own view as to what knowledge is he attempts to defer an answer. But then he is pressed on the matter, leading to a brief exchange:

> SOCRATES: Do you think it fair to say one knows something one does not know?
>
> ADEIMANTUS: Of course not, at least not as one "knows" it. But one ought to be willing to say what he "believes," as his belief.
>
> SOCRATES: What?! Have you not noticed that beliefs (*doxas*) apart from knowledge (*epistēmēs*) are reproachful? The best of such are blind—or do you think that those who offer a true belief without understanding are somehow different from those blind folk who just happen to select the right path?[77]

The blindness of *doxa* means that it at best *imagines* or *supposes* what is real—just like a blind person seeking a path. It might be right, correct, and true at times, but there is no certainty that it so. Belief wanders in shadows.

Plato's Pistis (Πίστις)

Yet Plato is interested in exposing more fully the nature of belief and toward that end he considers aspects of it caught better by a different word than *doxa*. The word in question is πίστις (*pistis*), which has as its verb complement πιστεύω (*pisteuō*). The Greek noun *pistis* is most associated with the Christian New Testament where it is given new prominence in a specifically religious context. While the verb *pisteuō* is translated as "believe," the noun *pistis* is regularly rendered as "faith" rather than "belief." The rendering "belief," though, was common in English until the word "faith" was introduced in the 14th century and rapidly replaced "belief" in Bible translations.[78]

In our exploration of the philosophical discussion of the relationship between knowledge and belief *pistis* takes a backseat to *doxa*, but that hardly makes it insignificant. In order to capture a more complete picture of "belief" we need to seriously reckon with this word *pistis* and that requires first of all attaining an appreciation of its range of meaning as well as whatever core sense we might discern. In brief, *pistis* in an active sense can mean:

- Trust
- Confidence or assurance
- Persuasive arguments
- Evidence or proof

Pistis is the kind of noun that can actually express an action like a verb does. When used in an active sense *pistis* signifies *trust* placed in something (whether a person or thing); it is *relational*. This meaning of trust constitutes the foundational sense of *pistis* and, arguably, colors all of its other senses. The word reflects *confidence* and *assurance*, often as the result of persuasion—an idea linking

---

[77] Plato's *Republic*, VI.506b-c. The quote is from 506c. Socrates' opening question uses *eidota* (εἰδότα, fr. οἶδα (*oida*)) for "knows" and *mē oiden* (μὴ οἶδεν, again a form of *oida*) for "does not know." The phrase "without understanding" here is meant to suggest that the kind of true belief that lacks *logos*.

[78] See Bolich, *Honest Belief, Credible Faith*, 14-18.

pistis to both feeling and thinking. Much of our confidence is derived from intellectual persuasion, so the idea of *pistis* as being *persuasive arguments* that reassure and increase confidence is logical enough. The term can refer as well to giving *evidence* and at times it is even pressed to the sense of constituting *proof*.

There is a passive sense as well and thus *pistis* also can mean:

- Trustworthiness
- Honesty

- Credibility
- Loyalty

In a passive sense, the core meaning of *pistis* as trust becomes *trustworthiness* so that both trust given and merit for trust received are key elements of the word's legitimate range of meaning. With respect to trustworthiness, as applied to persons, there exists a sense of their *honesty* or *credibility*; of things it refers to the *credit* they merit. Not unexpectedly, we find *pistis* referring to those people, ideas, and objects that arouse trust and confidence because they seem honest, credible, and reputable. This is why, for example, we hear talk about 'pledges of good faith' or phrases like 'good faith and credit.'

Fundamental Differences between "Knowledge" and "Belief"

In a work earlier than the *Republic*, the *Gorgias*, this word *pistis* is employed by Plato to offer a fundamental distinction between knowing and believing.

> SOCRATES: Now let us review this point. Is there something you would name "acquired knowledge"?
> GORGIAS: Certainly.
> SOCRATES: And also "acquired belief"?
> GORGIAS: Yes.
> SOCRATES: Concerning these two, do you regard "acquired knowledge" and "acquired belief" to be the same, and so also "knowledge" and "belief" (*pistis*), or are they different?
> GORGIAS: In my estimation, Socrates, they are different.
> SOCRATES: Certainly so—and there is a way you can know. For if someone were to ask you, "Gorgias, is there both false belief (*pistis pseudēs*) and true (*alēthēs*)?" I should think you would say, "There is."
> GORGIAS: Yes.
> SOCRATES: Well then, is there also false knowledge (*epistēmē . . . pseudēs*) and true (*alēthēs*)?
> GORGIAS: Absolutely not!
> SOCRATES: Clearly, then, knowledge and belief are not the same.
> GORGIAS: You speak truly.[79]

---

[79] Plato, *Gorgias*, 454c-d. The phrase "acquired knowledge"—i.e., "learning"—translates the verb μεμαθηκέναι (*memathēkenai*, fr. *manthanō*); "acquired belief" translates πεπιστευκέναι (*pepisteukenai*, fr. πιστεύω (*pisteuō*)). Both verbs are perfect active infinitives—verbs that signify a completed action with ongoing effects (perfect tense), and that can function as verbal nouns (infinitive form). The word for "knowledge" here is μάθησις (*mathēsis*), the kind of knowledge acquired through instruction (i.e., education). The verb for "know" in Socrates' 4th remark is γνώσῃ (*gnōsē*, fr. *gignōskō*), with the sense of being sure or proving what is being supposed.

In this exchange Socrates first links "acquired knowledge"—i.e., "learning"—with "knowledge" in the sense of an "education" (using here the Greek word *mathēsis*)—in other words, knowledge acquired through instruction. Is this different from the Greek *epistēmē* ("knowledge") that we have been focusing upon? Note that he shortly after chooses *epistēmē* and contrasts it with *pistis* ("belief") the same way he had before contrasted *mathēsis* with *pistis*. What Socrates is doing, simply, is establishing that knowledge (*epistēmē*) can be acquired, just as belief (*pistis*) can be, but where belief can be either true or false, knowledge is ever only true. This last point is a very fundamental one and points to why knowledge is preferable to belief.

However, the above exchange is part of a larger conversation and what immediately follows is an important working out of the above logic.

> SOCRATES: Yet those who have acquired knowledge, just like those who have acquired belief, continue to be persuaded.
> GORGIAS: That is so.
> SOCRATES: Are you willing, then, that we posit two kinds of persuasion— one yielding belief (*pistin*) without having knowledge, and the other offering knowledge (*epistēmēn*)?
> GORGIAS: Yes, for so it is.[80]

Both knowledge and belief are persuasive, and each produces a sense of conviction and feeling of confidence. But *knowledge takes time*. The persuasion that accompanies belief can be produced in a short period of time. Clearly, this difference between knowledge acquired over time through instruction and belief acquired quickly following persuasive speech is, for Plato, a very consequential one.

Now at this point it would be fair to wonder why Plato's Socrates chooses to use the word *pistis* rather than *doxa*. In the later dialog *Theaetetus*, where a similar discussion about belief and persuasion occurs, Socrates uses *doxa*.[81] If nothing else, this suggests that Plato could at times envision *pistis* and *doxa* as referring to the same kind of "belief," namely, that which produces persuasion.[82] The term *pistis*, with its inherent affinity for the sense of persuasion or conviction, is a perfect choice for "belief" as something acquired.[83]

---

[80] Plato, *Gorgias,* 454e-455a. "Acquired knowledge" here translates μεμαθηκότες (*memathēkotes*, fr. *manthanō*)—i.e., what they know has been learned. The phrase "acquired belief" translates πεπιστευκότες (*pepisteukotes*, fr. πιστεύω (*pisteuō*)). Both of these are pluperfect participles. The phrase "without having knowledge" (ἄνευ τοῦ εἰδέναι, *aneu tou eidenai*) uses the perfect active infinitive of the verb *oida* (οἶδα). In Socrates' 3rd remark, *eidenai* is used synonymously with his preceding use of *epistēmē*.

[81] Plato, *Theaetetus,* 201a-c.

[82] It may be that because persuasion is the lead idea in this portion of the *Gorgias*, that *pistis* is selected over *doxa* because of its linguistic relation to the Greek noun πειθοῦς (*peithous*, "persuasion"), derived from the verb πείθω (*peithō*, "persuade").

[83] Overall, *pistis* is a word used sparingly by Plato, so when it occurs in epistemological connections it merits careful attention.

The first time *pistis* occurs in the *Republic* is shortly before the exchange between Socrates and Adeimantus that we read earlier. They are discussing the Good, something they agree is the highest of all objects of study.[84] There is one thing they think people can agree upon:

> SOCRATES: Isn't it obvious that . . . when it comes to the Good, no one settles for having the mere appearance of it, but all seek the reality itself? Here, in this latter case, the mere belief (*doxan*) that Good appears is dishonorable.
> ADEIMANTUS: This is very much so.
> SOCRATES: The Good, then, is what every *psyche* chases after, and for its sake does all that it does, being driven by the intuition of what the Good *is*, yet simultaneously baffled by the Good's nature, unable to grab hold of it, or even declare a confident belief (*pistei*) about it like the *psyche* can do with other things. . . .[85]

The situation, when we put everything together, looks like this:

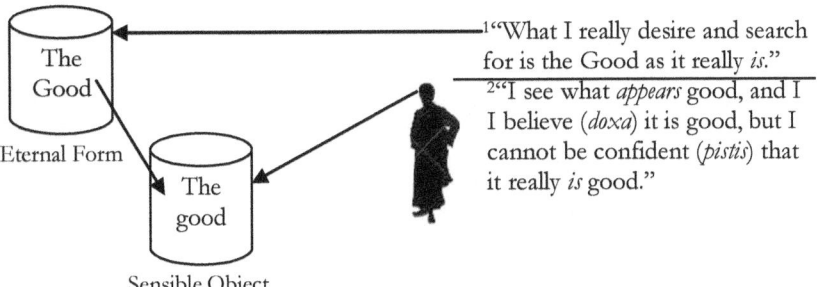

The *psyche* yearns for knowledge of the eternal Intelligible Forms, especially the Good, and mere belief on such an important matter is insufficient. Both *doxa* and *pistis* express the concept of "belief," but with different shades of meaning. In the instance of *doxa* the belief is a judgment or estimate of Good being present, while in the case of *pistis* the idea of belief highlights its inherent confidence—which in this situation is lacking.

The Line Fixed between Knowledge and Belief

The above thinking reinforces the basic Platonic theme that a significant difference between knowledge and belief exists. Socrates, still with the Good in mind, remarks that in the discussion he and his companions are having they refer to both the "Good" (one thing) and the "good" (many things). The eternal Idea, or Form (Good), is unified and real, but gives rise to many imperfect copies (good). While the Form called Good can be *thought* about, it can't be physically *seen*; what we see are the transient and imperfect copies that also bear the name of "good."[86] The Good and the good belong, as it were, to different

84 Plato, *Republic*, VI.505a-d.
85 Plato, *Republic*, VI.505d-e. Here I am translating the form of *pistis* with two words: "confident belief." One might instead construe *pistis* here as expressing "reliance."
86 Plato, *Republic*, VI.507a-c.

realms. The eternal Idea that can be thought about exists in an Intelligible realm (i.e., one open to the mind). The things we call good that we can see belong to the Sensible world (i.e., the world perceived by the senses). This observation, that there is a difference in how the human mind operates toward each, leads Socrates to work out what such a difference means.

Here is his basic picture:

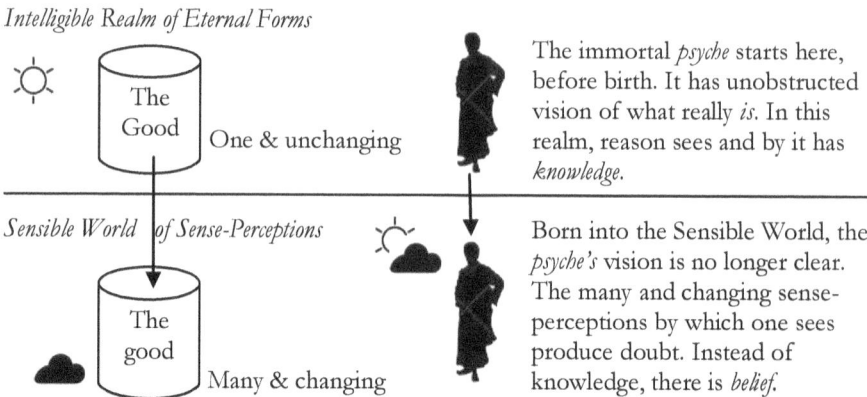

Intelligible Realm of Eternal Forms

The Good — One & unchanging

The immortal *psyche* starts here, before birth. It has unobstructed vision of what really *is*. In this realm, reason sees and by it has *knowledge*.

Sensible World of Sense-Perceptions

The good — Many & changing

Born into the Sensible World, the *psyche's* vision is no longer clear. The many and changing sense-perceptions by which one sees produce doubt. Instead of knowledge, there is *belief*.

Plato's Socrates begins by noting that we rely on vision to see visible things (e.g., the visible things we call "good"). Through sense-perception we engage the Sensible world. Though all human senses matter, vision is extolled above the rest. But it is highly dependent on something external to itself: light. The sun provides this light. Obviously the sun is not vision, but without its light there is no seeing of visible objects. For Socrates this suggests an analogy: the relation of the sun in the Sensible world to vision and visible objects is like the relation of Good in the Intelligible realm to the mind with its understanding of invisible but intelligible things.[87]

The organ of vision in the Sensible world is the eye; the organ of sight in the Intelligible realm is the *psyche*. This leads Socrates to remark:

> Take what we have said about the eyes with reference to the *psyche*: when the *psyche* fixes upon what is illuminated by truth and what is real, it apprehends, and knows, and appears to possess understanding. But when it fixes upon what is mingled with darkness, on what comes into being and then passes away, it believes and its sight is dimmed; it bounces among beliefs (*doxas*) and appears to have no understanding.[88]

---

[87] Plato, *Republic*, VI.507c–508e. The key term is νοῦς (*nous*), "mind" as mental acts of perception and thinking. It can, depending on context, be translated "intellect," or "intelligence," or "understanding."

[88] Plato, *Republic*, VI.508d. The word translated "apprehends" is ἐνόησεν (*enoēsen*, fr. νοέω (*noeō*)); "knows" translates ἔγνω (*egnō*, fr. γιγνώσκω, (*gignōsko*)); "understanding" translates νοῦν (*noūn*, fr. νοῦς (*nous*) in both places. The word "believes" translates δοξάζει (*doxazei*, fr. *doxazō*).

The *psyche* when oriented to the Intelligible achieves knowledge; when fixed in its gaze on the Sensible world it tosses and turns from one belief to another.

This line of thinking then leads Socrates to declare, "The reality providing truth to things known and yielding power to those who know is the Idea of Good. And it must be held responsible for the existence of both knowledge and truth, even as it is itself intended to be known."[89] The eternal Idea, the Form called Good, makes knowledge and truth possible, and is their proper object. It is a remarkable declaration, and one that in Platonic thinking makes epistemology and ethics inseparable.

The Good is supreme, above knowledge and truth, as glorious as each is. Still elaborating his analogy, Socrates remarks that just as the sun provides light for vision it also is the source responsible for bringing forth, growing, and nourishing the things of the Sensible world. In a similar manner, the Good makes real the objects that can be known in the Intelligible realm. However, just as the sun causes generation but is not itself "generation," so Good causes knowledge and truth to come into being without itself being "being."[90]

Urged to complete his analogy, Socrates then contrasts the Sensible world ruled by the sun with the Intelligible world ruled by the Good by establishing his famous divided line with its stages of cognition. It looks like this:

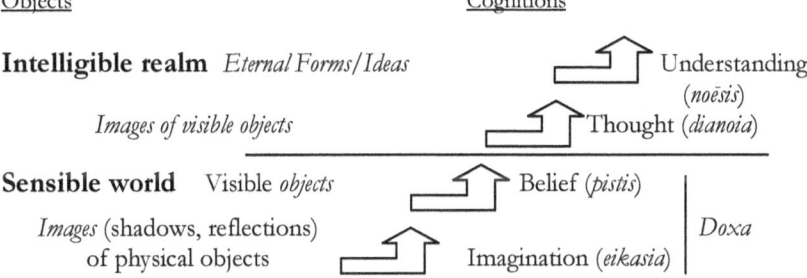

But before we hear what Socrates actually says, a word of caution seems in order. Though the notion of 'stages' might suggest a kind of continuum where one stage blends into the next (especially since these are pictured in an ascending order, rising from the least to the best), we probably do better to think of 'steps.' Each is distinct and qualitatively different from the others. One ascends by stepping up. This sense of the stages as discrete steps is in harmony with the sharpness of the line drawn between the Sensible and Intelligible.

Socrates describes the line as dividing the Sensible world from the Intelligible realm into two unequal sections. Each of these, in turn, is itself subdivided

---

[89] Plato, *Republic*, VI.508e. The phrase "things known" translates γιγνωσκομένοις (*gignōskomenois*), and "those who know" translates γιγνώσκοντι (*gignōskonti*); both from *gignōsko*. "Knowledge" translates ἐπιστήμης (fr. *epistēmē*); "to be known" translates γιγνωσκομένης (*gignōskomenēs*, fr. *gignōsko*).

[90] Plato, *Republic*, VI.509a-b. The Greek word behind "generation" is γένεσιν (*genesin*, fr. γένεσις (*genesis*)), while that for "being" is οὐσίας (*ousias*, fr. οὐσία (*ousia*)). We cannot here examine this famous set of remarks further.

49

into separate segments. All of these are arranged in accord with their relative degree of visibility—i.e., how clear they are as we engage them. If these are thought of as ascending steps, then the bottom two are in the Sensible world and the remaining ones—above the line—belong to the Intelligible realm. The first step in the Sensible world is the cognition of images such as the shadows or reflections that physical objects cast. Above it is the cognition of the physical objects themselves through sense-perception. We can picture this by blending our two previous illustrations:

Sensible World of Sense-Perceptions

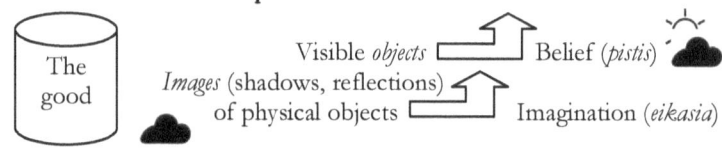

Many & changing

The Sensible world is one of darkness or, at best, shadows. No wonder, then, that *doxa* is a taking up of an *uncertain* position, one limited in confidence (*pistis*).

At this point Socrates asks, "Would you be willing to affirm that, with respect to what is truth and what is not, the division proportionally expresses the difference like this: as a believed object is to a known one, so is the likeness of a thing to the thing itself?"[91] In other words, the shadow or reflection—the image or likeness of an object in the Sensible world—is not the truth compared to the reality of the thing itself. To get at the reality of the thing itself requires us to step higher.

Having differentiated the segments of the Sensible world, Socrates next turns to the Intelligible realm. It also has two parts. Again we can combine earlier images:

Intelligible Realm of Eternal Forms

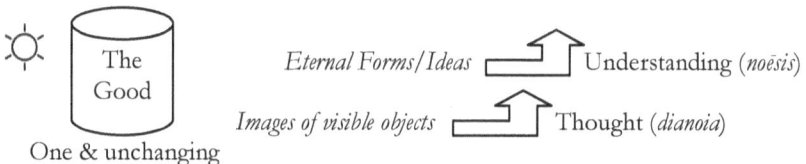

One & unchanging

In this realm of light and clear vision, the lower step is where the *psyche* considers the physical objects of the Sensible world as mere images of their higher, truer, more real eternal Forms. The mental operation of the *psyche* is reasoning, but reasoning that proceeds from certain assumptions to their logical conclusions. Socrates illustrates this by appealing to mathematics. In geometry, for

---

91 Plato, *Republic*, VI.509c-510a. Socrates' question is at 510a. The phrase translated "believed object" is δοξαστόν (*doxaston*, fr. δοξαστός (*doxatos*), an adjective derived from *doxa*); the phrase rendered as "known one" is γνωστόν (*gnoston*, fr. γνωστός (*gnostos*), an adjective). The translation intends to capture the sense of these terms as adjectives.

example, certain angles and shapes are taken as "givens"—as starting-points beyond debate. From these initial premises mathematical problems are logically pursued to yield predictable conclusions. The thinker is not interested in a particular physical shape *per se*, but the Form behind it. The highest step of cognition finally dispenses with dependence on images. It also uses reason, initially forming hypotheses and then using the Socratic process of dialectic to investigate and test in order to get at the truth itself—the *real* thing—to reach the Idea (Form) that is the First Principle itself. From there the mind proceeds to operate using the Ideas themselves to reason and derive conclusions.[92]

Socrates sums up the discussion of the divided line as follows:

> So there are four portions of our line corresponding to four conditions in the *psyche*. The mind's understanding is the highest; thought occupies the second step; the third is given to belief; and the last is mere imaging. Arrange these in ascending order and proportion according to their degree of clarity corresponding to the degree their respective objects are real and fit truth.[93]

This portion of the *Republic* is justly renowned as especially important for understanding Plato's epistemology. In a few lines it sets forth a basic division that not only separates ostensible kinds of knowing, but arranges them according to clarity and corresponding trustworthiness.

Socrates' summary of the line and stages is briefly remembered in the third instance of the term *pistis* in the *Republic*. Socrates says:

> It will be useful, then, to retain what we previously set out, that the foremost part we call "knowledge" (*epistēmēn*), the second we name "thought" (*dianoian*), the third we term "belief" (*pistin*), and forth we name "imaging" (*eikasian*).[94]

We must note immediately that the "knowledge" (*epistēmē*) named here is equivalent to the "mind's understanding" (*noēsis*) that was used the first time these four things were named. The other three terms remain the same.

Socrates immediately adds:

> "Belief" (*pistin*) and "imaging" should be understood together, as "wider belief" (*doxan*); and "knowledge" and "thought" together as "intellection." Whereas belief (*doxan*), widely construed, concerns things *becoming*, intellection concerns *being*. In the same way that *being* is to *becoming*, even so is intel-

---

92 Plato, *Republic*, VI.510b-511d.
93 Plato, *Republic*, VI.511d-e. "Belief" here is a form of the Greek *pistis*. The phrase "mind's understanding" translates νόησιν (*noēsin*, fr. νόησις (*noesis*)). "Thought" translates διάνοιαν (*dianoian*, fr. διάνοιας (*dianoias*), which can carry the meaning of having a notion (i.e., like an opinion or belief), and thus sits naturally between "understanding" and "belief." It is translated by some as "understanding," as in the discerning of an intention or purpose or meaning of something. But "thought"—a more general term—seems to better fit the sense here, especially since it follows *noesis*, a better term to express the kind of understanding that is often conceived of as "knowledge." Finally, "imaging" translates εἰκασίαν (*eikasian*, fr. εἰκασία (*eikasià*)), a noun denoting the likeness or representation of something.
94 Plato, *Republic*, VII.533e-534a.

51

lection to belief (*doxan*). The same comparative proportionality continues, in that as intellection is to belief, so is knowledge (*epistēmēn*) to belief (*pistin*), and thought to imaging.[95]

I have distinguished "belief" here as simply 'belief' and as 'wider belief' in order to better convey the difference drawn by Plato between *pistis* and *doxa*.

Knowledge, Belief & Practice

The final occurrence of *pistis* occurs in the last book of the *Republic*. Socrates points out that for all of the various crafts people engage in there are three kinds of 'art' or 'skill' involved: producing, using, and imitating (i.e., in the sense of replicating or reproducing it). Socrates observes that not only with respect to crafts, but also for living beings and actions, it is *use* that determines how goodness, beauty, and correctness are judged.[96] This then leads to the following:

> SOCRATES: Of necessity, then, the user is the person who has the most experience and can inform the maker about the good and bad aspects of something based on its actual use. For instance, a flute-player reports to the flute-maker which flutes perform well and enjoins the flute-maker as to what kind of flute to produce, which the flute-maker will do.
>
> GLAUCON: You are right, of course.
>
> SOCRATES: Then, is it not the user who *knows* (*eidōs*) that provides useful feedback as to which flutes perform well and which poorly, and the flute-maker *believes* (*pisteuōn*) the user and makes them accordingly?
>
> GLAUCON: Yes.
>
> SOCRATES: Thereby the flute-maker has correct belief (*pistin*) concerning the flutes being well-made or poorly made, but it is still the one who uses the flutes who has knowledge (*epistēmēn*).
>
> GLAUCON: Quite so.
>
> SOCRATES: But what about the person who by imitation replicates a thing? Does such a person have knowledge (*epistēmēn*) from use whether what is being portrayed is or is not beautiful and correct? Does the imitator have correct belief (*doxan*) about such replicas merely because of being compelled to associate with the one who knows (*eidōti*) in order to make replicas?
>
> GLAUCON: Neither is the case.
>
> SOCRATES: So an imitator, concerning whether a replica is well or poorly done, will neither *know* (*eisetai*) nor correctly *believe* (*doxasei*).[97]

---

[95] Plato, *Republic*, VII.534a.

[96] Plato, *Republic*, X.601d. The Greek word translated as "art" or "skill" is τέχνας (*technas*, fr. τέχνη (*technē*)), a word of some importance in philosophical discussions.

[97] Plato, *Republic*, X.601d-602a. The first "knows" translates εἰδώς (*eidōs*, fr. οἶδα (*oida*)); "believes" translates πιστεύων (*pisteuōn*, fr. πιστεύω (*pisteuō*), the verb counterpart to the noun *pistis*); "correct belief" translates πίστιν ὀρθὴν (*pistin orthēn*)) the first time and (*doxan orthēn*) the second. The "knows" in Socrates' fourth comment translates εἰδότι (*eidōti*), and like the final "knows," which translates εἴσεται (*eisetai*), comes from οἶδα (*oida*). The final "believes" translates δοξάσει (*doxasei*), which could also be rendered here as "correct belief." The translator's choice is between render-

The one who knows is the one who uses a thing, not the maker of it, nor the imitator of it. The maker occupies the higher end of the belief stages—*pistis*—while the imitator is confined to the shadows of a wider *doxa*. Only the user has knowledge—and it should guide the maker's belief.

This is a point I have not yet highlighted but one well worth reflecting on for a moment. Rather than just consider the question whether belief might ever become knowledge—in Platonic terms, a bottom-up perspective—Plato at times focuses on a top-down perspective where knowledge is not only superior to belief but also meant to guide it. The goal remains knowledge itself, but the knowledge someone else possesses can guide the belief of one who does not yet possess knowledge. This is an ultimate goal of learning through dialectics.

In an interesting passage in the dialog *Meno*, Socrates raises the point that from a practical standpoint, at least in many matters, there may not be any advantage to possessing knowledge over belief, provided the belief is "true." For example, suppose one wants to know the way to a certain destination. Two people present themselves as guides. One has actually been to the place and "knows" the way there; the other has not been there, but possesses a "true belief" about how to reach the place. In such a case, what difference does it make whether one knows or believes? In either case the traveler who follows directions will get to the destination.[98]

Why then, wonders Meno, pursue knowledge? Socrates points to the quality decisive for knowledge: *certainty*. In this case, what he has in mind is something *securely fastened* so that it sticks around. It is *certain* in that it is *secure*. True beliefs, he points out, are wonderful for as long as they endure; but they don't stick around unless to them is added grounds that transform them into knowledge.

We might picture the situation like this:

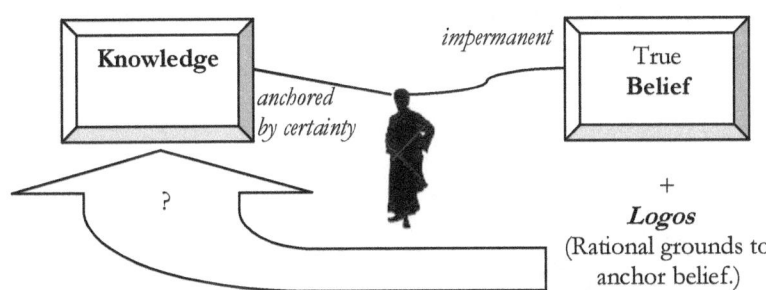

In this remark Socrates seems to endorse Theaetetus' third definition, but Socrates being who he is cannot resist adding a moment later, "Of course, I do

ing the line so that two verb forms appear, or mix a verb form with a noun because "correct" (*ortha*) is an adjective.

[98] Plato, *Meno*, 97a-c. The same Greek words are in play: *doxan* (δόξαν) for "right belief" (this time being modified by *orthēn* (ὀρθὴν), "right" or "correct," rather than *alēthē* (ἀληθῆ), "true'; and, *epistēmēn* (ἐπιστήμην), for "knowledge."

not know this; I am only making a conjecture. On the other hand, that 'right belief' is other than 'knowledge' is an altogether different matter; I am not guessing about that! If I am to claim I 'know' anything—and I don't suppose that about much—this is one such matter."[99] And so we are left with the *possibility* that belief might occasionally be knowledge, but no certainty on the matter.

Much like a Kansas girl in Oz, Plato's searcher after knowledge attempts to peek behind the curtain to find the wizard pulling his ropes and levers. In his effort to find certainty and stability he opts to posit eternal Forms that the truly wise can discern. But his effort comes at a cost; the Sensible world cannot be ultimately trusted. This inherent doubt about the first and most immediate part of human experience always has met with some resistance. Many respond by asking, If we cannot trust our senses, what can we trust? Plato's answer of reason, though often endorsed, still must explain how reason then relates to sense-perception. Plato's answer, most famously set out in the *Republic*, satisfies some, but for many others just generates new questions.

Indeed, Plato's Socrates continues to raise more questions than offer secure answers. Plato himself seems to have more confidence in finding answers than his mentor, but as mentioned earlier, distinguishing Plato's positions from any he represents as his teacher's remains an uncertain proposition. The overall impression one receives from both of them is that neither ever stops stretching toward knowledge. They both seem to possess the kind of restless mind that attracts people to pursue philosophy, where a love of wisdom is paired with a willingness to tolerate ambiguity and which chooses to stay open to possibilities. Although Plato offers a way to conceive of both knowledge and belief that relates them to one another—even to the point where in some instances belief might also be knowledge—he never quite fully assures us that such happens. So we must continue to explore, looking next to one of Plato's contemporaries.

---

[99] Plato, *Meno,* 98a-b. What secures true belief is *logismō* (λογισμῷ, from λογισμός), an account or reason why for believing. The quote is from 98b, where again we have "right belief" (*ortha doxa*) and "knowledge" (*epistēmē*) using familiar words.

6

Isocrates's Dissent

No philosopher is ever universally adored or endorsed by either peers or the public—and people today generally remain willfully oblivious to philosophical debates. But in ancient Greece there was a livelier interest in what wise men were saying and their ideas were taken seriously. Not infrequently the ideas propounded led not merely to debate, but controversy and censure. For example, Protagoras' ideas apparently landed him in enough trouble to drive him to seek a voluntary exile, while Socrates was condemned to die for his 'corrupting' influence. Plato is no exception to the rule. Though his ideas exercised influence, both in his own time and since there have been fierce critics.

One of these critics is the rhetorician Isocrates (436-388 B.C.E.), a contemporary of Plato. The pair knew one another, of course. Isocrates had at one time been a follower of Socrates, though he also studied under Gorgias of Leontini—the expert rhetorician we met in the previous chapter dialoging with Socrates. Plato's Socrates, in the dialog *Phaedrus*, remarks that Isocrates, then but a young man, is a gifted writer of speeches and a person of good character, who loves wisdom and—hopefully—will one day turn his attention to even higher things.[100] What Isocrates thought of this rather left-handed praise is unknown. However, Isocrates and Plato appear to have been at least on cordial grounds personally, with Plato hosting Isocrates for conversation.[101]

Plato and Isocrates were professional rivals, each leading a school, and Isocrates seems to have been the more popular figure with a larger following. To what, if any, extent this disparity in acclaim affected their relationship can only be speculated about. It is clear they had some sharp differences. They split on various matters not only of thought but of practice. For example, Isocrates accepted a small fee for his services while Plato refused the same—and criticized Isocrates for doing so.[102] We know from attention that Isocrates gave to the matter of collecting a fee—a practice he condemns in the Sophists—that

---

[100] Plato, *Phaedrus*, 279a.

[101] Diogenes Laertius, *Lives of Eminent Philosophers: Plato*, III.3 [*Plato*, 2] states Isocrates was a few years older than Plato. In III.8 [*Plato*, 9] he says the pair were friends and cites an older source that Plato entertained Isocrates at a country estate. Note: references are to Greek book and section. Some English translations use a slightly different system [indicated in brackets].

[102] Riginos, *Platonica*, 118 (anecdote 74).

the topic was a sore subject for him. He goes to great pains to distinguish what he does in accepting payment from what others around him were doing.

Isocrates on "Philosophy"

In their lifetimes, the labels 'philosopher' and 'Sophist' were pitted against each other, despite both groups professing a love of wisdom. As we saw in chapter 3, the Sophist had been, in Protagoras' generation, a professional teacher of how to speak persuasively, live well, and develop good character. The art of persuasive speech was central to their enterprise, but the other goals mattered, too. But in Isocrates' lifetime the Sophists were to become increasingly associated with clever but vain speech for personal gain. Socrates wants to displace such speech with the probing question-and-answer process of dialectics. Both Plato and Isocrates oppose the Sophists and both disdain any application of the label to themselves—a label each was liable to because of their own use of oratory and rhetorical devices in their writings. Indeed, there are indications Isocrates sees in Plato a kind of Sophist![103]

Both Isocrates and Plato style themselves 'philosophers,' though they mean very different things by the title. Plato's sense of philosophy was an innovation at the time, though his idea of a philosopher eventually prevailed. He prioritized the individual pursuit of wisdom and the private search for knowledge in ways Isocrates found objectionable. For Isocrates the term "philosophy" refers to the general study and education by which one cares for the *psyche* and inculcates culture; a "philosopher" is a teacher, particularly of the art of persuasive speaking for the public good.[104] At the age of 82, in offering a defense of himself, he addresses what he means by the words "wisdom" (*sophias*) and "philosophy" (*philosophias*), the latter being a term, he contends, much misused by some.[105]

> Now my view is simple enough to understand. Given that it is not in human nature to have knowledge such that we can *know* what is to be done or said, it follows that the one who is wise is the person who by *belief* in actual practice aims for and typically hits the best target in most matters. So philosophers are those persons who most diligently apply themselves to those studies by which they will most quickly acquire such wisdom.[106]

This understanding of the philosophic enterprise is foundational to Isocrates' epistemology, which is interested in *practical* reason rather than *theoretical*.

---

[103] See, for example, Isocrates, *Helen,* 1-5, where both Protagoras (by name) and Plato (by implication), among others, are criticized.

[104] Although Plato's sense of philosophy prevailed among philosophers, Isocrates' sense of it remains very much alive in fields like educational philosophy.

[105] Isocrates, *Antidosis,* 270.

[106] Isocrates, *Antidosis,* 271. The word translated "knowledge" is our familiar term ἐπιστήμην (*epistēmēn,* fr. *epistēmē*); "know" translates εἰδεῖμεν (*eideimen,* fr. οἶδα (*oida*)); "belief" renders δόξαις (*doxais,* fr. *doxa*). Cf. *Antidosis,* 272 for Isocrates' awareness of the novelty of his own understanding of 'philosophy' and 'philosopher.' The "wisdom" is practical in nature (*phronēsis*). Again, I have used italics to provide my own emphasis to highlight a distinction.

As we will see, the image of taking aim at a target is a fundamental one for Isocrates—and easily illustrated:

Belief is aiming for—and
usually hitting—a target.

As this illustration indicates, Isocrates sets out what he sees as a modest, practical, and attainable epistemological goal.

Isocrates' Critique—and Answer

We should not find it hard to imagine that part of Isocrates' appeal to many of his fellow citizens was his shared dislike with them of pointless debates by 'professionals' that seemed designed to feed the ego of the speaker and line his pockets with money. Isocrates seems also (doubtlessly like many fairly well-educated people of his day) to disdain academic hair-splitting. He proclaims to side with the ordinary, nonprofessional thinker, who listens to public debates and watches the debaters, and then draws his or her own conclusions about their value. Isocrates writes:

> When, accordingly, ordinary individuals add up everything, observing that those who 'teach wisdom' and 'provide bliss' themselves lack much and receive little from those they instruct, that they are on guard against contradictions in words while unseeing of the same in deeds, and, in addition, that they feign to know the future but concerning right now they are unable to say anything relevant or provide any counsel, but that, in great contrast, those who actively assert their beliefs (*doxais*) are more consistent and more successful than those who loudly announce their knowledge (*epistēmēn*), then I think these folk have good cause for judging as idle and frivolous these teachers' pursuits and as not being at all the proper care of the *psyche*.[107]

In another place he takes a similar stance against such Sophists, but adds his remedy:

---

[107] Isocrates, *Against the Sophists*, 7-8. The word "belief" translates δόξαις (*doxais*, fr. doxa). I have rendered χρωμένους (*chrōmenous*, fr. χράω (*chraō*)) as "actively asserts" to highlight its contrast with ἐπαγγελλομένους (*epangellomenous*, fr. ἐπαγγέλλω (*epangellō*)), "loudly announces." The former is authoritative in action while the latter is just a public show.

All the same, these fellows have clearly exhibited that it is easy, on any matter set before them, to artfully construct a false *logos*, yet they continue to waste time doing so! They ought to give up this hair-splitting nonsense, which pretends to convince by clever words but which long since has been convincingly refuted by their deeds. They would be better pursuing truth and the practice of those matters about being a citizen, and training their students to gain experience in such, all while pondering how much better it is to capably *believe* (*doxazein*) useful things than to exactly *know* (*epistasthai*) useless ones, and to be a little better in important matters than far better in the many small, useless things of life.[108]

Deeds, not speeches, define a person—and training others in righteous living means encouraging the acquisition of useful beliefs.

As all three of our excerpts have shown, Isocrates offers a far different contrast between knowledge and belief than Socrates and Plato. Isocrates argues for the benefit of *doxa*—taking up a position—because *epistēmē* is out of reach, or unnecessary, or impractical. We need to see why he reasons so.

Belief—The Natural Response to Life's Uncertainties

To understand Isocrates' championing of *doxa* we have to remember his conviction about what philosophy aims to do. Its purpose is to help a person master culture, including speaking well, in order to be a useful, productive citizen who contributes to the well-being of the community. Philosophy has a pragmatic aim of promoting practical wisdom. It is, in a very important sense, about acquiring an education in being a good person who is a good citizen. For him, private life always has public service in mind.

But consider the nature of life as a citizen, especially in a vigorous democracy. One constantly encounters diverse viewpoints—competing views about what is the best direction for the State to steer its course. Life in the community is not one well-served by navel-staring while contemplating esoteric truths about eternal Ideas. It is about entering into the practical moment-by-moment, day-by-day fray of working and living alongside others who like oneself struggle to do their best to get by and help the world be a little bit better place for their efforts. In such a life belief (*doxa*) is inescapable, omnipresent, and valuable.

If the core sense of *doxa* is taking up a position, which we can call "belief," we must remember that any taking of a position reflects a decision, and so words like "opinion," "supposition," "conjecture," or "judgment" are also popular choices to render *doxa* into English. Some sense of each of these other choices must inform our sense of what Isocrates means by *doxa*. What he desires is an honest reckoning for what people actually do as they meet what con-

---

[108] Isocrates, *Helen*, 4-5. The phrase "clever words" translates λόγοις (*logois*). I have rendered it thus to better fit the preceding use of *logos* and convey that the Sophists use the same process in words and reasoning alike to form their clever but empty speeches. The word "believe" translates δοξάζειν (*doxazein*, fr. δοξάζω (*doxazō*)). The word "knows" renders ἐπίστασθαι (*epistasthai*, fr. ἐπίσταμαι (*epistamai*)), a kind of knowing especially associated with knowing how to do something.

temporary psychologists call 'ill-defined problems' or problems possessing 'fuzzy boundaries'—i.e., problems characterized by uncertainty. If we are honest, the majority of life problems are such, and all of the more important ones— such as whom to spend one's life with, or what do to make a living, or where life's best meaning resides—are problems with more than one possible solution.

The *real* world, in other words, is a messy and uncertain one, a world where knowledge may be coveted—because who does not want truth and certainty?— but one where knowledge cannot be had for most things, including the critically important ones. Isocrates accordingly thinks the most appropriate course for epistemology is one that proves practical for everyday living. He finds his inspiration in the realm of the so-called *stochastic* arts. Such arts include things like navigating a ship, practicing medicine—or running a country. These are all arts of the imprecise, where conjecture rather than certainty prevails, and *doxa* reigns. Something stochastic has inherent in it an element of uncertainty so that the best one can do is deal with probabilities. One makes a best guess as to what will work. Like an archer taking aim at a distant target, trying to calculate distance, wind, and other variables, the most one can do is sight well, sigh, and release the arrow. It may not hit the bullseye, but most of the time a close placement suffices anyway.

In short, Isocrates is satisfied with the kind of outcome illustrated here:

The target is hard to hit as distance, wind, and other factors all must be judged. The archer takes aim as best he or she can and lets fly the arrow. A 'good enough' outcome is hitting the target, even if not a bullseye.

Isocrates describes the situation this way and offers his advice:

> Those who are intelligent, with respect to those things they *know*, do not need counsel (for it would be overly careful), but instead act as those who do know; but where they do take counsel, they ought not to hold that they already know what the result will be, but actively assert their *belief* though they admittedly are unknowing what might come about.[109]

It may be hard for some people to not view the advice as plain common sense; if you know what to do, do it, and if not, get sound advice instead of pretending to be a know-it-all. If this is, in fact, 'common sense,' Isocrates has no quarrel with it at all. He sees *doxa* as that practical endeavor by which people,

---

[109] Isocrates, *On the Peace*, 8. The first "know" translates ἴσασι (*isasi*, fr. οἶδα (*oida*)); the second renders ἐγνώκασι (*egnōkasi*); the third translates εἰδέναι (*eidenai*, fr. οἶδα). "Belief" renders δόξῃ (*doxē*, fr. *doxa*). The word "unknowing" translates the verb ἀγνοοῦντας (*agnoountas*, fr. ἀγνοέω (*agnoeō*)), an addition made to the Greek text later), related to our English noun "agnostic."

when not possessing knowledge upon which to act with certitude, must simply form the best belief they can (preferably in consultation with others). In short, Isocrates *prescribes* what many merely *describe*—the human tendency to rely on beliefs to pursue whatever seems the most immediately expedient course of action. As this practice generally gets people by, they persist in it. And why not? It seems to him that when backed up by sound, thoughtful beliefs, forthright assertions and action overcome the uncertainty of not knowing and provide a way forward.

Of course, folk vary in how well they form sound, actionable positions. Some do well in forming beliefs that advantage themselves and others, while some do poorly. Isocrates, a little later in the same work we just read, remarks:

> The situation looks like this. It seems to me that while everyone sets their heart on their own advantage and wants to have more than others, they do not *know* the manner of practice that brings such results, but they take up different *beliefs*—with some having suitable beliefs capable of hitting the mark, and others completely missing their target.[110]

This does not mean that some people are always smart in their beliefs and others hopelessly stupid. In another place Isocrates pointedly comments, "Those who are 'wise' occasionally miss the practical course to take, whereas occasionally some nobody who is generally looked down upon hits the target as to how to proceed and is judged to have given the best counsel."[111]

In light of the above information we can slightly alter our picture.

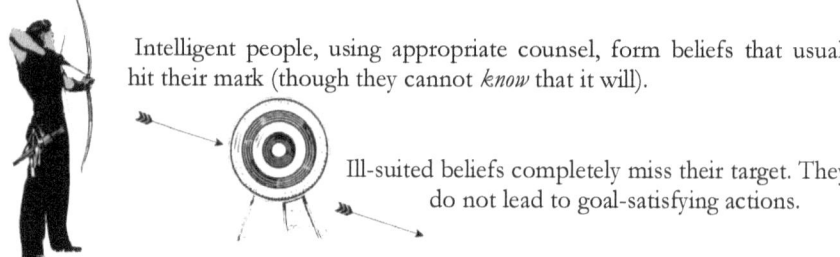

Intelligent people, using appropriate counsel, form beliefs that usually hit their mark (though they cannot *know* that it will).

Ill-suited beliefs completely miss their target. They do not lead to goal-satisfying actions.

In either case, a person uses belief *as if* it were knowledge, proceeding with confidence and taking actions. Beliefs are proved by their outcomes, with well-suited beliefs typically (but without guarantee and so not always) hitting their target.

Isocrates is mindful of the difficulties posed by *doxa* and proposes that rather than either pretend to a knowledge one does not possess or throw one's hands up in despair, a thoughtful person instead does the best he or she can and lives with the result. However, he also feels that the odds of being correct can be strengthened. He takes a stance between the Sophists like Protagoras and the

---

[110] Isocrates, *On the Peace*, 28. The word rendered "know" is εἰδέναι (*eidenai*, fr. *oida*); the word translated "beliefs" is δόξαις (*doxais*, fr. *doxa*).
[111] Isocrates, *Panathenaicus*, 248.

school of Plato. For him the key again can be found in stochastic arts like politics or navigation, where a course and its outcomes can and should be carefully plotted, though they never can be predicted with certainty.

In navigating life, beliefs should be plotted carefully,
like sailors steering a ship by the north star.

Thus for Isocrates the epistemological goal changes from a generally unreachable outcome (knowledge) to a more practical aim (well-considered belief).

In a letter written when he was 80 years old, Isocrates recounts what he has spent his career teaching, which he also thinks appropriate counsel for his letter's recipients:

> My normal practice is to tell those following this philosophy that the first thing to hearken to is this: the object of what ought to be accomplished by a discourse in whole and by its parts. When we find this and have precisely examined it, I say we should seek the shape through which we can bring to completion the end we have purposed. Now while I point out this for speech-making, it is really a rudimentary principle for all things, and that includes your own actions. Nothing can be intelligently achieved unless with foresight you first fully think through and deliberate how to spend the time you have left, and the kind of life you propose to lead with the reputation you are reaching for, and which honors really matter to you—those freely given by your peers or those involuntarily wrested from them. After you have marked off the general shape of your life, then you should reflect upon each day-by-day part with its actions to see how they will contribute to your original plan. And if in this way you search and philosophize, then you will take aim by your *psyche* at the target advantageous to you and you will be more likely to hit your mark. But if you lack such a plan, instead wandering haphazardly in your actions, then you will surely miss your mark in many things.[112]

In other words, Isocrates thinks that not merely in the crafting of a speech but in the shaping of a life should a person pursue a thoughtful and purposeful course of action. There are no guarantees, but this is the manner by which one most often hits whatever target in life is being aimed at.

---

[112] Isocrates, *To the Children of Jason*, 8-10.

This sentiment is underscored in a letter he writes to the son of Philip of Macedon, the young man remembered by us as Alexander the Great. Pleased to learn that Alexander has decided to study rhetoric, Isocrates tells him:

> Through this course you will in the present be likely to form suitable beliefs (*doxazein*) concerning things to come and so enjoin your subjects with no lack of intelligence about what each group should do, knowing (*epistēsei*) how to correctly judge (*orthōs krinein*) concerning what is noble and just—and what is opposite these things—and as well reward and punish each group as it is proper.[113]

The key to ruling well—to in effect come to *know* what is right to do—is to dedicate oneself beforehand to forming that education and set of beliefs conducive to sound rule.

Concluding Note

Modern philosophy and contemporary psychology increasingly have come to devote attention to stochastic situations. Ill-defined problems with all their uncertainty are common and we all must acquire adaptive skills to handle both their uncertainty and our imprecision in responding to them. Isocrates seizes upon the very quality of belief that so many other thinkers find disquieting—its variability—and sees in it *adaptiveness*.

Isocrates' dissent from Plato often is overlooked in philosophical examinations of the relation of knowledge to belief. Perhaps that is because his conception of philosophy lost, while Plato and his heirs came to be seen as the 'real philosophers.' Nevertheless, Isocrates' basic perspective has remained a popular enough alternative among the masses. Moreover, it bears some resemblance to a distinctively American approach called Pragmatism.

Yet from the standpoint of philosophy in the way it has come to be understood, Isocrates' approach is too limited. Sandwiched between Socrates and Aristotle, while vying with Plato, Isocrates's epistemology looks so simple as to be simplistic—or at least underdeveloped. What he had to say on the matters of knowledge, belief, and their relation was soon overshadowed by the giant whose name is Aristotle.

---

[113] Isocrates, *To Alexander,* 4.

7

Aristotle's Spectrum

Isocrates was hardly the only one to find Plato and his mentor unsatisfying. There is little wonder that so many Greeks found Plato's Socrates an irritant. His dialectical process seems to stir up many more questions than it elicits satisfying answers. Plato may advance arguments about how we can know, but his path to Eternal Forms seems obscure to many people, who prefer what they see as the more down-to-earth perspective of Isocrates. Yet Isocrates' reliance on a stochastic approach is shown by Plato to have its problems, too,[114] and for many the notion that in most things the *best* we can hope for is belief rather than knowledge remains unsettling. So by the middle of the 4th century B.C.E. there existed a number of distinctive ideas about knowledge that concerned how belief may or may not figure into how we know. None of these satisfied everybody.

So it is we arrive at the doorstop of another Greek philosopher, Aristotle, the student of Plato, in a debate that remained unsettled as to whether belief might under some conditions qualify as knowledge. Where scholars have wondered and argued for centuries to what extent Plato's ideas diverge from his teacher Socrates, the divergence of Aristotle (384-322 B.C.E.) from Plato is more marked and clear.[115] This is true despite the difficulty of Aristotle's works, made so by the roughness of so many being mostly notes, often partially completed, and those not always in full agreement with each other. Together, Plato and Aristotle have commonly been presented as the two great poles of ancient Greek philosophy, the former a champion of rationalism and the latter a stalwart advocate of empiricism. Such characterizations are easy to remember though they often come to stand in the way of better, more nuanced understandings. For example, Aristotle, too, extols the power of reason and his empiricism is of a different nature than that of empiricists today.

---

114 See, for example, Plato's Socrates' scathing remarks in *Gorgias*, 463a-464e that practices like oratory draw minds that are bold and clever, and prone to making hunches; guessing supplants knowing.

115 Aristotle's opposition to certain ideas of Plato, especially his theory of forms, seems to have been the focus of Book II of the now lost *On Philosophy*.

Let us begin our examination of Aristotle by picturing how he appropriates the tradition received from Socrates through his teacher Plato and then elaborates upon it. Like Plato, who acknowledges that Protagoras is not entirely wrong, Aristotle accepts that Plato gets some things right. For example, both Protagoras and Plato see starting with sense-perception as a rather obvious and sensible step. Aristotle also agrees that sense-perceptions require mental operations to fully function in our efforts to engage reality. But where Plato appeals to reason as providing an *a priori* (i.e., before experience) set of eternal Ideas or Forms that provide a context within which to understand sense particulars, Aristotle opts for a different explanation. Making use of memory to hold on to sense perceptions, the human mind can apply reason *a posteriori* (i.e., after experience). Abstract thinking using a process called *induction* logically gathers, classifies, and systematizes sense perceptions. This process is shown in the 1-2-3 steps at the left of the illustration below.

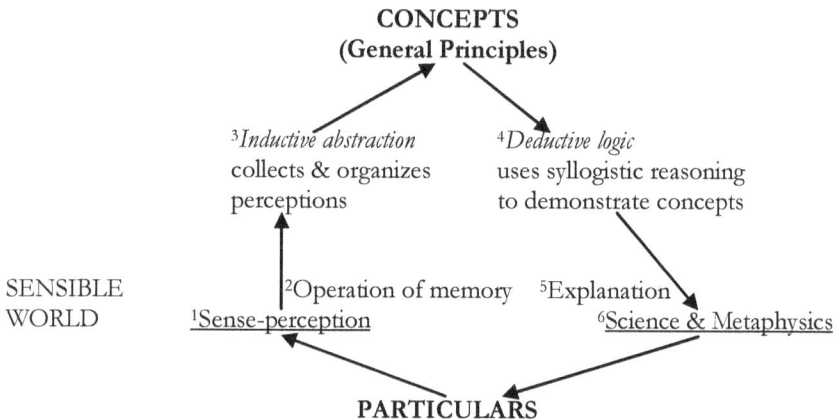

The right side of the illustration shows that arriving at concepts, or general principles derived from the mind's logical operations on sense-perceptions, is not the end goal. It is a critical way station on the road to knowledge (*epistēmē*). The ultimate goal for Aristotle is knowledge of reality, which means both metaphysics and science. Where the mind uses inductive logic to derive concepts from sense-perception, it employs a different kind of logic, called *deduction*, to demonstrate concepts. In other words, deduction does not establish general principles but shows how they explain the particular things that give rise to sense-perceptions. Thus the illustration displays a process that begins and ends with the particulars of reality. Steps 4-5-6 indicate how concepts are used to explain particulars in the manner of science, which uses both sense-experience (empiricism) and reason. In sum, Aristotle wants to *know* reality and such knowledge must *explain* itself.

We began this book by approvingly quoting Aristotle's conviction that "All people by nature stretch themselves toward knowledge."[116] But a key question is whether "knowledge" is something we can speak of relatively, or instead must be seen as categorical—an absolute that one either has or does not have.

Cognition, Reason, & Thinking

At a very broad level, we can speak of human *cognition*, the wide reach of the human intellect to employ thinking and reason toward the attainment of knowledge and understanding. At times, Aristotle uses the Greek word *gnosis* (one of the basic words for "knowledge") to signify "true cognition."[117] As the qualifier 'true' indicates, Aristotle, like Plato, recognizes not all cognition is of the same character.[118] Today psychologists studying reasoning involving belief note that two distinct cognitive styles can be distinguished. We can picture Aristotle's view and a modern one this way:

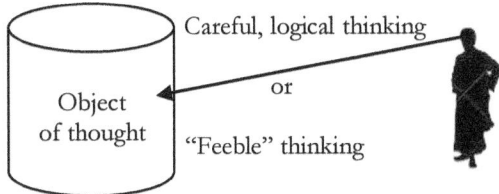

Careful, logical thinking = analytic cognitive style (deliberate, conscious, follows rules)

or

Object of thought

"Feeble" thinking = implicit cognitive style (swift, intuitive, uses shortcuts)

Like Aristotle's careful reasoning, an *analytic cognitive style* is deliberative in nature, taking time and conscious effort to follow established rules of thinking. Like Aristotle's more casual—'light'—reasoning, an *implicit cognitive style* is intuitive in character, seizing upon answers quickly and with less conscious attention, often relying on mental shortcuts (what psychologists term 'heuristics') and any apparent associations between things.

In the way Aristotle talks about it, the intellect (*nous*) and *thinking* (*noien*) are as inseparable as a noun expressed by a complementary verb; human intellect is incomprehensible apart from the act of thinking. Through thinking the mind operates on sense-perceptions to advance toward understanding (as seen on the left side of the first illustration). Intellect is in one sense like the Taoist's uncarved slab of stone—pure potentiality. But that is a passive sense of intellect.

---

[116] Aristotle, *Metaphysics,* 980a21 [I.1]. There is more than one way to reference Aristotle's works and because translations may employ only one or another, the two most common are both used here to aid the reader in finding material. However, line indications, less useful in English translations, have been left aside.

[117] Aristotle's use of *gnosis* is not completely uniform. Sometimes it seems to simply bear the sense of knowledge of some particular thing.

[118] Aristotle has *logical* reasoning συλλογίζωνται (*sullogizōntai,* fr. συλλογίζομαι (*sullogizomai*)) in mind. Aristotle, *Rhetoric,* 1396a-b [II.22.10]: "whether they reason with careful precision (ἀκριβέστερον, *akribesteron,* fr. ἀκριβής (*akribēs*)) or feebly (μαλακώτερον, *malakōteron,* fr. μαλακός (*malakos*))."

The active intellect, through thinking, can and does carve the block. Yet the intellect remains capable of thinking about anything; it has a universal reach and retains its potentiality no matter how much thinking goes on. It is even capable of thinking about itself (what psychologists term 'metacognition').[119]

While most of us say rational thinking is preferable to irrational thinking, we recognize the latter exists. Reasoning is no more identical to thinking than reason is to irrational thoughts. Conceived of as a division of thinking—a kind of thinking—reason is the highest form. Like Socrates and Plato, Aristotle has confidence that human beings are capable of knowledge because they are capable of reason; it is a part of being human by nature.[120] With respect to the right side of our first illustration, when we use "reason" (a cognitive operation) we produce an "account," "answer," "computation," or "reckoning" (all cognitive products) so that we provide an "explanation," make a "case," or offer an "argument." In short, knowledge attained by reason expresses itself in propositions. Or to put it somewhat differently, knowledge is a product of reason as a process and as a product of reason is expressed through reason in the explanatory form of an argument. Picture it this way:

Knowledge

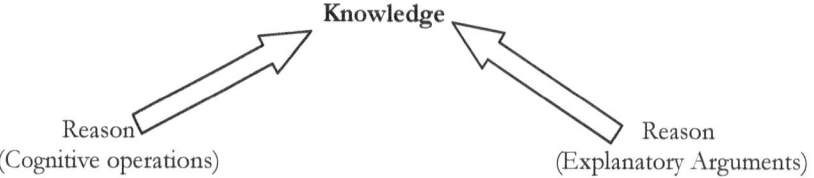

Reason
(Cognitive operations)

Reason
(Explanatory Arguments)

Reason stands before and after knowledge. In relation to our first illustration, knowledge stands at the top, the consequence of those processes that lead to "knowing" general principles. But the picture is incomplete if we stop here.

Human Rationality & Knowledge

The rational part of the human *psyche* itself divides into two abilities, one capable of knowledge in the purest sense (*epistēmonikos*), and one capable of skilled reasoning that yields knowledge in a practical manner (*logistikos*).[121] The former leads to *epistēmē*, often referred to as 'theoretical knowledge'; the latter leads to a practical reason yielding knowledge of the same kind. These are sometimes distinguished from each other by the labels *contemplative* (pure reason engaging the First Principles, or concepts) and *calculative* (practical reason engaging particular things that vary from one another).[122] But perhaps the most useful way to distinguish them is offered by Aristotle himself in his *Eudemian Ethics*

---

[119] For Aristotle's presentation on thinking, see *On the Soul* (*De Anima*), 429a-430b [III.4-6].

[120] Aristotle, *Nicomachean Ethics*, 1097b-1098a [I.710-15]. He adopts the view that the *psyche* has both a rational and irrational part—see 1102a (end) [I.13.9-10].

[121] Aristotle's epistemology is not nearly so simple as the presentation here makes it appear.

[122] Aristotle, *Nicomachean Ethics*, 1139a [VI.1.5-6]. Key terms: ἐπιστημονικόν (*epistēmonikon*, fr. ἐπιστημονικός (*epistēmonikos*); λογιστικόν (*logistikon*, fr. λογιστικός (*logistikos*)).

when he says that sometimes we talk about knowledge as something we *have* and sometimes as something we *use*.[123]

We can illustrate all of this as follows:

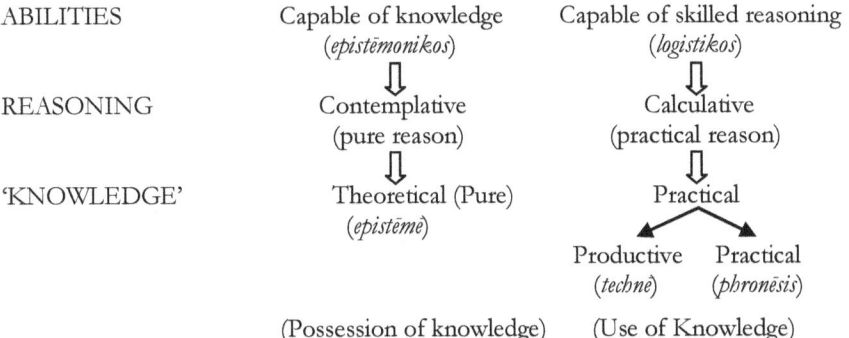

ABILITIES	Capable of knowledge (*epistēmonikos*)	Capable of skilled reasoning (*logistikos*)
REASONING	Contemplative (pure reason)	Calculative (practical reason)
'KNOWLEDGE'	Theoretical (Pure) (*epistēmē*)	Practical

Productive (*technē*)   Practical (*phronēsis*)

(Possession of knowledge)   (Use of Knowledge)

The highest form of knowledge (*epistēmē*) is the possession of a body of sufficient and certain information about reality that aims at what is eternal (metaphysics) and what is entailed in the natural sciences. The use of practical reason is wide enough to embrace arts and skills (*technē*), as well as prudent ethical practice (*phronēsis*). What unites both is their action-orientation, and the simple fact that they are not contemplative (i.e., not aimed at theoretical knowledge). These two—*technē* and *phronēsis*—can also be described as enough separate so that three kinds of knowledge result: theoretical, productive, and practical.[124] The essential distinction between theoretical knowledge and the other two is well-captured in Aristotle's comment in his *Metaphysics*:

> It is correct to call philosophy knowledge (*epistēmēn*) of the truth (*alētheias*). The purposed end of theoretical knowledge is truth; the intended end of practical knowledge is action. Even if they consider how things *are*, practical folk still do not contemplate what is eternal, but only what is now and in relation to other things.[125]

What Aristotle does is resist the idea that everything we call "knowledge" has to be *certain*. On the one hand, *epistēmē* is characterized by such certainty, which is why it is knowledge in the purest sense—i.e., exactly what we might expect in our English sense of possessing information sufficient, certain, and true. It is the knowledge of reality as it is and as such is the ultimate prize.

---

123 Aristotle, *Eudemian Ethics*, 1225b [II.9.4]. It is worth noting, too, that in this place Aristotle correlates "knowledge" (οἶδα, *oida*) with "understanding" (ἐφίσταμαι, *ephistamai*).

124 Aristotle, *Nicomachean Ethics*, 1139b [VI.2.5]. Key terms: τέχνη (*technē*); φρόνησις (*phronēsis*). On *phronēsis* also see the comment of Philodemus, *On Rhetoric* (*Rhetorica*), II, §2b, about Epicurus' remarks on it.

125 Aristotle, *Metaphysics*, 993b [II.1]. The word θεωρητικῆς (*theōrētikēs*) refers to "speculative," hence "theoretical" reflections. The phrases "purposed end" and "intended end" both translate τέλος (*telos*).

On the other hand, Aristotle recognizes the point made by someone like Isocrates that in ordinary experience there are many things where such certainty cannot be had.[126] This is knowledge at the level of the actual experience of things. But the proposed alternative to resign ourselves to mere opinions, as though these are all of equal truth and value, or all we can achieve, is repugnant to him. So he adopts a view that some "knowledge" is practical in that it reflects our actual experience of a thing even though in terms of any certainty that it reflects the way that thing really *is* can only be *probable*. Formally, it may be "belief," but at its best it coincides with knowledge, even if we lack the means to demonstrate that such is the case. Instead, practical knowledge explains a thing adequately based on actual experience but with the desire and expectation that such an explanation most likely reflects *epistēmē* rather than some false *doxa*. The rational mind always strives for a dependable, certain body of knowledge (*epistēmē*), but it is also rational to do the best we can to reach toward certainty in the uncertain practice of knowledge found in *technē* and *phronēsis*.

We can simplify the preceding illustration to show the ascendant nature of Aristotle's conception:

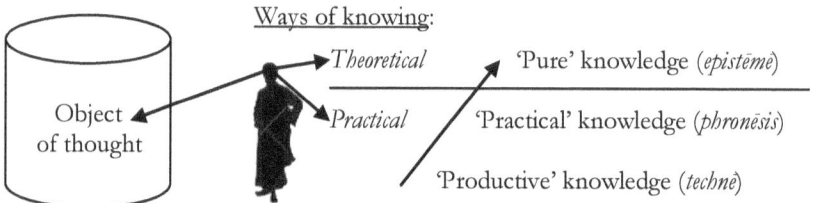

Both kinds of knowledge have their place; reasoning is at work in both theoretical and practical knowledge. In his *Rhetoric* Aristotle suggests that reasoning entails analytic (i.e., breaking things into their parts) and synthetic (i.e., seeing how the parts fit together) abilities. For any subject, he argues, one must have some familiarity with the elements of whatever question is at hand so that an understanding sufficient to reach some conclusion is possible.[127] Reason is able to both see the relevant elements and their relationship to one another.

Logos, Logic, & Argumentation

Reason properly belongs to knowledge (*epistēmē*).[128] Its methodological tool is logic. Aristotle, the father of logic, spends considerable time explaining reasoning's logical nature, especially deduction. As we saw in our original illustration, the goal is science—and science is knowledge by explanation. But rational explanation—*logos*—presents itself in particular manner. *Logos* drives logic. Aris-

---

[126] Aristotle, like others, had to reckon with Isocrates as a prominent figure articulating a distinct view on the nature and practice of rhetoric. Though a critic of Isocrates' views, Aristotle certainly recognized their influence. His early lost work *Gryllus* (c. 360 B.C.E.), on the subject of rhetoric, perhaps in the form of a Platonic dialog, apparently took Isocrates to task.

[127] Aristotle, *Rhetoric*, 1396a [II.22.4]).

[128] Aristotle, *Posterior Analytics*, 100b [II.19].

totle distinguishes two kinds of logic: inductive and deductive, though the latter is what historically is most often identified with logic.[129] We can start a brief review of logic with an elaboration of our first illustration:

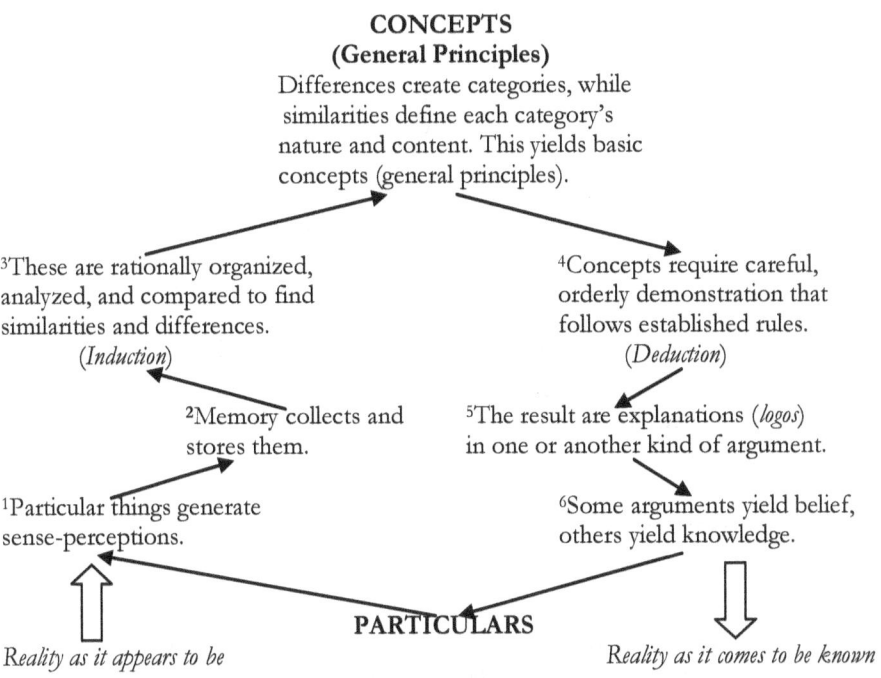

CONCEPTS
(General Principles)
Differences create categories, while similarities define each category's nature and content. This yields basic concepts (general principles).

³These are rationally organized, analyzed, and compared to find similarities and differences.
(Induction)

⁴Concepts require careful, orderly demonstration that follows established rules.
(Deduction)

²Memory collects and stores them.

⁵The result are explanations (*logos*) in one or another kind of argument.

¹Particular things generate sense-perceptions.

⁶Some arguments yield belief, others yield knowledge.

PARTICULARS

Reality as it appears to be   *Reality as it comes to be known*

Logic, in induction and deduction, is central to the whole enterprise. It exudes the very nature of *logos* and yields *logos* as the product of its twin processes.

Induction (ἐπαγωγή, *epagōgē*), as we saw in our first illustration, is a process drawing upon the experience of particular sense-perceptions to infer some general conclusion about them. *Deduction* (ἀπαγωγή, *apagōgē*) proceeds in the opposite direction, from the general to the particular. Deductive logic makes use of syllogistic reasoning, meaning that a presentation called a *syllogism* is formed to conduct an argument of explanation about some particular. A simple syllogism presents initial premises, one of which is 'major' and the other 'minor.' A conclusion is shaped based on these premises. Thus the basic form is: All *x* is *z*; *y* is *x*; therefore, *y* is *z*. This is easier to understand by illustration. For instance, using a famous example, here is a syllogism:

> All men are mortal.
> Socrates is a man.
> Therefore, Socrates is mortal.

---

[129] On induction not being reasoning in the manner deduction is, see Aristotle, *Topica*, 105a [I.12]. For a brief summary of induction and deduction see Aristotle, *Nicomachean Ethics*, 1139b [VI.3], with reference to the *Posterior Analytics*.

The first premise is the major one, broadest in scope and presenting the idea which is the object of the conclusion. In this case it is the idea of mortality. The second is the minor premise, which presents a particular instance of the general condition (i.e., "men"). The conclusion derives the particular idea of mortality for the particular instance of one man—Socrates—who belongs to the whole of mankind. This manner of reaching a conclusion from two premises is what we learn in school as deductive reasoning.

The hinge between induction and deduction are the concepts at the top of our first illustration. Induction *derives* them; deduction *demonstrates* them. The deriving of concepts depends on an ability to see both likenesses between things and their differences. The demonstration of concepts depends upon the ability to draw valid conclusions based on true premises through following rules. Reason shows that the premises of an argument are deduced from higher premises already established as true. But this process suggests an endless regression of deductive logic, always seeking true premises. The only way out of this dilemma is to posit certain "givens"—basic, universal, eternal truths—that require no proof. These are the fundamental first principles undergirding all reality.[130]

Logical reasoning produces *arguments*. All arguments are, in one way or another, efforts at explanation. An argument starts with at least one premise (or 'premiss') and, ideally at least, follows logical rules to reach a conclusion.[131]

Arguments

An argument is either valid or invalid, and its conclusion either true or not. Aristotle enumerates three kinds of arguments. Let us revisit a previous illustration and add in how the three kinds of argument fit:

ABILITIES	Capable of knowledge (*epistēmonikos*)	Capable of skilled reasoning (*logistikos*)
	⇓	⇓
REASONING	Contemplative (pure reason)	Calculative (practical reason)
	⇓	⇓
'KNOWLEDGE'	Theoretical (*epistēmē*)	Practical
		Productive (*technē*) Practical (*phronēsis*)

ARGUMENTS		
(Rational)	Demonstrative	Dialectical & Contentious
(Pseudo-rational)		Contentious (some)

First, a scientific argument is a *demonstration* (ἀπόδειξις, *apodeixis*) and is interested in explaining Nature (i.e., reality). Using deductive logic it demonstrates a

---

[130] Unlike Plato, Aristotle's "forms" are not pre-existent ideals but reside in physical Nature. On his arguments for first principles, see Aristotle, *Metaphysics*, I-IV.

[131] The terms: premise (πρότασις, *protasis*); conclusion (συμπέρασμα, *sumperasma*)

previously unknown truth—the logical conclusion of the line of argumentation built upon sound premises. The aim of scientific explanation is causation, in the broad sense of providing a rationale (*logos*) for why a particular thing belongs to the classification in which we have put it.[132] In other words, demonstration yields an explanation that justifies placing a particular thing in relation to a concept (e.g., calling Fido a dog). Such explanation is thereby knowledge (*epistēmē*) and requires no effort at persuasion.

A second kind of argument is *dialectical*. It starts from questions rather than answers (propositional statements). Some arguments about Nature are of this kind, as are ethical and logical ones. By investigating likenesses and differences, and carefully forming definitions, one gets to some logical conclusion. Dialectical arguments can be either inductive or deductive. These yield belief and are the kind of argument most and best suited to good belief.

Finally, there is the *contentious* argument, which also produces belief (opinion). It needs to be persuasive because it starts from what *seems* at first to be generally accepted, but upon examination shows that it isn't. Because the matter isn't certain it can be debated; because it can be debated persuasion is in play as each party contends to establish its own position as the most plausible.[133]

Belief

What we have been examining shows that for Aristotle the notion of knowledge entails separable intellectual abilities leading to two kinds of reasoning and producing two or three distinguishable kinds of knowledge, each possessing its own label. Of these various kinds of "knowledge"—which we might better call kinds of *knowing*—only one is labeled *epistēmē*, the kind of knowledge with all its certainty that remains our focus. Similarly, Aristotle distinguishes different kinds of belief. He employs a variety of terms, two of which—*doxa* and *pistis*—we have met already. To them we will add ὑπόληπψις (*hupolēpsis*)—an especially challenging word—and ἔνδοξα (*endoxa*), the most important of the four terms in Aristotle's discussion of belief. Let's start with the terms we are familiar with from before.

Doxa & Pistis

Aristotle retains the basic sense of *doxa* as the taking up of a position—thus, an "opinion" or "belief." *Doxa* does not share with *epistēmē* the quality of certainty. In the *Metaphysics* he employs the three states Plato had named—ignorance, belief, and knowledge—calling attention to the absolute nature of knowledge (as *epistēmē*), that it cannot sometimes be knowledge and sometimes

---

132 Traditionally, four causes are named: *material* (i.e., the actual physical properties that make up a thing and also make it different from other things); *formal* (i.e., the 'form' discerned in the particular substance; its observable structure or pattern); *efficient* (i.e., the agent behind the thing's existence); and *teleological* or *final* (i.e., the *telos* (ultimate purpose or end) toward which a thing moves).

133 Aristotle, *Topics* (*Topica*), 100b-101a [I.1]. The terms: demonstration (ἀπόδειξις, *apodeixis*); dialectical (διαλεκτικοὶ, *dialektikoi*) and contentious (εριστικό, *epistiko*)."

ignorance; it is an all-or-nothing proposition. To this he contrasts *doxa*, which he says can vary: "But it is belief (*doxa*) that takes upon itself that which is otherwise than what it is."[134] Some "knowing" is contingent—it *might* be true. While it lacks the certainty of *epistēmē*, "knowing" associated with *doxa* can coincide with what is true, but it is "belief" because it 'might be otherwise.'

It looks like this:

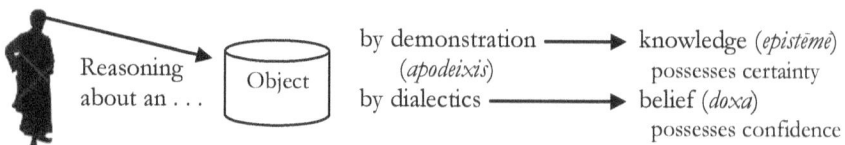

The ideas of certainty and confidence are pivotal for distinguishing knowledge from belief. The former is about certainty; the latter about confidence. Certainty supports confidence, but confidence can flow from other sources—most notably persuasion. So with *doxa* Aristotle turns to probing the relation of persuasion and confidence (or conviction) to the taking of a position.

For Aristotle, *doxa* is linked with both *logos* and with *pistis*. In a well-known passage in his *De Anima* (*On the Soul*) Aristotle coordinates them as follows: "Every belief position (*doxē*) implicates a belief conviction (*pistis*), belief conviction likewise with persuasion, and persuasion with reason (*logos*)."[135] Human beings, in the positions they take up (belief as *doxa*), demonstrate a process of conviction (belief as *pistis*) following persuasion (a concept we've seen closely linked to belief), and that implicates reason (*logos*) at work. It is easy to sketch:

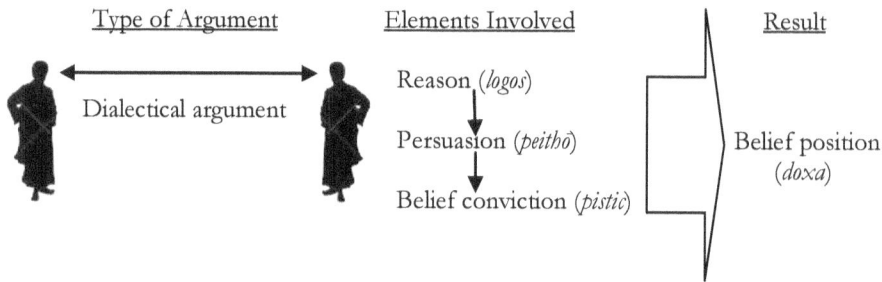

Thus, *doxa* implies rationality—*reasoned* belief (even if not necessarily *reasonable* belief). The situation, that we often accept as knowledge what follows persuasion and then uphold our position with conviction, indicates both thinking and the conscious effort of rationality to supply an account, give a reason, or provide an argument for our position. But that by no means guarantees that the

---

134 Aristotle, *Metaphysics*, 1039b (end) [VII.15].
135 Aristotle, *On the Soul*, 428a [III.3]. Rather than render both the forms of *doxa* and *pistis* as 'belief,' I have used phrases: "belief position" for δόξη (*doxē*), and "belief conviction: for πίστις (*pistis*). Obviously, there are other ways to render the text. Many use "opinion" for *doxē*, and a choice like "conviction" (used alone) for *pistis* in order to tease out the same senses I aim at with my phrases.

thinking is correct, the logic flawless, or the conclusion true. After all, people are persuaded to conviction on all sorts of lousy ideas showing very poor logic.

The critical role of *pistis* is hardly undervalued by Aristotle. Elsewhere he links belief conviction to reason in a manner that yields *epistēmē*. He writes, "When a fellow is convinced (*pisteuei*) in a certain way and the First Principles are certain to him, then he *knows* (*epistatai*); for if these principles are not better known than the conclusion, then his knowledge (*epistēmēn*) is merely by coincidence."[136] But note that while Aristotle joins conviction and certainty, it is the certainty of the First Principles that makes for knowledge. Otherwise, he may have, factually, the *content* of knowledge but only by chance; the person may be confident but certainty is absent. Where certainty is absent, what appears to be knowledge might be so by accident, but is more accurately labeled "belief."

Hupolēpsis

A third Greek term that is relevant to us is the noun ὑπόληπψις (*hupolēpsis*). What makes the term so intriguing is that its core sensibility links it to both *doxa* and *epistēmē*. Consider, with respect to *doxa*—with its basic sense of taking up a position—that the corresponding verb to *hupolēpsis* is ὑπολαμβάνω (*hupolambanō*), which literally means, "to take up by getting under." It is not hard to see, then, that in some contexts *hupolēpsis* conveys a sense like our word "belief." Like both *doxa* and *epistēmē*, which entail rational cognition and decisions, *hupolēpsis* generally represents what we would call a cognitive judgment, so that *hupolēpsis* seems to be a kind of thinking entailing judgment or "apprehension" (i.e., "grasp"), as in "taking something to be the case." Thus it can be conveyed in English as "supposition," or "assumption."

In the *Nicomachean Ethics*, Aristotle uses *hupolēpsis* as our "notion" or "belief" about what is good for us or in our own best interests.[137] In the *Metaphysics* a more technical use seems present; in discussing how *technē* is produced from experience, Aristotle contrasts multiple conceptions of experience with a single universal judgment (*hupolēpsis*) applied to like objects.[138] Put together, Aristotle's usage suggests that *hupolēpsis* might be seen (at least at times in certain contexts) as a cognition employing reason to render judgments so that both *doxa* and *epistēmē* might be subsumed under it. In other ancient literature *hupolēpsis* is sometimes used to mean "weak opinion" and we should remember that, too.

Endoxa

Despite the important roles terms like *doxa*, *pistis*, and *hupolēpsis* play, one other term emerges as the most significant for Aristotle: ἔνδοξα (*endoxa*). The relation to *doxa* is obvious, but *endoxa* is a clearly separable term and not merely a modified *doxa* (though it can be classed as a kind of *doxa*). While translated in different ways into English, the basic sense of it as intended by Aristotle is made

---

[136] Aristotle, *Nicomachean Ethics*, 1139b [VI.3 (end)].

[137] Aristotle, *Nicomachean Ethics*, 1140b [VI.5].

[138] Aristotle, *Metaphysics*, 981a [I.1].

plain by his own words: "the strongly endorsed beliefs held by all, or by most people, or by the wisest (i.e., philosophers), or simply put, those beliefs endorsed by all, or by most, or by the most notable of people."[139] Thus, *endoxa* refers to the beliefs held not by individuals *against* the crowd, but those endorsed *by* the crowd, or at least by a sizeable number, or at the very least by those we would term 'most in the know.' I have elected to render *endoxa* as "strongly endorsed beliefs" but a simpler translation like "reputable beliefs" works well, too. There is a presumed credibility in *endoxa*, but Aristotle is sensible enough to know it might be falsely imputed.

Endoxa refers to a strongly endorsed belief by any or all of the following:

The Masses

The Most Learned

Both Masses & Most Learned

We today might call these "informed beliefs" (or opinions), though there is no guarantee that even a universally held belief is necessarily an informed one. *Endoxa* are both more stable than *doxa* and more reputable; thus they are preferable. A substantial portion of Aristotle's confidence in *endoxa* is his own belief that human beings are naturally predisposed toward truth.[140] If so, then it seems probable that a majority opinion is more likely to be true than the view of a solitary individual.

Philosophically it occupies a fundamental place in his epistemology. Think back to our basic illustration of Aristotle's epistemology. We might think of sense-perception as "reality as it appears to be." It is the reality of everyday experience. But everyday experience presents us with puzzles to mentally sort out, which we do with the help of others. Whether natural phenomena, or socially constructed ones, our perceptions are substantially shaped by shared beliefs. As Aristotle puts it in the *Nicomachean Ethics*, when discussing certain virtues:

> It is needful to do as we have done with other things, to set out things-as-they-appear-to-be (*phainemona*) and first deal with the questions they raise and in so doing bring to light as much as possible all the strongly endorsed

---

[139] Aristotle, *Topics*, 100a [I.1]. Cf. 105a [I.14]. *Topics*, quoted later in this chapter.
[140] See Aristotle, *Rhetoric* 1355a; cf. *Metaphysics*, 980a (line 21); also see 993a30-b4.

beliefs (*endoxa*) about these matters of experience—and if not all such beliefs, then the greater number of them, or the most important ones. For if we are able to resolve the questions such that strongly endorsed beliefs (*endoxa*) endure, it is enough.[141]

The process by which this occurs is dialectical argument.

Aristotle's adoption of *endoxa* makes possible an important distinction between propositions that are merely beliefs that any number of people might hold, including a solitary individual, and those that are widely held and by that virtue are more credible *prima facie*. The old familiar *doxa* is a wide, even generic term; *endoxa* offers a more precise and limited range that Aristotle can easily adopt as a technical term, one fixed and regular in sensibility.

To these we might add two other terms: *adoxa* and *paradoxa*. These terms are not widely used by Aristotle, but both occur in the *Topica*, where Aristotle makes the most generous use of *endoxa*. They thus invite us to see them in relation to it. Both are kinds of belief that contrast sharply enough with *endoxa* as to be seen in opposition to it. Yet both share something with *endoxa*, too. On the one side, *adoxa* is like *endoxa* in that it can be the belief of large groups. But it is unlike *endoxa* in that it lacks credibility; *adoxa* is, as it were, the strongly endorsed belief of children or fools—the common people (*hoi polloi*) at their worst. On the other side, *paradoxa* is like *endoxa* in that it can possess *logos* and so cannot be rejected out of hand. It is unlike *endoxa* in exactly the way its name suggests: it represents the minority viewpoint, the one against the majority, and so is a position not strongly endorsed.

Although a questionable consistency with which Aristotle uses these terms makes it risky and highly debatable trying to picture how they relate, it might be worthwhile to attempt doing so in order to get a broad view of the matter. The following illustration may help us see the terms in 'the big picture.'

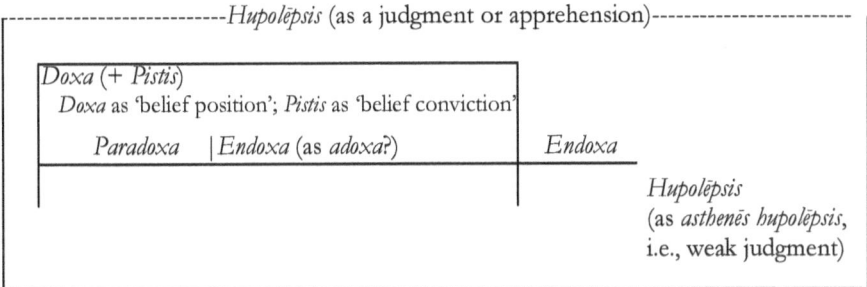

In this picture, all *doxa* and *endoxa* are kinds of *hupolēpsis* in the sense of that word as a broad cognitive operation. In turn, *endoxa* can be seen as a kind of *doxa* since the latter term is broader. Yet, in Aristotle's usage there is enough distinction to warrant seeing some *endoxa* as a contrast to *doxa*. Perhaps one way

---

[141] Aristotle, *Nicomachean Ethics*, 1145b [VII.1.5]. The relation of *endoxa* to *phainomena* has been a matter of some debate, which we cannot enter into here.

to view this is to see *adoxa* as a pseudo-*endoxa*. Or we may instead simply recognize that while formally *endoxa* can be called a species of *doxa* it is, for Aristotle, a special and superior one. *Paradoxa* is a kind of *doxa*. Finally, *hupolēpsis* can also exist as a kind of *hupolēpsis*—an 'inferior' *hupolēpsis* to the 'superior' form.

Belief & Thinking

We must now see how these different terms fit into what Aristotle says about thinking in *De Anima*. The intellect's thinking (*noien*) includes both imagination (*phantasia*) and belief judgment (*hupolēpsis*) as elements.[142] Shortly before, Aristotle had noted that imagination is especially connected with *hupolēpsis*—which here seems meant in its broadest sense—and which entails some degree of imagination. Aristotle then immediately turns to contrasting *phantasia* with believing (*doxazein*), which thus seems to function as a species of *hupolēpsis*. Believing simply seizes us; it is involuntary. Such believing rouses emotion, whereas simply imagining a thing does not.

Aristotle wants knowledge (*epistēmē*). That means he desires the kind of right thinking that leads to it. But since knowledge is characterized by a certainty that belief (*doxa*) lacks, intelligence (*nous*) is needed. The intellect (*nous*) can attain to knowledge, but merely because we think we understand something does not mean we have attained knowledge no matter how persuaded we might be, and not even if that persuasion is strongly shared (*endoxa*).

The Role of Belief in Reasoning & Argumentation

In *Topica* Aristotle expressly declares, "Now reasoning is an argument in which, certain things being laid down, something other than these necessarily comes about through them."[143] In other words, premises set forth lead to a conclusion not obvious when the argument commenced; a deduction leads to insight. To best get at how Aristotle treats the relation of knowledge and belief we must take a step back and return to the matter of how statements— "propositions"—are set forth in argumentation so that human reasoning can get at the matters people discuss. In his *Topica* (*Topics*) Aristotle sets for himself the following goal:

> Our present treatise purposes the discovering of a method by which we shall be able to reason from strongly endorsed beliefs (*endoxōn*) about any problem put before us, and also be able as we support an argument to avoid saying anything that will not support our position.[144]

Aristotle then immediately sets out reasoning as the presentation of arguments, as we already have said. As he elaborates them, it seems that they represent different orders of reasoning, with the argument of demonstration being the highest order. The kind of "strongly endorsed beliefs" (*endoxa*) he mentions

---

[142] Aristotle, *On the Soul*, 427b (end) [III.3.5 (end)].
[143] Aristotle, *Topics*, 100a [I.1.25].
[144] Aristotle, *Topics*, 100a [I.1 (beginning)].

above belongs to the second kind of argument—the dialectical argument. The third kind of argument, the contentious one, ranks lowest for only some of its reasoning is genuinely so. Both the dialectical argument and the contentious argument take their start from "strongly endorsed beliefs."[145]

Aristotle asserts that the method of argumentation is only fulfilled when sufficient skill, such as needed by a public speaker or by a physician, is reached, which in practice requires every means available to the person actually be used.[146] This then leads to considering both the nature of arguments (their kinds, bases, and subjects) and how a person properly equips him- or herself for argumentation. Every argument starts with, and is based on, "propositions." The subjects being reasoned about through propositions are "problems." Every proposition can be made into a problem by altering how it is posed.[147] Following this Aristotle turns his attention specifically to dialectical arguments, the kind associated with "strongly endorsed beliefs."[148]

Dialectical Arguments

Aristotle expressly states that "reasoning is *dialectical* which reasons from generally accepted opinions (*endoxōn*)." These provide a starting point regardless of whether they also prove to be a sound foundation. "A dialectical *problem*," he says, "is an investigative inquiry leading either to selecting or avoiding something, or to truth and knowledge—and does so as its own interest or as an aid in solving some other problem."[149] Problems arise when:

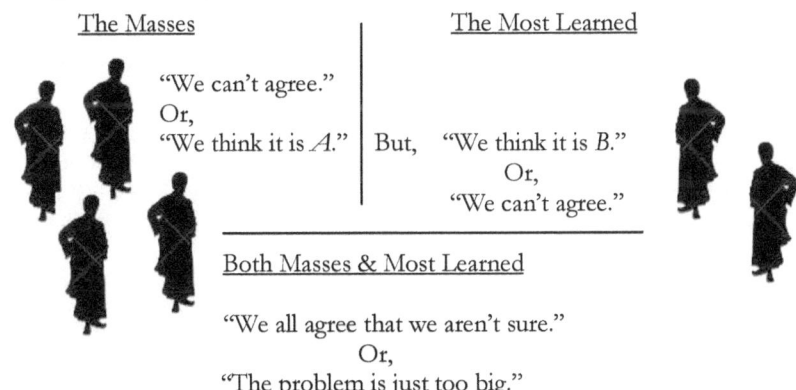

The Masses	The Most Learned
"We can't agree." Or, "We think it is *A*."	But, "We think it is *B*." Or, "We can't agree."

Both Masses & Most Learned

"We all agree that we aren't sure."
Or,
"The problem is just too big."

---

145 Aristotle, *Topics*, 100b-101a [I.I].

146 Aristotle, *Topics*, 101b [I.3].

147 Aristotle, *Topics*, 101b [I.4]. The terms: method (μέθοδον, *methedon*); propositions (προτάσεων, *protasiōn*); and problems (προβλήματά, *problēmata*) On the last point he provides an illustration. If we say, "Is not a definition of man, 'walking biped animal'?" we have formed a proposition; change it to, "Is a definition of man, 'walking biped animal'?" and our proposition has become a problem.

148 Aristotle, *Topics*, 104a [I.10].

149 Aristotle, *Topics*, 104b [I.11 (beginning)]. The word translated "knowledge" here is γνῶσιν (*gnōsin*, from γνῶσις (*gnōsis*)).

As the illustration shows, a 'problem' may arise within the starting point of "strongly endorsed belief" itself, either because there is no majority opinion or consensus, or the general opinion of the masses is at variance with the most knowledgeable folk, or the latter group cannot agree among themselves. But problems can also arise because there is room for doubt, with compelling arguments capable of being mounted on either side of the issue (e.g., *paradoxa*). Sometimes problems emerge simply because the question at hand is so immense that coming up with reasons adequate to support an argument is too elusive.

Dialectics entail a give-and-take process. Their fundamental difference from arguments of demonstration is that they ask questions rather than simply present statements. But Aristotle's sense of dialectic is not exactly like Plato's. Socrates employs dialectical reasoning to get at reality, and Plato thinks it can lead to the eternal Forms. Aristotle, on the other hand, employs dialectical arguments with a suspension of what is certain. Rather than beginning with what it *known* to be real, such arguments start with what all people, or most of them, or the most learned, *suppose* is real. Dialectical arguments must start with questions because answers that are certain and sufficient cannot be presumed.

Dialectical arguments are still logical in form. Their structure is like that of arguments of demonstration in making use of syllogisms. But the latter employ different kinds of premises—what we might term 'higher order' premises because they are necessary and true. In dialectical arguments, where uncertainty prevails, the premises are not self-evident, but must be accepted. And that is precisely where Aristotle finds *endoxa* invaluable. If one must discuss matters that are uncertain, why not start with what all people, or most of them, or the most learned believe?

As we saw in an earlier figure, dialectical arguments belong to practical knowledge (*technē* and *phronēsis*); they *use* or *practice* knowledge in a world of experience where the certainty of *epistēmē* may hover in the background, but cannot be simply assumed to do so merely because the premises from which one starts are strongly endorsed (*endoxa*). Thus there is a sense in which dialectical arguments not only aim at knowledge, but seek to express it. Nevertheless, even where they incidentally coincide with *epistēmē* they still cannot be labeled more than *endoxa*. The premises of dialectical arguments are contingent, rather than necessary. That means they can change; belief is about things that seem to be, but might be otherwise.

How Beliefs Can Be Both True and False

Aristotle points out how a propositional belief can be both true *and* false.

The same proposition (*logos*) can be thought both true and false. Consider, for example, the proposition 'he is sitting.' This may be true; but when that person rises, this very belief, if retained, becomes false. And so it is with beliefs (*doxēs*). For one may believe truly that a person is sitting, and when that person rises then believe falsely, if the belief (*doxan*) the person is sitting is still held. . . .

But the proposition (*logos*) and the belief (*doxa*) have themselves remained unchanged in all respects. The contrary quality—change—comes about through an alteration of the facts in the case. The actual proposition 'he is sitting' remains unchanged, but according to the actual case we call the proposition true in one circumstance, false in another. What pertains to propositions also applies to beliefs.[150]

In short, a propositional statement or belief is fixed in content and form, but the reality it addresses can change. Therefore the statement, remaining the same, can be true in one instance and false in another because actual circumstances which the proposition addresses have changed. All beliefs (*doxa*), then, are both contingent and circumstantial.

Aristotle's Ladder

It remains for us now to see if we can put things together in a manner that shows the 'forest' of Aristotle's epistemological thought rather than trying to name every 'tree' in it. Let's start by an implicit contrast to Plato's line. We can still envisage 'steps' but the fixed line between a Sensible world and a real of Eternal Forms is absent; all takes places in the Sensible world.

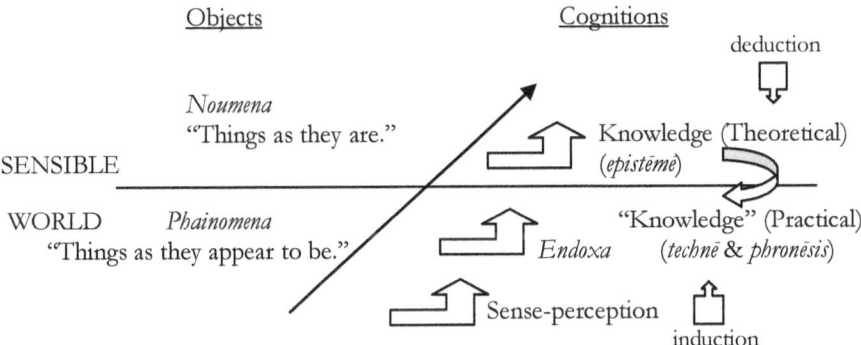

In Aristotle's ladder the separation of phenomena (*phainomena*) into both perception and belief may remind us of Plato's divided line, where the Sensible world is divided into images and visible objects and Plato sets out *doxa* as embracing both *eikasia* ("imagination") and *pistis*. But Aristotle has more confidence in what perception can yield and he extends that confidence to *endoxa*. Moreover, for Aristotle there is no appeal to an invisible, insensible world. There is just reality, and through reason we can apprehend it quite well enough. Induction is like an escalator going up, from particular perceptions to general concepts; deduction reasons like an escalator going down, proceeding from concepts to explain the nature of perceptions.

Knowledge here straddles Plato's more definite separation of belief and knowledge. For Aristotle strongly endorsed belief (*endoxa*) is a reasonable jump-

---

150 Aristotle, *Categories of Interpretation* (*Categoriae et de interpretation*), 4a-b [ch. 5]. "The same proposition (*logos*) can be both true and false" (4a, line 24).

ing off point on all uncertain matters—and such are the province of practical knowledge. But practical knowledge aims at more than *endoxa*. It seeks to use and apply what *epistēmē* possesses. In a sense, *technē* and *phronēsis* are a translated dialog between *endoxa* and *epistēmē*.

Aristotle's Spectrum

As we have seen, Aristotle has much to say about both belief and knowledge and their relationship. Aristotle's Greek terms translated as "belief" are numerous. The adding of *pistis* to the mix with *doxa* and *epistēmē* provides a richer way to envision things. Now we can speak of "opinion" (*doxa*), the weakest belief, modified to the better by "the best opinion" (*endoxa*) and distinguished from "belief" (*pistis*), rational conviction. Neither opinion nor belief are "presumption" (*hupolēpsis*) either. Yet belief is not "knowledge" (*epistēmē*). There remains some distance between convincing 'proofs' that commend themselves and an actual certainty belonging to knowledge alone.

Knowledge & Belief

Let us begin this section with an illustration of how knowledge and belief might relate to one another.

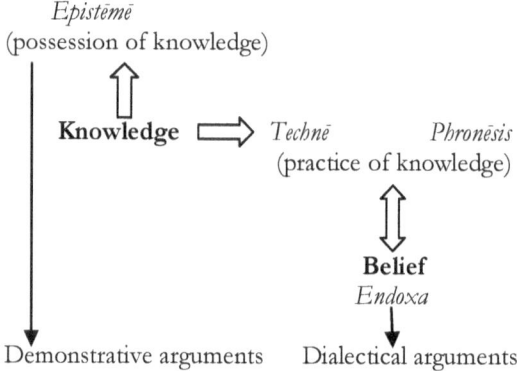

This more simply means:

Use of knowledge = Belief

and it does so because the practical application of knowledge in life experience, whether through the practice of an art or skill, or the practice of politics or virtue, is fraught with uncertainty. *Endoxa* guides where *epistēmē* is absent. But, as we have discussed above, *epistēmē* lurks ever in the background. While practical knowledge must content itself with probabilities rather than certainty, the body of theoretical knowledge remains and its necessary truths steer people who are, Aristotle thinks, reaching toward knowledge and predisposed toward truth.

In the *Posterior Analytics*, Aristotle distinguishes knowledge (*epistēmē*) from belief (*doxa*) as having different objects. Knowledge is about objective universals, such as classes of objects that can be established with certainty. Such are expressed by 'necessary' propositions, which simply means they express matters that have to be this way and no other; they are *certain*. On the other hand, *doxa* concerns propositions that might be true and real—but do not have to be; they could also be false or merely imaginary.[151] Put even more simply, knowledge expresses itself in statements about things that have to be the way they are and it is evidentially so that they are this way and no other. Matters of *doxa* are expressions of things that are before us right now and that seem to be this way from our present perspective, but they are always *contingent*, meaning they do not have to be this way for certain and for always. The bottom line is this: beliefs must have some degree of uncertainty, otherwise they aren't beliefs, but pure knowledge (*epistēmē*).

Aristotle writes:

> The object of knowledge and knowledge (*epistēmē*) itself differ from the object of belief and belief (*doxēs*) itself. This is because knowledge is of the universal and the necessary, and the necessary cannot be otherwise than what it is. But other things—even though both true and actually existing— are capable of being otherwise. Obviously, knowledge cannot be about such matters for if so such things would be certain and no longer capable of being otherwise. Nor can these other things be the object of intellect itself (*nous*) (by which I mean the beginning of knowledge), nor of a knowledge that cannot be demonstrated (for that is the apprehension of immediate premises). Truth has only three paths—*nous*, *epistēmē*, and *doxa*—and the accounts by which they are disclosed. Of these *doxa* alone concerns things that can be otherwise and so true or false; put differently, *doxa* involves the apprehension (*hupolēpsis*) of premises that are immediate, but not necessary.
>
> Now, what has been presented accords with what we might expect from experience, for belief—like anything that can be otherwise—lacks certainty. No one thinks he is "believing" when considering something certain; he "knows" it. On the other hand, when one thinks of something that it is a particular way, but might be otherwise, there is a recognition this is "believing"—because belief involves things of this nature, whereas knowledge is always about things that *must* be as they are.[152]

---

[151] Aristotle's *Posterior Analytics*, 88b30-34 (I.33). Cf. Aristotle's *Nicomachean Ethics*, 1139b (VI.3).

[152] Aristotle, *Posterior analytics*, 89a [I.33]. My choice of "intellect itself" for νοῦς (*nous*) is admittedly very debatable. As I have pointed out elsewhere, *nous* is a versatile noun rendered variously depending on context. Often translated "mind" it refers thus to mental acts of perception and thinking; sometimes the choice of "thinking" or "thought" well fits the sense of a form of the word in a particular place. But sometimes its meaning is even broader, encompassing feeling, judging, and/or deciding. The sense of it at times communicates intention or purpose. It can, in some uses, be translated "intellect" or "intelligence." Sometimes its sense coincides with "reason" (as the mind's faculty rather than the act itself). This last—"reason"—is one choice here, but somewhat misleading; better is "intuition," which in a technical sense fits well but wasn't chosen because its common construal by people today would again be misleading. I chose "intellect itself" to convey the parenthetical meaning—that of the mind's most basic operating, which is where knowledge begins.

Aristotle here provides his own dividing line: *epistēmē* belongs to things that are necessary (*have* to be), while *doxa* belongs to what is contingent (does *not* have to be). Or, as we have heard earlier, *doxa* concerns things that 'can be otherwise.' Knowledge—that is, *epistēmē*—is only with respect to the universal and certain principles, not about contingent things that can change. We can venture a hypothetical representation of Aristotle's ideas in the form of a spectrum:

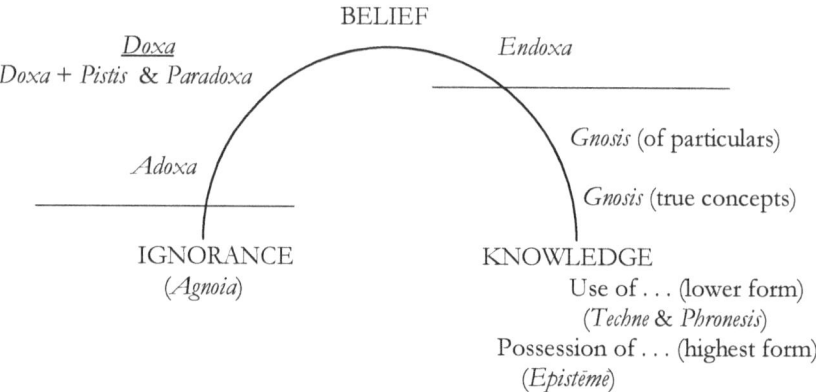

As can be seen, there are dividing lines separating the three states. The middle state—belief—has the most diversity. The extremes are ignorance (*agnosia*)—literally, the absence of knowing and knowledge—and at the far opposite of it, the possession of a body of knowledge (*epistēmē*).[153]

Aristotle is quite aware that some people argue that the same thing can be the object of both knowledge and *doxa*, and further contend that they "believe" everything they "know." Aristotle maintains that they are mistaken, having confused how they attained a fact and the reason for it.[154] He concludes that it is impossible to simultaneously hold both a belief and have knowledge, though he allows it is possible for one person to know something while another merely holds an opinion or belief about it.[155] Aristotle does not allow for *doxa* and knowledge to ever be the same—a rejection of the idea that knowledge is true, justified *belief*. But he does allow that belief (*doxa*) can be true, and in fact be highly credible (*endoxa*). One might even argue that belief leads right up to the door of knowledge and politely knocks. But only knowledge is inside.

The ultimate aim for Aristotle is neither *doxa* nor *endoxa*. He wants *epistēmē* with its certainty and grasp of reality, or at least as close as we are able to come to such through a thorough understanding. At best, even *endoxa*—credible, reputable belief—falls significantly short of the kind of knowledge most desired. That does not mean belief is worthless. It just means it has a lesser place in the better results of human thinking.

[153] It is worth noting that Aristotle spends some time discussing ignorance, too. See his famous and much discussed section in *Eudemian Ethics,* 1225b (II.9).

[154] Aristotle's *Posterior Analytics,* 89a12-38 (I.33).

[155] Aristotle's *Posterior Analytics,* 89a39-40-89b1-6 (I.33(end)).

8

The Epicurean Alternative

Something seems to have changed in the tenor of discussion leading to the birth of the schools of thought we turn to in this and the next two chapters. Increasingly Greek philosophy[156] turned away from theoretical musing to a preoccupation with the practical, especially ethics—and did so with religious fervor. Indeed, for many the Greek philosophical paths of Epicureanism, Stoicism, and Skepticism became a kind of salvation in the face of life's uncertainties.

There were changes, too, in the realm of epistemology. A discernible shift in focus from the *nature* of knowledge to the *possibility* of it occurred. There was no longer the presumption that knowledge must be attainable and a real question whether it can be. If nothing else, the vigor of the earlier debates about knowledge had aroused an increasing measure of skepticism—a skepticism embraced by some, but vigorously contested by others.

Pride of place historically belongs to the Epicureans. The founder, Epicurus of Athens (342-270 B.C.E.), developed a complete system of philosophy that over time proved to be both a starting-point and a serious opponent to Stoicism as well as a significant alternative among the competing schools of philosophy to which a Greek or Roman might turn.[157] But as our interest lies with epistemology, it is with that aspect of Epicurean thought we shall concern ourselves.

Both Epicurus' life and his work are known to us principally through the material presented by Diogenes Laertius in his *Lives of Eminent Philosophers*. Tradition says he established his school of philosophy at age 32, and as it was conducted on property known as 'the Garden,' that name eventually attached itself to his philosophy.[158] A prodigious writer—noted for his penchant of eschewing citations of others in favor of staying strictly with his own thoughts—he is said to have written some 300 volumes (i.e., scrolls).[159]

---

[156] With Epicurus, the Stoics and the Skeptics we now enter into a period of ancient Greek philosophy more commonly referred to as "Hellenistic" philosophy.

[157] Besides Epicurus, Hermarchus (Epicurus' successor), Metrodorus of Lampsacus, and Polyaenus should be mentioned as instrumental in the promotion and spread of Epicureanism.

[158] Diogenes Laertius, *Lives of Eminent Philosophers: Epicurus*, X.10, 17 [*Epicurus*, 5]. Also, Cicero, *On Moral Ends* (aka *On Ends, Good and Evil*; Latin *De finibus*), V.3 [V.1]: *in Epicuri hortis*. The first citation format for Cicero is to book and section in the Latin text; the second is to book and chapter. Some English translations offer both, others only one or the other.

[159] Diogenes Laertius, *Lives of Eminent Philosophers: Epicurus*, X.17 [*Epicurus*, 7].

When exactly he turned to philosophy and under whom he may have studied remains uncertain. Nevertheless, one tradition relays that Epicurus' work *The Canon* (or, *On the Criterion*) was based on an earlier work titled *Tripod* by Nausiphanes, a Democritean philosopher under whom Epicurus is alleged to have studied.[160] Given the attention to epistemology in *The Canon*, which serves as the first part of Epicurus' own triad for philosophy (together with physics and ethics), and the ties to Democritean thinking on physics, it seems reasonable to see Epicurus' epistemology in some continuity with that perspective.

Democritus

The views of Democritus (c. 460-c. 370 B.C.E.) about reality stand in the background of Epicurus's own thinking about reality and inform the development of his epistemology. Although Epicurus disavows being influenced by any predecessors—including Democritus—it seems clear enough that he is no more capable of operating in that manner than anyone else is.

Democritus won fame for his advocacy of the theory that reality is comprised of atoms (very miniscule bits of indivisible matter) and the emptiness between them (the "void").[161] But our interest lies in epistemology and in that respect the famous saying of Democritus—"By agreed convention, a thing is 'cold' or a thing is 'hot,' but in truth there are only atoms and emptiness."[162]—is where we must start. What does Democritus mean?

It may be that Democritus is contrasting the certainty of what actually *is*— atoms and void—with what *seems to be*, which remains a matter of perception. Similar to his contemporary Protagoras, Democritus recognizes individual differences in sense-perception; these create a subjective experience—and that thereby creates epistemological uncertainty. However, unlike Protagoras, who accepts each variant perception as a matter of belief, but true, Democritus assumes a more skeptical stance. As understood by Epicurus, Democritus is viewed as having denied the reality of anything other than atoms and void, which means that the realm of knowledge (*epistēmē*), of what can be known as true and certain, is significantly limited.

The writer who offers the most extended presentation of Democritus' epistemology is Sextus Empiricus, the Skeptic philosopher. He notes, for example, the apparent similarity between Democritus and the Skeptics in the way perceptions are spoken about, but observes that while the words may be the same their meaning is different, for when Democritus talks about differences in perception he means to highlight them as that which is uncertain against the certainty of atoms and void. On the other hand, when a Skeptic reflects on such differences what is meant is an uncertainty about whether any perception accurately reflects something real.[163]

---

[160] Diogenes Laertius, *Lives of Eminent Philosophers: Epicurus*, X.14 [*Epicurus*, 8]. Also see X.30-31.
[161] Diogenes Laertius, *Lives of Eminent Philosophers: Democritus*, IX.44 [*Democritus*, 12].
[162] Diogenes Laertius, *Lives of Eminent Philosophers: Pyrrho*, IX.72 [*Pyrrho*, 8]. Cf. IX.45.
[163] Sextus Empiricus, *Outlines of Pyrrhonism*, I.30.213-214.

In one place Sextus Empiricus presents Democritus' view as follows:

> Democritus at times throws out the things that appear (*phainomena*) to sense perception (*aisthēsei*) and instead says that nothing appears in accord with truth (*alētheian*), but only in accord with belief (*doxan*), since true things are those that actually exist—the atoms and the void. For he says, "By agreed convention, a thing is 'cold' or a thing is 'hot,' but in truth there are only atoms and emptiness." In other words, the things of sense-perception (*aisthēta*) are supposed (*nomizetai*) and believed (*doxazetai*) to actually exist, but this is not the truth because they do not actually exist, because only atoms and the void do. In his *Confirmations*, despite promising to establish believability (*pisteōs*) to the senses, he is found condemning them! For he says, "But we in reality do not comprehend anything as it actually is, but only what shifts around according to the body's disposition and of things both entering it and resisting it." And once again he remarks, "Now that we do not comprehend how each thing *is* or *is not*, has been made evident quite often." And in his book *Concerning Ideas*: "It is necessary that one know," he says, "that a person by this ruling principle is separated from what is actually real." And once more, "This argument again makes clear that of actual reality we have no knowledge (*ismen*) but is in every case what belief (*doxis*) draws up." And finally, "It will be obvious that to know (*gignōskein*) each thing as it really *is* is extremely difficult."[164]

In sum, Democritus seems to regard only the atoms and the void as certainly real and the foundation of all things. But what appears to human senses cannot be regarded as *certain* and therefore is not "knowledge." Human minds in perception rework things as the situation of their physical being changes so that as a result we are left with "belief" (*doxa*), which is a kind of redrawing of reality to fit a given moment and personal situation. So, unlike Protagoras, Democritus is unwilling to reduce *everything* to belief, and account it all true. Instead, what is certain and true is very limited in scope. This is why he can also say, "And truly we can know nothing, for truth is in a deep sea."[165]

---

[164] Sextus Empiricus, *Against the Dogmatists: Against the Logicians* (*Pros logikous*), I.135-137. My citation, though cumbersome, is to indicate that his large work *Against the Professors* (*Pros mathēmatikous*) is itself divided into parts, each with their own conventional title. *Against the Logicians* is books VII-VIII of the whole, but often included with books IX-XI as part of a volume titled *Against the Dogmatists*, where it is books I-II. As we repeatedly see, words like *phainomena* (φαινόμενα) and *aisthēsis* (αἴσθησις) are important philosophical terms. The verb "appears' renders φαίνεσθαι (*phainesthai*, fr. φαίνω). My choice of "believability" for *pisteōs* (πίστεως) is debatable, as the sense here should be construed as 'believable' as in 'worthy of trust.' I want to highlight the connection with *doxa*; matters of sense-perception are not seen as warranting the sense of trust that knowledge with its certainty commands; they remain articles of belief. The phrase "ruling principle" translates κανόνι (*kanoni*). The phrase "actually real" renders ἐτεῆς (*eteēs*), which might more simply be put as "reality," but I want to emphasize the distinction being made between what really *is* (actual reality) and what *seems to be* (i.e., commonly taken as reality). The word "knowledge" translates ἴσμεν (*ismen*, fr. ἴσμη).

[165] Diogenes Laertius, *Lives of Eminent Philosophers: Pyrrho*, IX.72 [*Pyrrho*, 8].

Democritus retains utter confidence that reality can be known by reason; it is a matter of necessity. Sextus Empiricus explains it this way:

> But in the *Canon* he says there are two kinds of knowing (*gnōseis*): on the one hand, through sense-perceptions (*aisthēseōn*), and on the other hand, through the mind (*dianoias*). Of these he calls knowing through the mind "authentic," testifying that it is trustworthy (*piston*) in the judgment (*krisin*) of truth (*alētheias*). But to the other, knowing through sense-perception, he gives the name "illegitimate," denying it reliability in the discernment of truth. He then says, "Of the two ways of knowing (*gnōmēs*) that exist, one is authentic and the other illegitimate. To the illegitimate belongs seeing, hearing, smelling, tasting, touching; but the authentic is different from this."[166]

The position of Democritus might be illustrated in this manner:

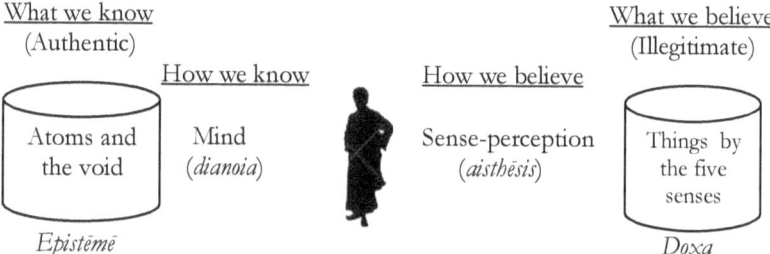

What we know (Authentic)	How we know		How we believe	What we believe (Illegitimate)
Atoms and the void	Mind (*dianoia*)		Sense-perception (*aisthēsis*)	Things by the five senses
Epistēmē				*Doxa*

Democritus contrasts the certainty of a basic reality known by reason with the uncertainty of "knowing" by the senses—which is really just "believing."

Epicurus & Knowledge: Canonic Epistemology

Methodologically, Epicureans espouse a disdain for dialectics.[167] Nevertheless, while calling for the use of ordinary terms in philosophic discourse, Epicurus in developing his *Canon* establishes his own 'rules'—principles to guide Epicurean thinking. In a letter to Herodotus, which Diogenes Laertius preserves, Epicurus explains the importance of adhering to basic rules:

> Certainly one must proceed by returning to the main principles, constantly fixing them in memory in order to achieve an authoritative conception of things and with exactness discern a correct knowledge (*akribōma*) of specific things, which follows when these principles are well-embraced and remembered. [168]

---

[166] Sextus Empiricus, *Against the Dogmatists: Against the Logicians*, I.138-139. Also see Aëtius, *Opinions of the Philosophers* (*De placita philosophorum*), I.25.4 [Stobaeus, *Anthology* (*Eclogues*), I.4.7]. As always, trying to decide how best to render a form of διάνοια (*dianoia*) is a challenge, since in English words like "mind," "intellect," or "understanding"—all viable choices in translation—carry different connotations.

[167] Diogenes Laertius, *Lives of Eminent Philosophers: Epicurus*, X.31 [*Epicurus*, 20].

[168] Epicurus, *Letter to Herodotus*, in Diogenes Laertius, *Lives of Eminent Philosophers: Epicurus*, X.36 [*Epicurus*, 24]. The word for "knowledge" here is ἀκρίβωμα (*akribōma*), meaning a "precise accounting" or "exact knowledge" of the matter under consideration.

The foundational criterion (*canon*) is the judgment of things as 'true' or 'false'—i.e., real or not—by sense-perception.[169] Sextus Empiricus writes:

> Now Epicurus says that all sense-perception (*aisthēsis*) is about things both true (*alēthē*) and real (*onta*). For there is unbroken continuity between a thing being 'true' and saying that 'it exists' (*huparchon*). And so in writing about truth and falsity, he says, "Truth is the same as having the being it is said to have." And, "Falsity is the same as not having the being it is said to have." He further says that sense-perception (*aisthēsin*), apprehending the things offered to it, neither taking away nor adding to nor changing anything (by virtue of being apart from reason (*alogon*)), is thus always being truthful and offers up things as they really are. But whereas all the things of sense-perception (*aisthētōn*) are true, the things of belief (*doxasta*) are different: some are true and some false, as has been shown earlier.[170]

Epicurus argues that precisely because sense-perception's immediacy is unmediated by reason, it avoids the manipulations of reason (the taking away, adding on, and changing that happens when reason is engaged), and thus can be trusted to present real objects as they really are. Or, to put it in a simple formula:

$$\text{Sense-perception} = \text{truth and reality (things as they } are\text{)}$$
$$(aisth\bar{e}sis) \qquad (al\bar{e}th\bar{e}) = (onta)$$

Put simply, as Diogenes Laertius writes, "With respect to making pronouncements on unknown matters, they start by observation of sense phenomena."[171]

Epicurus' epistemology is grounded in physiology. Perception is a physical process whereby certain atoms associated with an external object are an "image," or "idol" of that object. These atoms, arising from the object, represent it faithfully. An object, made of atoms, has a 'skin' or 'frame' of atoms, hollow and incredibly thin, that preserves the exact likeness and shape of the object.[172] Much later, the Roman Epicurean poet Lucretius (c. 99-55 B.C.E.), writes simply of "the existence of what we call 'images' (*simulacra*); an image (*imago*) has the appearance and contour resembling something like a kind of skin (*membranae*) at the surface of the body of a thing, which is torn away to flit about from here to there through the air."[173]

This image almost instantaneously crosses the void separating object from person, and enters through the senses. As Epicurus puts it: "Now we must also consider that it is by the entering of something arising from objects outside our-

---

[169] For a more expansive view of the role of the "criterion" (κριτήριον, *kritēriom*) in ancient Greek philosophy, see Sextus Empiricus, *Against the Dogmatists: Against the Logicians*, I.29-37.

[170] Sextus Empiricus, *Against the Dogmatists: Against the Logicians*, II.9. Immediately after this, Sextus goes into the Stoic view on the same matter.

[171] Diogenes Laertius, *Lives of Eminent Philosophers: Epicurus*, X.32 [*Epicurus*, 20].

[172] Epicurus, *Letter to Herodotus*, in Diogenes Laertius, *Lives of Eminent Philosophers: Epicurus*, X.46 [*Epicurus*, 24].

[173] Lucretius, *On the Nature of Things* (*De rerum natura*), IV.37-41.

selves that we see their shapes and think of them." There is an "impact" so that a *phantasia* ("appearance") arises, which is a representation of the image whether apprehended by the mind or the senses.[174] It looks like this:

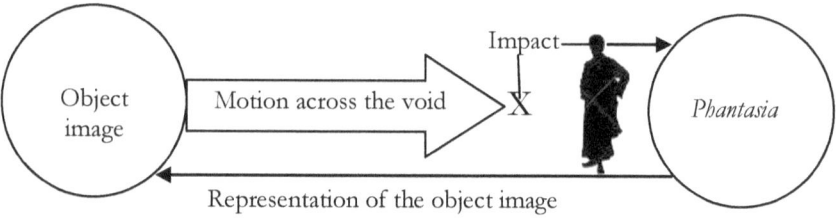

Representation of the object image

Lest we immediately object that sensory illusions make of this idea a *prima facie* absurdity, we must note that all Epicureans maintain is that in sense-perception there exists a faithful representation of the *image*, not of the object itself. While the image originates as a true representation of the object, it is just an image and so subject to manipulation. Lucretius patiently tries to dissolve apparent difficulties, offering a number of different situations, such as how a distant city can appear to have rounded towers when they are actually square; the distance the image has to travel wears at it and smoothes its angles.[175] But more fundamentally, such cases bring us to the role of reason.

Reason: A Subordinate Function

Epicurus consistently subordinates reason to sense-perception. Diogenes Laertius summarizes, or paraphrases, the teaching of Epicurus this way:

> Nor is there anything that can refute them. For a sense-perception (*aisthēsis*) cannot do such to another, for either they are similar and alike in validity, or different in kind and incomparable because they discern different things. Likewise, reason (*logos*) cannot refute them because reason depends upon the sense-perceptions (*aisthēseōn*).[176]

Reason (*logos*) follows *after* sense-perception (*aisthēsis*).

One of the important qualities of sense-perception for Epicurus is that it is *alogos*—apart from, or 'without' reason. If the immediacy and directness of sense-perception (*aisthēsis*) means it can apprehend objects truthfully, as they are, the remoteness of reason—forever at a remove from the object—means it can (and often does) add, subtract, or change the image that comes into contact with it.

---

[174] Epicurus, *Letter to Herodotus*, in Diogenes Laertius, *Lives of Eminent Philosophers: Epicurus*, X.46-50 [*Epicurus*, 24]. The key terms are: "image" (εἰκών, *eikōn*); "idol" (εἴδωλον, *eidōlon*); "impact" (ἐπερεισμός, *epereismos*); "mind" (διανοία, *dianoia*); and "senses" (αἰσθητηρίοις, *aisthētēpiois*).
[175] Lucretius, *On the Nature of Things*, IV.353-362.
[176] Diogenes Laertius, *Lives of Eminent Philosophers: Epicurus*, X.31 (end)-32 [*Epicurus*, 20].

So the situation actually looks like this:

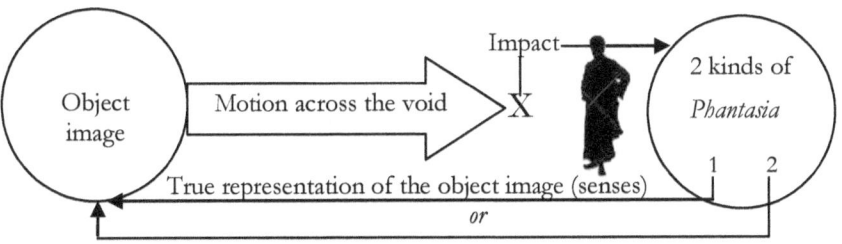

True or false representation of the object image (reason)

Epistemological *uncertainty* is associated with reason, which means that unlike the Stoics and others, the Epicurean cannot count on reason for knowledge.

It is not that reason is unable to provide truth. But because it has the ability to add, subtract, and change, it is constantly prone to do so. This accounts for most of what we regard as 'mistakes' in perception. Lucretius, after recounting many such instances which, he confesses, seem to exist to shake confidence (*fidem*) in sense-perception,[177] adds by way of explanation:

> For the most part we are tripped up by beliefs (*opinatus*) of the rational soul (*animi*), which of itself makes additions, so that we "see" what is not actually there in the sensation of sight. Nothing is more difficult than to separate out the manifest facts from the dubious ideas tacked on afterwards by the rational soul.[178]

This does not mean we should discount reason entirely. Indeed, reason matters to Epicurus and his followers,[179] even though the specifics on the matter are among the more difficult features of the philosophy. The key component is an idea about how reason best builds upon repeated sense-perceptions.

Prolēpsis: A Cognitive Anticipation

Prolēpsis—an "anticipation" or "preconception"—is a term for a key concept in Epicurean thinking. A *prolēpsis* is a cognitive "pre-notion" of something not yet actually present. It is the product of repeated sense impressions registered and stored in memory. Thus a *prolēpsis* is a mental composite built and held within memory based on an accumulation of sense-perceptions. In short, it is the epitome of how reason follows from sense-perception.

Diogenes Laertius remarks on the crucial place in the Epicurean system held by *prolēpsis*. He writes, "Now, in the *Canon*, Epicurus says the criteria for truth are sense-perceptions (*aisthēseis*), preconceptions (*prolēpseis*), and emotions

---

[177] Lucretius, *On the Nature of Things*, IV.462-463.
[178] Lucretius, *On the Nature of Things*, IV.464-468.
[179] See Diogenes Laertius, *Lives of Eminent Philosophers: Epicurus*, X.144 (Maxim 16) [*Epicurus*, 31]: "Chance events rarely affect the Wise, for reason (*ho logos*) is the greatest and supreme governor of his life now and over its entire course."

(*pathē*). But Epicureans in general also include the presentations held in the mind."[180] He then goes on to elaborate on the idea of *prolēpsis* in Epicureanism:

> About *prolēpsin* they speak of it as if it is a 'direct apprehension' (*katalēpsis*), or a 'correct belief' (*doxa orthēn*), or a 'notion' (*ennoian*), or a 'general understanding' (*katholikēn noēsin*) being stored; that is to say, it is an advance recollection of external things that have many times appeared to us. An example: "Such and such a thing is a human being." As soon as we say 'human being,' immediately a *prolēpsin* of such an image is thought of, as directed by sense-perceptions (*aisthēseōn*). In fact, the principal referent for everything we name is already implied and plain; we could not even seek what we search for without first having knowledge (*egnokeimen*) of it.[181]

A *prolēpsis*, then, is something supplied by the rational mind from the storage of memory. But it remains dependent on the sense-perceptions that have preceded it and which build it in the first place. However, once built it then can guide the process of sorting sense-perceptions and making sense of them. Among the ways Diogenes Laertius says that the Epicureans speak of *prolēpsis* is as *doxa orthēn*—"correct belief"—and by the company it keeps such *doxa* is rational in character.

Belief

Belief belongs to the rational part of the *psyche* and is tied to *prolēpsis*. In the sense of a *prolēpsis*, a belief is 'correct' because it is formed in memory from many prior sense-perceptions upon which it depends. Accurate mental pictures and concepts must be formed or human cognition is hopeless. But while a *prolēpsis* in itself—as a composite mental representation—is a correct belief, that does not mean every belief is also correct. A given belief (*doxa*) can be a misapplication of a correct belief (*prolēpsis*), as for example, when a person mistakes a cow for a horse. The person may have very accurate mental pictures of both animals yet mistake one for the other.

This stems from the fact, says Sextus Empiricus, that belief (*doxa*) though also associated with the *phantasia* ("appearance") of an object is different:

> According to Epicurus there are two things existing in close association with one another—appearance (*phantasias*) and belief (*doxa*); of these, the appearance (*phantasian*), which is called 'evident' (*enargeian*), is by its nature always true (*alēthē*). . . .

---

[180] Diogenes Laertius, *Lives of Eminent Philosophers: Epicurus*, X.31 [*Epicurus*, 20 (start)]. There is no easy way to translate *tas phantastikas epidbolas tēs dianoias*. A *phantastikos* is a representation of an "appearance" (*phantasia* or *phantasma*) held in the "mind," or "intellect" or "reason" (*dianoia*).

[181] Diogenes Laertius, *Lives of Eminent Philosophers: Epicurus*, X.33 [*Epicurus*, 21]. In a body-based philosophy like Epicureanism *noēsin* (fr. νόησις) refers to a faculty of the *psyche* that, like sense-perception, is able to perceive the "images" (*eidola*) produced by things, but differently than as done in immediate sense-perception. *Noēsis* is an understanding built upon previous sense-perceptions that in *prolēpsis* preserves and presents a general concept.

Also, with respect to objects lying close to hand we must reason likewise. So a thing seen not only appears (*phainetai*) visible, but actually is as it appears (*phainetai*); and a thing heard not only appears audible, but actually is the same in truth (*alētheiais*)—and such is also the case with the remaining senses. Appearances (*phantasiai*), whenever they happen, are true (*alētheis*).[182]

As such, a belief is subordinate to and derived from sense-perception, but unlike sense-perception it is prone to error. Sextus writes:

> Of beliefs (*doxōn*), according to Epicurus these may be either true (*alētheis*) or false (*pseudeis*). Those that are true are confirmed by evidence, and not disconfirmed, having the quality of being self-evident (*enargeias*); those that are false are disconfirmed and not confirmed by evidence, lacking clarity (*enargeias*).[183]

Diogenes Laertius writes similarly:

> Now "belief" (*doxan*) they also call "supposition" (*hupolēpsin*), and they say it can be either true (*alēthē*) or false (*pseudē*). For if it is supported by confirming evidence and not contradicted by the same, it is true; if it is not supported by confirming evidence or is contradicted by it, then it is false. Because of this they introduced the watchword "waiting"—as in, waiting to draw closer to a thing to learn if the way it appears is truly the shape of a tower.[184]

Sextus Empiricus explains the nature of the confirming evidence needed: "Confirming evidence is direct apprehension (*katalēpsis*) through the self-evident (*enargeias*) that what is being believed (*doxazomenon*) is the same as it was believed (*edoxazeto*) to be. . . ."[185] In our example, by waiting the observer may find out if the tower really has a rounded shape or not.

This, we might say, is the Epicurean version of the idea of a 'justified true belief.' If sense-perception (*aisthēsis*) supports belief (*doxa*), then it is knowledge. The alternative term *hupolēpsis*—an "assumption" or "supposition"—fits well with the sense of a belief that is also a *prolēpsis*. A preconception may have validity based on the evidentiary store of sense-perceptions upon which it rests, but it is still a "belief" until, by "waiting" (*prosmenō*) further, immediate sensory confirmation makes it "knowledge."

---

182 Sextus Empiricus, *Against the Dogmatists: Against the Logicians*, I.203 (1st paragraph) and I.204 (second paragraph). Also see I.205-221 for broader context and commentary on this view.
183 Sextus Empiricus, *Against the Dogmatists: Against the Logicians*, I.211. The phrase "confirmed by evidence" renders ἐπιμαρτυρούμεναι (*epimarturoumenai*,fr. ἐπιμαρτυρέω), which might also be translated "supported" (by evidence or testimony); "disconfirmed by evidence" translates ἀντιμαρτυρούμεναι (*antimarturoumenai*, fr. ἀντιμαρτυρέω).
184 Diogenes Laertius, *Lives of Eminent Philosophers: Epicurus*, X.34 [*Epicurus*, 22].
185 Sextus Empiricus, *Against the Dogmatists: Against the Logicians*, I.212.

We might illustrate the matter this way:

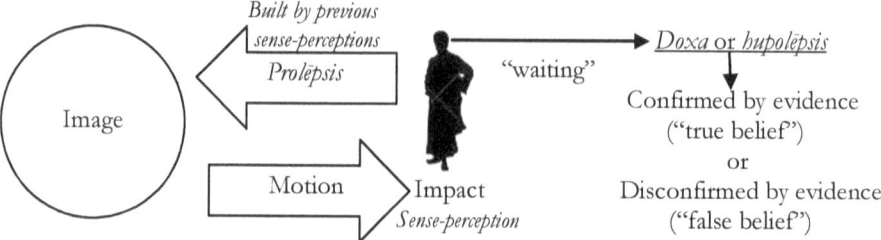

Diogenes Laertius makes the point that *prolēpsis* offers "clarity" (*energēs*)[186]—a way by which thinking can make full use of a store of experience to form judgments and test their veracity. In short, *prolēpsis* helps toward knowledge.

In his letter to Herodotus, Epicurus offers his own elaboration:

> Now, that which is false (*pseudos*) and faulty belief (*prosdoxazomen*) always occurs while 'waiting' (*prosmenontos*) upon confirming evidence, or at least the absence of disconfirming evidence. (Then, neither confirmed nor disconfirmed, we still experience a movement within ourselves connected with an act of perceptual representation (*phantastikè*), yet different from it, and it is from this which error (*pseudos*) arises.)
>
> For the likeness of mental images (*phantasmōn*), being as if the images (*eikoni*) of actual things, whether they come from the sleeping mind, or other conscious thoughts (*dianoias*), or some other criteria (*kritēriōn*), could never compare to the actual objects except such objects were actually perceived. And making mistakes would not happen except we receive a different movement within ourselves, connected with an act of perceptual representation (*phantastikè*), yet different from it; and it is from this movement, if it is neither confirmed nor disconfirmed, that error (*pseudos*) arises. On the other hand, when confirmed or not disconfirmed, then truth (*alēthes*) exists.[187]

Belief may be true or false, but it seems always to start as *impatient*. It forms as an internal motion that happens while waiting for supporting evidence, or for disconfirming evidence. While such evidence—or the lack of disconfirming evidence—may finally yield a true belief, where the mental conception matches closely enough the image of the real object and the object itself, there is a period in which its truth or falsity is indeterminate. Though in either case—whether the belief be true or false—it is associated with sense-perception having occurred before it, nevertheless the source of error is a judgment from this impatience. For instance, the belief that an object is a tower with rounded edges

---

[186] Diogenes Laertius, *Lives of Eminent Philosophers: Epicurus*, X.33 (near end) [*Epicurus*, 22].

[187] Epicurus, *Letter to Herodotus*, in Diogenes Laertius, *Lives of Eminent Philosophers: Epicurus*, X.50-51 [*Epicurus*, 24]. "Confirming evidence" renders ἐπιμαρτυρηθήσεσθαι (*epimarturēthēsesthai*, fr. ἐπιμαρτυρέω); "disconfirming evidence" translates ἀντιμαρτυρηθήσεσθαι (*antimarturēthēsesthai*, fr. ἀντιμαρτυρέω). Similarly, "confirmed" (ἐπιμαρτυρηθῇ, *epimarturēthē*) and "disconfirmed" (ἀντιμαρτυρηθῇ, *antimarturēthē*). Both are terms referring to the bearing of witness, testimony, or evidence for or against someone or something.

would be confirmed or disconfirmed if only the person waited long enough to draw close enough to receive confirming or disconfirming evidence.

We are left with a composite picture for cognition somewhat like this:

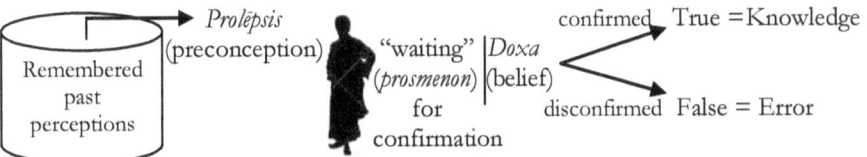

The rational faculty relies on sense-perception (*aisthēsis*), accumulating through the impact of sensations a store of remembered past perceptions. These are rationally grouped according to likeness—what we can call concept formation—to make available a mental picture that is an anticipation or preconception (*prolēpsis*). Such mental pictures are triggered by the mere mention of a word—'man,' 'cow,' 'horse'—and immediately present this composite of stored and sorted past perceptions for use with respect to incoming sensory data. A *prolēpsis* aids thinking while sense-perception is occurring by generating belief (*doxa*) or a supposition (*hupolēpsis*) about the sensory image (*eikōn*) contacting the mind. Epicureans advise "waiting" (*prosmenon*) for confirmation or disconfirmation that the *prolēpsis*-belief is true. A confirmation means a belief is true and accordingly adds to the person's store of knowledge. In sum, knowledge is a distal product of cognition following after sense-perception.

The Limitations of Knowledge

While belief (*doxa* or *hupolēpsis*) is prone to error, knowledge, as that which is both true and certain, is *limited*. Epicurus qualifies the reach of knowledge in a distinctive way. In a letter to Pythocles, Epicurus writes:

> To begin with, not unlike other matters, the goal (*telos*) of investigative knowledge (*gnōsiōs*) of celestial phenomena, whether in association with other matters or as its own object, is calmness and firm confidence (*pistin*)—just that and nothing else.[188]

Consistent with his desire to offer a practical, down-to-earth, sensible philosophy that both explains reality and helps a person live within it, Epicurus sets forward the notion that what we can know is enough to achieve peace of mind. This is harmonious with his goal of avoiding pain (e.g., fear), and promoting pleasure (e.g., a calm mind).

Near the end of his letter to Herodotus, Epicurus addresses the anxiety aroused in people by an imperfect knowledge of nature. Of course, he says, the desire to understand exactly the way things are is the goal of knowledge. But it is an elusive goal in a world where alternative explanations for events are possi-

---

[188] Epicurus, *Letter to Pythocles*, in Diogenes Laertius, *Lives of Eminent Philosophers: Epicurus*, X.85-86 [*Epicurus*, 25].

ble. What human beings do know has to be sufficient for achieving the true pleasure of a mind-at-ease, one free of fear. *Partial* knowledge, *imperfect* knowledge, is still *sufficient* knowledge. This is important because, he argues, people who experience anxiety arising from a lack of complete knowledge fall prey to outrageous claims—and he has specifically in mind the kind made in the name of religion. Epicurus contests what he sees as inconsistent and harmful beliefs about the gods associated with an imperfect understanding of the celestial bodies.[189] This is why in his *Principal Doctrines* he says, "It is impossible to let go one's fear about matters of most importance without understanding the nature of the cosmos for instead a person falls prey to myths."[190]

Concluding Note

We began our examination of Greek philosophy with the provocative proposal by Protagoras that sense-perception leads to personal judgments that are true for the person who believes them and that this constitutes personal knowledge. The subjectivity and relativism of this stance excited opposition. Figures like Socrates, Plato, Aristotle, and later the Stoics, all responded by both affirming an objectivity in knowledge and by asserting the importance of reason.

Epicurus, while not agreeing entirely with Protagoras, does agree that sense-perception is of fundamental importance. Epicureans find that those schools— the Academy, the Peripatetics, the Stoics—that prize reason so highly are promoting a standard that leads away from knowledge and toward error. They argue that if it were not for the rational faculty in us we would not form erroneous beliefs. So, as rational beings we must use reason, but our use must be carefully constrained. It must begin with a sober realization of its secondary and dependent position with respect to sense-perception. Then, used appropriately, true beliefs can be formed and these constitute a reliable "knowledge." It is an approach many applaud for its attention to sense-perception but which many others find naïve in its confidence. But no group has more confidence than the Stoics to whom we now must turn.

---

[189] Epicurus, *Letter to Herodotus*, in Diogenes Laertius, *Lives of Eminent Philosophers:: Epicurus*, X.78-80 [*Epicurus*, 24].

[190] Epicurus, *Mxims* (aka *Sovran* [*Sovereign*] *Maxims* or *Principle Doctrines*), 12, in Diogenes Laertius, *Lives of Eminent Philosophers: Epicurus*, X.143 [*Epicurus*, 31]. The word "understanding" translates κατειδότα (*kateidota*, fr. κάτοιδα).

9

The Stoic Sensibility

About the same time that Epicurus was formulating the philosophy that would bear his name, the philosopher Zeno of Citium (c. 334-c. 262 B.C.E.) was founding a new approach that would come to be known as Stoicism.[191] Though influenced by the ideas of Socrates and Plato,[192] Aristotle,[193] and even the Epicureans, the Stoics would quickly develop their own distinctive ideas, defending the possibility of achieving knowledge and engaging in vigorous philosophical debates with the other schools of the day, such as the Skeptics and Epicureans. As an influential school of philosophy, Stoicism flourished for centuries, even being steadfastly practiced by the 'philosopher-king' of Rome, the emperor Marcus Aurelius, in the late 2nd century.

Stoicism is a complex philosophy developed over a significant period of time by many creative and strong-willed thinkers, making it challenging to adequately present its epistemology, and all the more complicated by the generally fragmentary nature of our sources for all but a few of the later Stoics. Among the most prominent Stoic philosophers we may name (using the conventional scholarly divisions):

> ➤ Early Stoicism: Zeno, Cleanthes, Chrysippus, and Diogenes of Babylon;
> ➤ Middle Stoicism: Panaetius of Rhodes, and Posidonius; and
> ➤ Later Stoicism: Gaius Musonius Rufus, Seneca, Epictetus, and the emperor Marcus Aurelius.

To try to simplify our task we shall examine Stoicism by focusing in turn on each period and trying to highlight distinctive contributions. A rather greater share of attention will go to the early Stoics than to the later ones.

---

[191] The name is derived from the covered porch (*Stoa*) in Athens where the first Stoics gathered and began to teach. See Diogenes Laertius, *Lives of Eminent Philosophers: Zeno,* VII.4-5. Attribution of Zeno as founder can be found in Cicero, *Academics (Academica),* I.42 [ch. XIII].

[192] Though influenced by Platonic philosophy, Zeno and the Stoics strongly rejected Plato's theory of forms. Zeno wrote his own *Republic,* copying Plato's title but in opposition to Plato's ideas; it has not survived.

[193] The ancient geographer and historian Strabo (*Geography,* II.3.8) claimed of the prominent Stoic Posidonius that he did much imitating of Aristotle. Current opinions on Aristotle's influence vary.

In the days of the Late Roman Republic, Cicero—using the voice of the famed Roman Senator Marcus Porcius Cato Uticensis (Cato the Younger, 95-46 B.C.E.), a Stoic devotee—observes, "there is in Stoicism difficult reasoning (*ratio*) and a certain obscurity." This is attributed to the novelty of its ideas when they were introduced, and the accompanying vocabulary used. About this Cicero himself remarks that Zeno "with many things contrived unusual notions, and imposed them on things through a novel use of words."[194] Zeno, so to speak, constructed Stoic philosophy on the fly, appropriating existing words and investing them with his new meanings.[195]

Zeno arranged Stoicism into three divisions—logic, physics, and ethics—but these were closely intertwined and it is difficult to maintain that any one division consistently achieves priority.[196] One matter is clear: the Stoics, from the start, possessed complete confidence in reason. Cicero says of Zeno that, "Zeno, and most of the other Stoics, view *Ether* as the Supreme God, being endowed with *mentes*, by which all is directed."[197] The key term here is *mentes*, which can be translated as "mind," "intellect," "reason," "judgment," and so forth. The idea is of that faculty making possible the governing of the universe.

Cicero explains how Zeno understood reason:

> Whereas those who preceded him had not said that all virtue is in reason (*ratione*), but that some virtues have been perfected by Nature or by habit, Zeno fixed all virtue in reason (*ratione*). Whereas that earlier generation said those types of virtues I mentioned above could be separated, Zeno argued that it was in no way possible to do so, and instead judged that not merely the exercise of virtue was magnificent, but the virtuous character itself, and that it is impossible that virtue exist in anyone without that person constantly practicing it. Whereas his predecessors did not eliminate passion (*perturbationem*) from the rational soul (*animi*) that is in human beings, saying that it is human nature to suffer and desire and fear and experience joy, they also drew them together within narrow bounds, but Zeno taught that the wise is entirely free from all such 'diseases' as they might be termed. And whereas those men of old said that passions (*perturbationes*) are natural, and share nothing of reason (*rationis*), and so they placed passion (*cupiditatem*) in one part of the rational soul (*animi*) and reason (*rationem*) in another, Zeno could not give his assent (*assentiebatur*) to this. For Zeno, passions (*perturbationes*) were a matter of willing (*voluntarias*), and were caught up by a judgment of

---

[194] Cicero, *On Moral Ends* (*De finibus*), III.15. First quote (at beginning of 15).

[195] The Stoics seemed unconcerned by this practice; Chrysippus, according to Aulus Gellius, *Attic Nights* (*Noctes Atticae*), XI.12.12, "affirms that all words are by nature ambiguous, seeing that from the same word two or more senses are possible."

[196] Diogenes Laertius, *Lives of Eminent Philosophers: Zeno*, VII.39 [VII: *Zeno*, 33]. Cf. Cicero, *On Moral Ends*, IV.4: "The entirety of philosophy was divided into three parts, which partitioning Zeno saw should be retained."

[197] Cicero, *Academics*, II.126 [ch XLI]. Book II of the *Academics* is also known as *Lucullus*.

belief (*opiniosque iudicio*), and that a certain lack of moderation was the mother of all passions (*perturbationum*). [198]

Some key ideas in Stoic thinking surface in Cicero's account. First and foremost is the preeminence given to reason and its attachment to virtue. Stoic thinking became first and foremost about ethics—virtuous living. Second we might also note the incidental mention of "assent," which we shall examine later. Third, the place of feeling—especially strong emotions, or "passion" (*perturbatio*)—with all its disorder and chaos, was an ongoing concern in Stoic thought. We shall attend more to that matter in a moment. Finally, the role that belief (*opinio*) plays in all of this is intimated.

Phantasia & Katalēpsis

Despite the preeminence of reason the Stoics start with sense-perception. Diogenes Laertius, quoting Diocles the Magnesian, tells us that the Stoics prioritized sense-perception (*aisthēsis*) and the appearances (*phantasia*) of objects accompanying it. In Diocles' words:

> The Stoics resolve to place first an explanation of "appearance" (*phantasia*) and sense-perception (*aisthēseōs*), inasmuch as the criterion by which the truth of things comes to be known (*ginōsketai*) is itself a kind of appearance (*phantasia*), and because the matter of assent, and of direct comprehension (*katalēpseōs*), and of mental explanation, which precedes the rest, cannot be put together apart from appearance (*phantasias*). For appearance (*phantasia*) comes first, then thought, which is at once ready to express the affect of the appearance (*phantasias*) by presenting an explanation (*logō*). [199]

Cicero reports that Zeno contributed some novel notions about how things impress themselves on our senses. Zeno names as *phantasia* ("appearances") the actual physical impression made on the senses by stimuli,[200] then adds that the mind, by exercise of the will, assents to certain of these appearances. Thus, similarly to the Epicureans, the Stoics observe, "Although sense-perceptions are truthful, the *phantasia* they yield can be either true or false."[201] If Stoics, like Epicureans, start with sense-perceptions, they do not from there follow a similar path. One difference between the Stoics and others is captured by the late Stoic philosopher Hierocles, who writes, "For they think that sense-perception (*aisthēsin*) has been naturally provided for the apprehension of objects, but not

---

[198] Cicero, *Academics*, I.38-39 [ch. X].

[199] Diogenes Laertius, *Lives of Eminent Philosophers: Zeno*, VII.49 [*Zeno*, VII.36]. I have chosen to render νοήσεως λόγος (*noēseōs logos*) as "mental explanation" to better distinguish it from διάνοια (*dianoia*), which comes later.

[200] "Sense-impression" is a common way of rendering *phantasia* despite the fact that "appearance" is more accurate. *Phantasia* is not restricted to sense-impressions, but can be applied to thoughts, too.

[201] Pearson, *Fragments*, 61, as Zeno, fragment 8 [= Stobaeus, *Anthology (Ecologues)*, I.50.21 = Aëtius, *Placita*, IV.9.4 = Von Arnim, *Stoicorum Veterum Fragmenta* (SVF), II.278].

also for the apprehension of oneself."[202] That sentiment gives a clue to how the Stoic approach varies; it not only prioritizes the role of reason but appreciates a strong psychological referent in the self.

Let us break down Cicero's presentation, focusing on *phantasia*, the "appearance" of something presented to the mind. Sextus Empiricus starts his discussion of the Stoic view by simply noting, "*phantasia* is, according to them, an 'impression' (*tupōsis*) on the *psyche*."[203] Once more we have a word used in a technical sense: *tupōsis*, which can be variously rendered in English as "impression," or "moulding," or "imprinting," or the like; it carries a basic sense of a "forming" upon something. Given the apparently differing construals of the term by Zeno's successor Cleanthes and the later leader Chrysippus, the term may well serve as one of the 'obscurities' Cicero mentions. Chrysippus, after Cleanthes, apparently aims to escape the rather more narrow possibilities of adhering to Cleanthes'—and presumably Zeno's—sense of it as a physical pressing upon the *psyche*.[204]

Some, but not all *phantasia* are characterized by *katalēpsis*, a comprehension of the appearance being "self-evident." These Stoics call true, or "self-evident appearances" (*katalēptike phantasia*). This leads Zeno to a basic distinction: the quality of *katalēpsis* makes possible a perception that can't be doubted, and thus is knowledge;[205] *phantasia* lacking such a quality fosters belief and is ignorance, because it is feeble and cannot be distinguished from what is false or unknown.

We have as a basic picture the following:

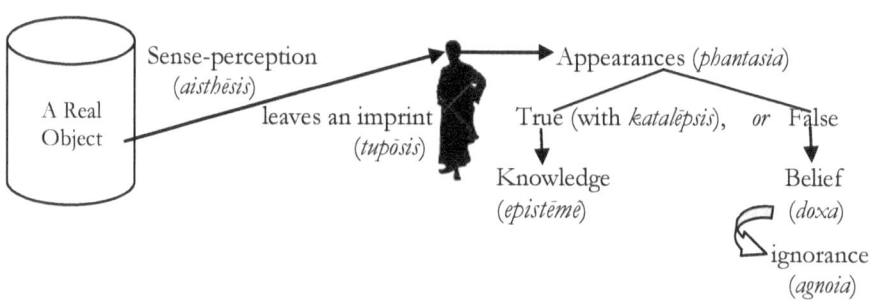

(The above may help explain Cicero's Cato calling Stoic reasoning "difficult"![206])

It will be helpful to grasp how *phantasia* separate into two kinds and Diogenes Laertius offers this description:

---

202 Hierocles, *Elements of Ethics*, I.44-45. Hierocles—not to be confused with the Neoplatonist of the same name—belongs to Late Stoicism and shares its emphasis on practiced virtue (ethics).
203 Sextus Empiricus, *Adversus Mathematicos: Against the Logicians*, I.228.
204 See Diogenes Laertius, *Lives of Eminent Philosophers: Zeno*, VII.50 [*Zeno*, 36].
205 On the Stoic sense of *epistēmē* see Stobaeus, *Anthology (Eclogues)*, II.74 [=Von Arnim, *Stoicorum Veterum Fragmenta* (SVF), III.112] (English translation of this passage in Long and Sedley, *Hellenistic Philosophers*, 256).
206 The question of how far to press the equivalence of ignorance and belief is one such difficulty.

Now an appearance (*phantasian*) is said to be an impression on the *psy-che*—the name having been carried over from the impression a seal makes upon wax. Of appearance (*phantasias*) there is the kind directly apprehended (*kataleptiken*) and the kind not so comprehended (*akataleptikon*). Of *katalep-tiken*, which they take to be the criterion of real things, it is that which comes about because of something real and corresponds to that real thing, and is the impression of the real thing. Of *akataleptikon*, it does not come about because of something real, or if it does, it is not a true correspondence to it, being neither clear nor an adequate representation.[207]

The key thing is the matter of whether or not the 'appearance' provides a direct comprehension of some real thing.

Assent

Remembering Cicero's description, we must factor in for both kinds of *phantasia* the possibility of "assent." Cicero's word is *adsensionem*, rendering the Greek term συγκατάθεσις (*sunkatathesis*).[208] The use of the word in this context is another of Zeno's innovations; he borrows a term derived from the democratic process of casting votes to say that the mind does the same. Stobaeus in his ancient *Anthology* writes, "The Stoics did not make sense-perception (*aisthesis*) a matter of appearances (*phantasia*) alone, but made its essence dependent upon assent (*sunkatatheseōs*); for sense-perception is assent to a sensible (*aisthetikè*) appearance, with the assent being set into motion by oneself."[209] Zeno not only formulated the notion but made it decisive and natural; the human mind naturally responds to appearances, weighing the evidence they present, and forming a judgment about them. Since Zeno the idea of assent has been important in philosophy, theology, psychology, and law.

Zeno thus calls attention to the role dictated by reason; the human mind has an indispensable role and one wherein reason must govern if truth and knowledge are to be achieved. There is a profoundly psychological element that comes into play, as Stobaeus' remark points out: assent represents a self-generated motion, a chosen activity by the individual affected by sense-

---

[207] Diogenes Laertius, *Lives of Eminent Philosophers: Zeno*, VII.45-46 [*Zeno*, 36]. The phrase "real things" translates πραγμάτων (*pragmatōn*, fr. πρᾶγμα (*pragma*)), "things," but in context "*real* things." The phrase "adequate representation" renders ἔκτυπον (*ektupon*), often translated as "distinct," but it is a word used in artistic work and here connotes an imprecise rendering in the mind because the *phantasia* does not present as an immediately forceful impression.

[208] The word derives from συγκατατίθημι (*sunkatatithēmi*). The form συγκατάθεσις is also found. To transliterate Greek into English, the Greek consonant γ has the English sound of 'n' when followed by certain consonants, such as κ, so this latter Greek form is quite understandable.

[209] Stobaeus, *Anthology*, I.49.25 (citing Porphyry's *De Anima*) [= Von Arnim, *Stoicorum Veterum Fragmenta* (SVF), II.74]. The word ὁρμὴν (*hormēs*, from ὁρμή), carries the core sense of "impetus" and appears to be an idea that originated with the Stoics. In Stoic thinking, *hormē* can cover both a reasoned, voluntary choice and an irrational impulse. See Cicero, *On Moral Ends*, V.17: "natural desire of the soul, which the Greeks call ὁρμὴν": *appetitum animi, quem ὁρμὴν Graeci vocant*. The idea predates Panaetius. Chrysippus' concern is to avoid any notion of an uncaused motion (whether in the *psyche* or not); the Stoics are firm determinists.

perception. Cicero says Zeno taught that *phantasia* "received by the senses are attached to the mind by assent, which is lodged in our will and so a matter of choice."[210] Assent decides a *phantasia* is true, and assent belongs to human will.

We can now add this notion of assent so that things fit together like this:

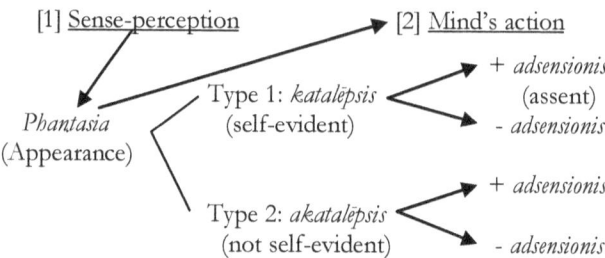

Any given *phantasia* may or may not receive the mind's assent, because such assent is always a choice of the intellect. It is, at least in adults, reason at work. But not every assent is equal in value, because some accompany directly apprehended, self-evident *phantasia*, and some do not. Thus the mind's decision-making—or vote-casting, if we like—is not guaranteed to be flawless; mistakes are made.

A key part in deciding to give assent is an appearance's "clarity" or "distinctness" (*enargeia*)—the "self-evidenct" quality that establishes its truth. The idea of *enargeia* is that objects naturally yield appearances to the senses that self-reveal the object. Sensory data typically presents itself in a clear, self-evident manner so that it can be used as a guiding rule in determining the truth of an appearance and, subsequently, whether it yields knowledge of an object (i.e., of the object as it *is* and not merely as it *appears to be*).

An appearance's *enargeia* is instrumental in *kataléptike phantasia*—the *katalépsis* is a direct comprehension of the *phantasia* made possible by its *enargeia*. Or, to put it into common English, the direct comprehension of the sense-perception is a result of being so clear as to be self-evident. That both *katalépsis* and *enargeia* convey in English the sense of being "self-evident" is telling. The former is a way of saying that the mind immediately grasps—comprehends—the appearance because of its clear, distinct, self-evident nature. But the comprehension is not merely of the *phantasia* but of the actual object itself. Thus the self-evident appearance (i.e., of the way a thing *appears* to be) can also yield knowledge (i.e., of the way a thing *is*). We may picture the matter in this manner:

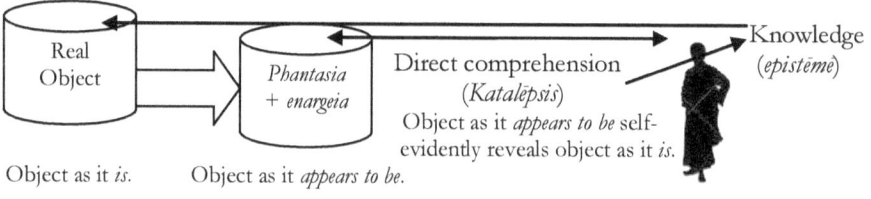

---

[210] Cicero, *Academics*, I.40 (end) [ch.XI]: *accepta sensibus, adsensionem adiungit animorum, quam esse volt in nobis positam et voluntarium.*

A "self-evident" appearance is one so clear it reveals an object as it *is*.

The importance of only giving assent to *phantasia* characterized by *katalēpsis* becomes obvious. It is so important a factor that it becomes the epistemological standard, or criterion, by which judgments of truth are made. But lest we get ahead of ourselves, let us complete our analysis of Zeno's scheme. The two kinds of *phantasia*, plus the presence of assent, leads to two possible outcomes: knowledge, or belief. With *katalēpsis* lodged between them, we have a complete spectrum, as we saw Cicero earlier indicate.

Zeno establishes his own continuum, one we might contrast with that set out earlier by Plato. Let us set them together in order to better compare them, with Plato's scheme on the left and Zeno's picture using Cicero's terms:

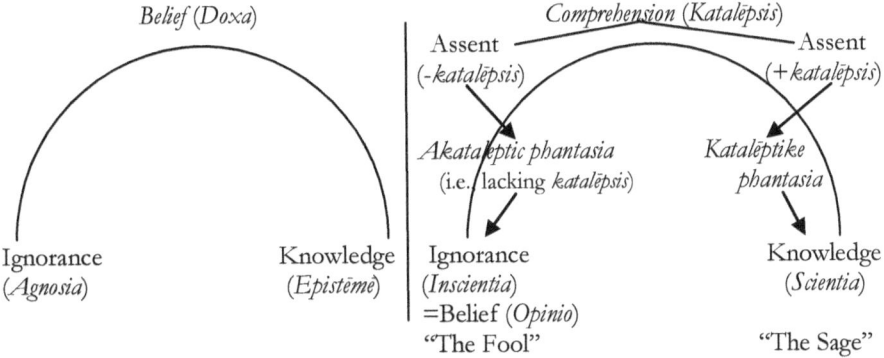

The Stoic picture is more complicated because of how assent interacts with *katalēpsis*. Following Cicero's lead, we have placed *katalēpsis* between ignorance and knowledge. But *katalēpsis* is "comprehension" and really leads to knowledge, not ignorance. So how can it be placed between knowledge and ignorance? To make sense of the illustration we have to see the role of assent. Sometimes, the Stoics argue, people give assent without comprehension and the result is the formation of belief, which reflects ignorance.

Still, our illustration is somewhat flawed in that the Stoic conception wants to identify *katalēpsis* with *self-evident* comprehension, that is, the kind of comprehension of an appearance that recognizes by the clarity and distinctiveness of it that here is a genuine peek at reality. So let us return to our earlier illustration on *katalēpsis* and assent and now complete it like this:

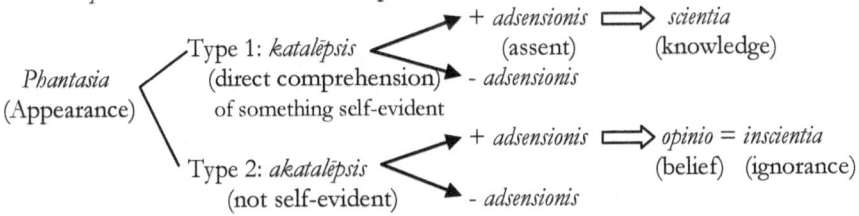

It is easy to see why, in this scheme, *katalēpsis*—lodged between *phantasia* and two very different outcomes—is so important to the Stoics.

Later, the Skeptic philosopher Sextus Empiricus (c. 160-c. 210 C.E.) characterizes the Stoic position in a manner that adds some important detail:

> They profess there are three things mutually linked: knowledge (*epistēmēn*), and belief (*doxan*), and between them, contiguous to both, comprehension (*katalēpsin*). Of these three, knowledge is said to be certain and stable and confirmed by reason. But belief is weak and a false assent. Comprehension, between these two, is assent attached to a direct apprehension of some appearance (*katalēptikes phantasias*); according to them, *katalēptike phantasia* is true and of such a kind that it cannot be false. They further claim that of these, knowledge is found only in the wise, while belief is found only in the worthless—but comprehension is found going both directions, and it is the criterion established for truth.[211]

The key here is that *katalēpsis* touches both belief and knowledge. Put simply, knowledge is strong because it is rational, dependable, and certain; belief is weak because it comes from a mistake in the assent process.

Now Sextus Empiricus' comment that "knowledge is found only in the wise" affords us a glimpse at another facet of the Stoic conception of knowledge. It is a *property* of mind—a stable set, or disposition. Elsewhere Sextus writes of *epistēmē* that it is "a particular state of the ruling part"[212]—and uses the metaphor of the hand making a fist to illustrate what he means.

The same image is in Cicero, who tells us that Zeno illustrates the states ranging from ignorance (the unwise) to knowledge (the wise) this way:

> And Zeno would perform gestures to illustrate: he would show his hand with outstretched fingers and say, "This is what an appearance (*visum*) is like." Then he would close his fingers a little and say, "This is what assent (*adsensus*) is like." Next he would press his fingers together so as to make a fist and say of it that it was like comprehension (*comprensionem*)—and with this illustration he for the first time used the word *katalēpsis* for that matter. At last he would raise his left hand, vigorously squeeze his right hand's fist, and then declare that this is what knowledge (*scientiam*) is like, which no one save the Wise possess; but who the 'Wise' are or have been none of the Stoics are accustomed to say.[213]

---

[211] Sextus Empiricus, *Adversus Mathematicos: Against the Logicians*, I, I.151-152. The word translated "certain" is ἀσφαλῆ (*asphalē*), which has the sense of being completely "secure." The phrase "confirmed by reason" translates ἀμετάθετον ὑπὸ λόγου (*ametatheton hupo logou*). The word translated "assent" is each time a form of συγκατάθεσις (*sunkatathesis*). The word "worthless" renders (*phaulois*), which suggests an ordinary person prone to wickedness; the term joins ethics to the epistemological thrust here. Also see I.38-44, where Sextus discusses the Stoic distinction between "truth" and "true."

[212] Sextus Empiricus, *Outlines of Pyrrhonism*, II.8.81. The same in slightly altered form occurs at *Adversus Mathematicos: Against the Logicians*, I, 39.

[213] Cicero, *Academics*, II.145.

We can now redraw our continuum using Cicero's story:

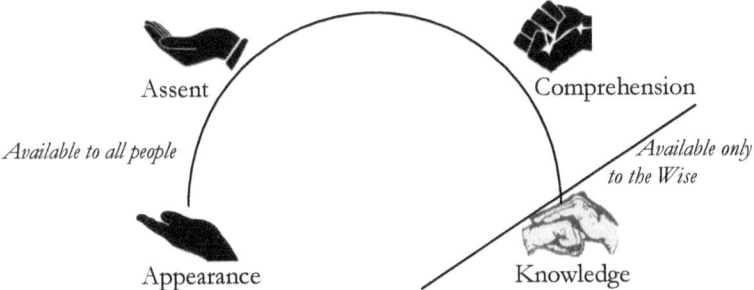

Assent

Available to all people

Comprehension

Available only to the Wise

Appearance

Knowledge

Like light against the darkness, knowledge is available only to the Wise.

However, in what we have been presenting we have been presuming that the equating of belief (*doxa*) and ignorance is a simple, straightforward matter. It is not. Some Stoics may have been content to adhere to such an idea, and an argument can be made that this view is the mainstream Stoic position. But most contemporary scholars think otherwise, though the nature of the evidence makes coming to a firm resolution presently impossible The issue turns on whether what is in view are general states of mind (e.g., belief versus knowledge), or a view of belief as a particular—and deficient—form of assent. Should we be looking at warring states of mind, or varying kinds of individual assent? Does Stoicism adopt a stark binary code which places most people in one state (i.e., the ignorant who hold beliefs), and only the Wise in another (i.e., with knowledge), so that each state leads to a predictable outcome? Or do the Stoics actually separate out belief from ignorance, so that the former is narrower than the latter—a difference of a certain kind of improper assent versus all kinds of errors? Anyway one looks at the issue it emerges as clear that the Stoics do not see belief and knowledge as ever being the same.

Knowledge & Belief

In the debate over whether there is any knowledge the Stoics answer with a strong affirmation. With respect to the relation of knowledge to belief, they set forth a completely negative relationship: belief (*doxa/opinio*) is the opposite of knowledge (*epistēmē*) so much so that it can be said to be ignorance. All people are prone to the cognitive mistake of believing false *phantasia* and what that means is they have given assent—i.e., judged what is false to be true—so that they have mistaken their belief to be knowledge. Only the wise, in their disciplined approach to appearances, spare themselves such errors and truly build up a body of knowledge. The rest of humanity is ignorant precisely because people are unable to sort out which of their judgments of assent are accurate; they believe both the true and the false. This means that even when they get it right—i.e., make an accurate assent to a self-evident appearance—they remain ignorant because they don't *know* they got it right; they can only *believe* they are right. This is why they can be said to "know" many particular things, yet never really have "Knowledge." The ignorant are forever stuck in the shadows.

Zeno's disciple and successor, Cleanthes, is recorded by Clement of Alexandria as having written in his *Poetics* the following verse:

> Do not look to belief, wishing to say "I have become wise,"
> nor fear the lack of judgment and shameless belief of the many;
> for the multitude do not have wise, nor righteous, nor good judgment,
> which is something discovered in few people.[214]

In short, one need neither endorse nor fear belief; what is needed is acknowledging the reality of its existence in order to avoid its limitations.

It might seem we have said all we need to say about the Stoic position. However, while the basic foundation has been set out, and the decisive matter of how knowledge and belief relate to one another has been explained, there still remain some matters of pertinence. We shall examine two such matters: the Stoic conception of belief that encompasses a role for emotion, and the Stoic convictions about what people can and should do about belief.

Belief & Feeling in Early Stoicism: Chrysippus

Chrysippus of Soli (279-206 B.C.E.), the successor to Cleanthes as head of the Stoic School, was a prodigious author and ranks beside Zeno as the most important of the early Stoic philosophers. The noted independence of thought for which various Stoic thinkers have been variously praised or criticized shows itself in Chrysippus. He modifies the central idea of Zeno and Cleanthes with respect to the meaning of *tupōsis*, often translated as "impression" or "imprint." Rather than specifying that an appearance (*phantasia*) forms like a ring's seal on wax, Chrysippus stays closer to the basic sense of the word *tupōsis* as an "alteration." So, Diogenes Laertius reports Diocles writing, Chrysippus in his book *On the Psyche* argues that a *phantasia* makes an alteration (ἀλλοίωσις, *alloiōsis*) on the *psyche* that is more like an ongoing process than a one time product, and so the image of a fixed seal on wax does not do it justice. The key to understanding the *phantasia*, he says, is this: "But the proper conception of *phantasia* is of that which starts from something real and in accordance with it an impression has been taken, and that impression stamped, and firmly sealed, in such a manner that there is no doubt it arises from a real object."[215]

Although Chrysippus united Stoic doctrine and more than any other figure established a kind of Stoic orthodoxy not all of his ideas were equally well-received. One of his more controversial proposals concerns the role of feelings. A logical consequence of the Stoic view of the universe and the role of reason leads to his idea, controversial even within Stoicism, about reason's relation to belief and the relation of *doxa* to feelings and emotion. According to Galen

---

[214] Cleanthes' *Poetics* as quoted by Clement of Alexandria, *Miscellanies*, V.3. The phrase "lack of judgment" translates ἄκριτον (*akriton*); the word "judgment" renders κρίσιν (*krisin*).
[215] Diogenes Laertius, *Lives of Eminent Philosophers: Zeno*, VII.50 [*Zeno*, 36].

(129-c. 200/210 C.E.), the notion that strong feelings impact cognitive judgments can be traced back to Zeno, though his is a more moderate position than that taken later by Chrysippus. [216] Chrysippus links belief to feeling in such a manner that the latter can be construed as a kind of the former.

"Generic" Feelings

In a work titled *On Affections* (*Peri Pathōn*, known only secondhand and in fragments), Chrysippus elaborates Zeno's ideas and in so doing makes his own contribution. He identifies four "affections"[217] that are often called "generic feelings" (γενικά παθῆ, *genika pathē*), and which commonly are judged as 'good' (desire and pleasure), or 'bad' (fear and pain). These pairs further divide along an orientation in time. One member of each pair relates to the present (pleasure and pain), and the other to the future (desire and fear).[218]

Appearance:	'Good' *Pathē*	'Bad' *Pathē*	
Time Orientation:	Pleasure	Pain	*Present*
	Desire	Fear	*Future*

What distinguishes Chrysippus' position, though, is his step in identifying feelings as beliefs (*doxan*). He has in mind exactly the basic sense of *doxa* as the taking up of a position; feelings, in his view, express judgments. What is remarkable (and controversial) in his position is that feelings belong to the rational part of the *psyche*.[219] Like beliefs derive from the rational mind, form judgments, and motivate behavior, so also emotions—strong motivators of action—are 'rational.' They are judgments about something as "good" (e.g., desire and pleasure), or "bad" (fear and pain). This alters our above illustration as follows:

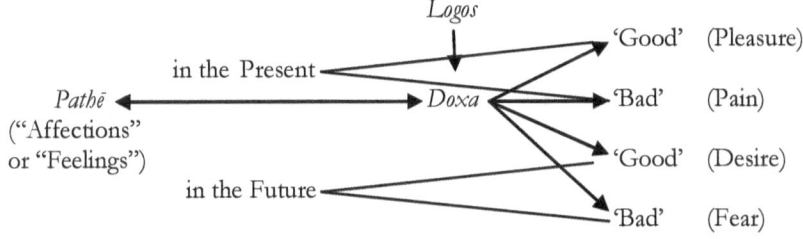

---

[216] Galen, *The Doctrines of Hippocrates and Plato*, V.478.
[217] "Affections" being understood here in the psychological sense of "affect," or as we more commonly say, "feeling" or "emotion."
[218] Stobaeus, *Anthology* (*Eclogues*), II.90-92 (utilizing chapter 6 of Pseudo-Plutarch, *Desire and Grief* (*De Libidine et Aegritudine*)), in *Stoicorum Veterum Fragmenta*, III.394. The four basic "affections" (πάθος, *pathos*) are: pain (or "distress": λύπη, *lupē*), pleasure (ἡδονή, *hēdonē*), fear (φόβος, *phobos*), and desire (or "appetite": ἐπιθυμία, *epithumia*).
[219] Galen, *The Doctrines of Hippocrates and Plato*, IV.2.2 (cf. V.1.4), claims that Chrysippus "judges that beliefs (δόξαν) and expectations arise in the rational part only" of the human soul. The phrase "rational part" renders λογιστικῷ (*logistikō*, fr. λογιστικός). See fragment 168 in Kidd's translation, *Posidonius, III*.

Feelings are a particular species of *doxa*—belief judgments of a feeling that something is good or bad, a present fact or a future expectation. In other words, emotions do not follow *from* beliefs but *are* beliefs.

Emotions as beliefs—or what we may cautiously name 'emotional beliefs'—are said by Chrysippus to have certain characteristics. These include:

> ➢ "Rationality" (*logistikos*);
> ➢ Judgment (*krisis*) as supposition (*hupolēpsis*);
> ➢ Erraticism, or exceeding motion (*ptoia*);
> ➢ Immediacy (i.e., "freshness" (*prosphatos*)); and
> ➢ Impermanence.

Let us consider each briefly.

"Rationality" (*logistikos*) here can easily be misunderstood, which is why I have put it inside quotation marks. A superficial reading of the Stoic position—or one motivated by an oppositional stance—can easily misrepresent it. Emotions can be spoken about as both 'rational' and 'irrational'—which may be more of a challenge for English minds than it probably was for Greek philosophers. Galen, who finds fault with Chrysippus as having a deficient perspective on the *psyche*, and accuses him of being contradictory, plainly recognizes that Chrysippus thinks belief (*doxan*) "belongs only to the rational part of the *psyche*"[220]—and yet is irrational. In Stoicism, *logos* reigns and the cognition of belief is ruled by reason, a function of the mind. This is not the same as *logos* being used normatively—guiding decisions, motivating actions, and serving as a foundation for evaluations. Instead, in that latter respect, emotions are *irrational* in that *doxa* replaces *logos*. Accordingly, Chrysippus may not be as contradictory as a critic wants him to be. Emotions may be beliefs rooted in the function of reason, but they do not thereby have to be rational in the sense of employing reason; they instead rely on *doxa*—and that leads us to the next characteristic.

Emotions are judgments. With respect to this, Diogenes Laertius writes, "They teach that emotions are judgments, as is said by Chrysippus in his *On the Passions*." Laertius then illustrates this point with Chrysippus' example of avarice, which is defined as a "supposition" (*hupolēpsis*) that money is good. As we saw earlier, *hupolēpsis* has a core sensibility linking it to *doxa*. It generally represents a cognitive judgment, such that *hupolēpsis* seems to be a kind of thinking entailing judgment (*krisis*), or "apprehension" (i.e., "grasp"), as in "taking something to be the case." Laertius goes on to note that this kind of 'judgment by supposition' is a feature common to all emotions.[221] Arius Didymus goes so far as to further characterize some as *asthenēs hupolēpsis*—'weak' *hupolēpsis*,[222] because emotions as cognitive judgments are often less enduring, and less trustworthy.

---

[220] Galen, *The Doctrines of Hippocrates and Plato*, IV.2.2. Also see IV.1-3.
[221] Diogenes Laertius, *Lives of Eminent Philosophers: Zeno*, VII.111 [*Zeno*, 63].
[222] See Stobaeus, *Anthology* (*Eclogues*), II.89: ἀσθενής ὑπόληπψις (*asthenēs hupolēpsis*).

The notion that emotional beliefs exhibit erraticism goes back to Zeno. According to Diogenes Laertius, Zeno regarded emotion (*pathos*) as "both irrational and contrary to the *psyche's* nature, being impulsive and of exceeding motion."[223] A pithy saying attributed to Zeno is that "emotion is a fluttering (*ptoia*) of the *psyche*."[224] He apparently likened this to the fluttering of wings. Though perhaps a bit enigmatic, it may suggest an instability, impulsivity, or erratic nature; to use a different analogy, it is like a breeze that comes unexpectedly and departs quickly and waxes and wanes in intensity. It is true that neither of my labels "erraticism" nor "exceeding motion" completely capture the idea, but both clutch at elements of it.

The immediacy and impermanence of emotional beliefs can be handled together. According to Chrysippus emotions are "fresh" (*prosphatos*) beliefs, by which he means they are "recent" beliefs. Their power comes in their temporal immediacy. Thus, pleasure and pain are judgments about something present: pain judges something as bad, while pleasure judges it as good. Similarly, fear and desire are judgments about things bad or good—but with a future expectation (e.g., desire is a judgment that something *will be* good). But as all of these judgments are recently formed ones, their intensity (as is true of emotions in general) wanes over time.[225]

It should not be hard to see how the characteristics of emotions correspond to those of many *doxa* that are not emotions. Beliefs often exhibit irrational reasoning but they are always judgments—expressions of a position that can be expressed propositionally. They can be erratic, impulsive, and impermanent. In short, it is easy enough to see how emotions and other beliefs are often alike.

Belief & Feeling in Middle Stoicism: Posidonius

The period of Middle Stoicism (2nd -1st centuries B.C.E.) shows both continuity and discontinuity with the views of Early Stoicism. Prominent figures of Middle Stoicism include Diogenes of Babylon, Antipater of Tarsus, Panaetius of Rhodes, and especially Posidonius of Apameia and Rhodes, the leading Stoic thinker of this period. Of these, our interest is in Posidonius.

A century after Chrysippus, Posidonius (c. 135-c. 50 B.C.E.) also wrote a work entitled *On Affections*. The later writer Galen quotes him as writing near the beginning of it, "For I think that concerning things good and evil, and concerning purposes and virtues, all depends upon a correct, close examination of emotions."[226] Galen goes on to quote Posidonius' view that emotions (which produce discord and unhappiness) have their origin in a failure to live in accord with reason.[227]

---

[223] Diogenes Laertius, *Lives of Eminent Philosophers: Zeno*, VII.110 [*Zeno*, 63].
[224] Arius Didymus in Stobaeus, *Anthology* (*Eclogues*), II.7 [=Von Arnim, *Stoicorum Veterum Fragmenta*, I.206].
[225] Galen, *The Doctrines of Hippocrates and Plato*, IV.7.12.
[226] Galen, *The Doctrines of Hippocrates and Plato*, V.6.2.
[227] Galen, *The Doctrines of Hippocrates and Plato*, V.6.4.

Mindful that emotional opinions can move us in strong and not always welcome ways, Posidonius advises that we cultivate a way of "living in advance." He distinguishes movements in the *psyche* as including both emotions proper and what we might call "anticipations," or anticipatory movements—a kind of pre-emotional state. It looks like this:

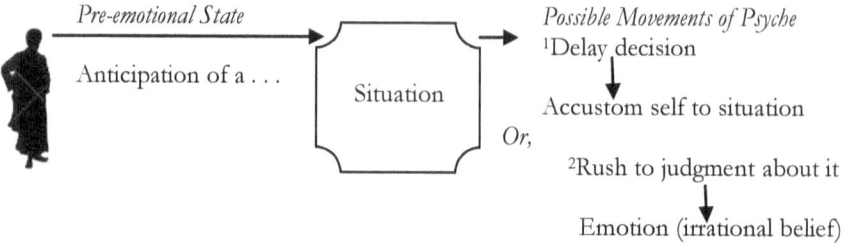

The mind imagines and a feeling might follow. But it does not *have* to follow. According to Galen, Posidonius advocates using this pre-emotional state to anticipate what might happen, accustom ourselves to it, and thus escape any sudden rush to judgment such as Chrysippus describes.[228] By mentally handling in advance matters as though they have already occurred we rob them of their power to surprise and overwhelm our judgment if they do actually occur at some point.

Like Zeno and Chrysippus, Posidonius aligns *pathos* (emotions) with *doxa* and characteristic of those who are not wise and who regularly fall prey to false appearances. In fact, remarks Galen, Posidonius says that the *psyche* of an unwise person still resembles that of a healthy person so long as it is "calmly removed from emotions."[229] Both knowledge and belief generate judgments, and these can be expressed propositionally, but they are *not* equal. Belief (*doxa*) falls significantly short of the fully cognizant reasoning that belongs to knowledge (*epistēmē*). This explains why emotions are a kind of belief—they are judgments lacking the support of knowledge.

Belief & Feeling in Late Stoicism: Seneca

Alongside this broad picture we need note as well further thinking about emotions. Lucius Annaeus Seneca, commonly referred to as Seneca the Younger (c. 1 B.C.E.-65 C.E.) contributed a substantial body of literature explaining, promoting, and elaborating Stoic philosophy. His moral essay *On Anger* (*De Ira*) will serve us for a glimpse into his Stoic epistemology and, especially, his innovations with respect to thinking about emotions.

---

[228] Galen, *The Doctrines of Hippocrates and Plato*, IV.7.7-8 (*Corpus Medicorum Graecorum*, V 4,1,2, p. 283).
[229] Galen, *The Doctrines of Hippocrates and Plato*, V.2.8.

In book II of *On Anger* Seneca addresses whether or not anger is a judgment (*iudicio*)—a decision roused from ignorance or knowingly.[230] He writes:

> That anger is roused by the appearance of an injury is undoubtable; but the question at hand is whether anger immediately follows an appearance, springing forth without assent of the rational soul, or whether it is set in motion with the rational soul's assent. Our position is that anger undertakes nothing on its own, but instead depends on the rational soul's approval. To take hold of an appearance as having received an injury, and add longing to avenge it, is to join under one yoke two things—that one ought not to have been injured and one ought not to withhold vengeance—and this is no mere impulse set in motion involuntarily. An impulse is a simple thing, but this is a complex matter comprised of many parts: someone has perceived something, has been offended by it, has condemned it, and now seeks to be avenged. None of this is possible unless the rational soul assents to the appearance which strikes it.[231]

The same sense of a double yoke is found in Cicero as he considers the teaching of Chrysippus on sorrow. Cicero attributes the cause of grief as follows: "It is nothing other than the belief (*opinio*) and judgment (*iudicium*) of a great and present evil."[232] The role of belief (*opinio*) is easily discerned:

> But when to the belief (*opinionem*) of a great evil is added the belief (*opinio*) that it is necessary, proper and dutiful to bear sorrow, then by these very things does emotion cause great suffering to fall upon one. From belief (*opinione*) are those various and abominable kinds of grieving—self-neglect, a womanish tearing at the cheeks, a beating of the breast, thighs, head. . . .[233]

Recalling our earlier illustrations, we can picture Seneca's description (and one for Cicero's would look much the same):

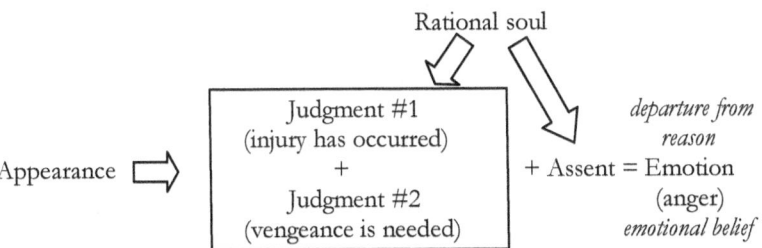

Something appears and it impacts the rational soul (*animus*). Judgments are stirred; these, as we recall, assess an appearance as either self-evidently true or as not so. Belief stemming from ignorance makes the faulty judgment that some-

[230] Seneca, *On Anger* (*De Ira*), II.1.1. The Latin text may read either *quae intra nos non insciis nobis oriuntur* or without the *non* (supplied by E. Hermes' 1905 text edition).
[231] Seneca, *On Anger*, II.1.3-5. The words translated "appearance" are forms of the word *species*. The word "position" renders *placet* (fr. *placeo*).
[232] Cicero, *Tusculan Disputations*, III.61 [III.25].
[233] Cicero, *Tusculan Disputations*, III.61-62 [III.26]. "Emotion" translates *perturbatio*.

thing not self-evidently true has been truly comprehended—in this case that injury has occurred and vengeance is justified—and assents to this belief. The result is not true knowledge but false belief (emotional belief).

Earlier in *On Anger* Seneca had pointed out the contrasts between reason and emotional belief. These contrasts include:

Reason	Emotion
Stable	Unsettled
Trustworthy	Treacherous
Healthy	Unhealthy
Resolute	Vacillating
Equable and balanced	Suggestible and short-lived
Desires justice	Desires justification
Focused on the relevant	Distracted by trivialities[234]

Three Movements

Now to this point there is nothing especially remarkable or new in Seneca's presentation, though there is a hint of what is to be developed. We recall that the orthodox Stoic position on emotions holds that they arise from the rational part of the *psyche* but are irrational in that they are mistaken beliefs that something presently is, or shall be, good or bad—and this judgment justifies the feeling that then rouses itself within. For Seneca the key question is whether an emotion like anger is a sudden, involuntary motion that grasps the mind and compels it to move in a certain way—apart from its will—or instead is subject to the rule of reason such that anger shows a decision based on faulty belief that then sets aside reason and knowledge.[235]

Seneca develops an understanding of emotions that extends the thinking set out by Chrysippus, and especially by Posidonius. He writes in *On Anger* the following:

> So that you may know (*scias*) in what manner ignoble passions begin, increase, and run wild, note that at first there is an involuntary internal motion—just a setting of the stage for ignoble passion and thus a kind of threat—which when joined with an act of the will, albeit not an unyielding one, convinces me it is necessary I require vengeance when I am injured, or that it is necessary another face punishment right here and now for some wickedness done. This third movement (ignoble passions run wild) is now uncontrollable which no longer as a matter of the will seeks vengeance, but simply does so because it has overwhelmed reason (*rationem*). There is no possibility of escape by reason (*ratione*) from the initial thrust that occurs in the mind, just as there is no escape from the blow it brings to the body. It is as involuntary as when we yawn because another does, or blink when some-

---

[234] Seneca, *On Anger*, I.17.2-18.2. The fourth pair comes from 17.3-4 The fifth pairings are from 17.5-6. The sixth pairings are from 17.7; the last from 18.1-2.

[235] See Seneca, *On Anger*, II.2.1. On the rational soul, perception, and impulse, cf. Hierocles, *Elements of Ethics*, IV.24-53 [= Ramelli, *Hierocles the Stoic*, 10-13 (Greek text and English translation)].

body thrusts fingers toward our eyes. Reason (*ratio*) is unable to be victorious in such cases, though perhaps by practice and vigilant attention we can reduce the power of ignoble passions. Different is that internal motion which has proceeded from judgment (*iudicio*) and has exalted it.[236]

This, too, can be pictured, as follows:

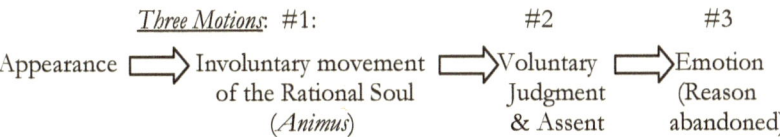

Three Motions: #1: #2 #3

Appearance ⟹ Involuntary movement ⟹ Voluntary ⟹ Emotion
of the Rational Soul   Judgment   (Reason
(*Animus*)   & Assent   abandoned)

Here we find the notion that the first discernible internal motion is anticipatory in nature; it is not itself yet emotion, but sets the stage for it.[237] But once the will improperly chooses to indulge the initial, involuntary motion through assent to it a very steep and slippery slope presents itself. Assent to erroneous judgments produces a departure from reason; the ignoble passions run riot and reason is nowhere in sight. Reason cannot control whether the initial motion occurs, but it is a human decision whether it then leads to emotion or not.

The Incompatibility of Emotion with Reason

Seneca concurs with other Stoics on the incompatibility of emotions with the reign of reason:

> Accordingly, reason (*ratio*) will never accept help from shortsighted and violent impulses, over which it itself has no authority, which it can never restrain, unless it were to propose opposing them with other impulses equal and of like nature, such as fear against anger, anger against idleness, dread against desire. May virtue be far from such evil that reason have recourse to vice![238]

Put more bluntly, *beliefs*—as emotions—oppose reason and knowledge. Emotional beliefs are what inflict us. But they have only the power our erroneous judgments grant them. What tortures us is the faulty *judgment* (belief).

---

236 Seneca, *On Anger*, II.4.1-2. The phrase "ignoble passions" translates *adfectus* a Latin correspondent to the Greek term *pathos* and especially used by Seneca in the sense of 'base' or 'dishonorable' emotions. The phrase "internal motion" renders *motus*, which corresponds here with the Stoic sense of how emotions are a movement within—a notion adapted by Seneca's next qualifying phrase (which is similar to Posidonius' thinking). The phrase "setting of the stage" renders *praeparatio*, a "preparation" that makes possible the subsequent development. The phrase "has exalted" translates *tollitur*, a term clearly parallel to *nascitur* (has proceeded) and in context seems to refer with it to the movement associated with emotion. Cf. II.3.1, "None of these things that move the rational soul by chance should be called ignoble passion; rather we should say the rational soul *endures* them, not causes *them*."
Cf. Marcus Aurelius, *Meditations,* V.19, on the *psyche*: "but it turns and moves itself alone."
237 Cf. Hierocles, *Elements of Ethics,* VI.17-20 [= Ramelli, *Hierocles the Stoic,* 16-17] with respect to *aisthēsis* as an "initiating" (ἀρχική, *archikē*) faculty.
238 Seneca, *On Anger,* I.10.1-2.

The philosopher Aëtius offers us a summary of Stoic philosophy:

> The Stoics stand firm on certain points, such as that wisdom (*sophian*) is knowledge (*epistēmēn*) of matters divine and human and that philosophy is the habitual practice of that skill (*technēs*) fitted to it which, first and foremost, is virtue. Virtues (*aretas*) are of three kinds: natural, ethical, and logical. This requires of philosophy a same threefold partition in things concerning nature, ethics, and logic. And when dealing with nature the focus is on the world and living things; in ethics the focus is on the conduct of human living; and with logic the focus is *logos* (*ton logon*), which they also call 'dialectic.'[239]

The Stoics envision the life of the wise as being the practice of virtue, which itself reflects the knowledge of both divine and human things.

Epictetus (c. 50-135 C.E.), born a slave in Hierapolis of Asia Minor, later as a freedman establishing a Stoic school in Greece at Nicopolis, is an outstanding representative of the late Stoic emphasis on practiced virtue. His *Discourses* begin with the great theme of the preeminence of reason. Epictetus proclaims that of all human faculties the "rational faculty" (*logikos*) alone is able to comprehend its own nature as well as that of everything else.[240] About it he also says, "Quite clearly it is the faculty able to appropriate whatever appears (*phantasiais*) to us."[241] A chief part of this handling of the *phantasia* we encounter is the process of judging, including the correct discernment of what is appropriate to use and how to use it appropriately;[242] "if you cultivate this, and place all in its keeping, you will never be hindered, never thwarted, never moan, never blame, never flatter anyone."[243] Trusting everything to the rational faculty offers the possibility of correct discernment and use of every appearance.

Epictetus lays out Stoic epistemology with a simple explanation:

> What is responsible for giving assent to anything?—that something appears to us to be the case. Because certainly it is impossible to assent to something that appears to *not* be the case! Why is this? Because this is the nature of thinking: to incline toward truth, to be displeased by falsity, and to withhold assent when uncertain.[244]

---

[239] Aëtius, *Opinions of the Philosophers*, I. Prooemium 2. My translation is based on the Greek text in Diels, *Doxographi Graeci*. The phrase "habitual practice" translates ἄσκησιν (*askēsin*, fr. ἄσκησις), which typically describes a way of life, or the rigorous regimen of an athlete.

[240] Epictetus in Arrian, *Discourses,* I.1.3.

[241] Epictetus in Arrian, *Discourses,* I.1.5. The word "appropriate" translates χρηστική (*chrēstikē*, fr. χρηστικός) which is the ability to know how to use something—in this case, the things that appear to the mind (whether sensory data or ideas).

[242] Epictetus in Arrian, *Discourses,* I.1.6. The word used referring to judging is διάκρινον (*diakrinon*).

[243] Epictetus in Arrian, *Discourses,* I.1.12.

[244] Epictetus in Arrian, Discourses, I.28.2. The word translated "assent" is συγκατατίθεσθαι (*sunkatatisthesthai*, fr. συγκατατίθημι (*sunkatatithēmi*). The word rendered "thinking" is διανοίας (*dianoias*), which is quite variously translated, as "intellect," "mind," or "understanding."

The rational faculty judges and assents; human decision-making is fundamental and a matter of the will. The things that appear to the rational faculty are just raw materials; it is by human choices they are made into good or evil.[245]

> If you ask me how you will conduct yourself, this much I can say: if you use the principles of correct judgments you will do well, but if not, you will do poorly. For in every case how one does depends on how well they use these principles of correct judgment.[246]

All of this can be pictured as a sequential process with outcomes:

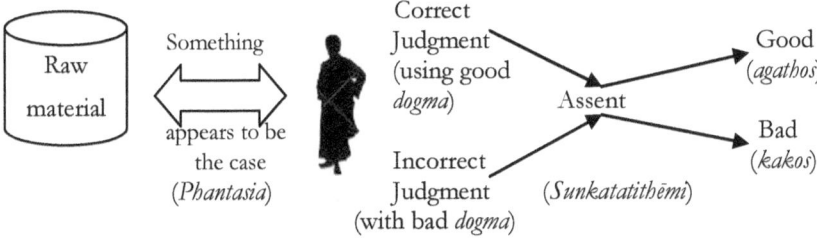

The raw material of the world and experience is there for everyone. What makes the difference is whether we correctly assess how things appear to be.

Right in the center of the above illustration is the fundamental term *dogma*, forms of which appear some 114 times in the *Discourses*. Epictetus uses *dogma* (pl. *dogmata*)—criteria for an authoritative, declared judgment—to reflect the decision-making basis of the rational faculty, which deduces principles upon which we act, and formulates decisions that may be richer or poorer for the quality of our thinking. A *dogma* is a "belief," but not like *doxa* is a belief. The latter are individual bits of ignorance, while *dogmata* form a collective body that offers a standard for judgment (*krisis*), guiding informed, rational assent.

---

[245] Epictetus in Arrian, *Discourses*, I.29.1-3: "The essence of the good is a certain kind of choice, as the essence of evil is a certain kind of choice. So, what then of things outside ourselves? They are the raw materials for deliberate choice, by which in handling them choice makes its own good or evil. How will it make the good? First, if it will not over-value the raw materials! For correct decrees about the raw materials make the choice be good, whereas incorrectly seen and distorted judgments make the choice be bad." The selection of "choice" (i.e., deliberate choice) to translate προαίρεσις (*proairesis*), instead of the more common rendering "will" is to emphasize the active, purposeful decision-making of the rational faculty rather than convey a sense of some independent moral agency ('the will') different from this faculty. The phrase "raw materials" translates ὕλαι (*hulai*); "correct decrees" renders δόγματα (*dogmata*, fr. δόγμα), a word often translated as "opinions," but which in the period of Imperial Rome carried the sense of Senatorial decrees, i.e., 'official opinions,' or 'judgments' (and see next note). The idea is that the rational faculty makes an authoritative decision by decreeing a matter as such or so. My rendering of "incorrectly seen and distorted" for στρέβλα (*strebla*) and διεστραμμένα (*diestrammena*) reflects that both terms are used of poor vision so that the sense is that the raw materials are not seen for what they are and so a false judgment of their use occurs, leading to what is bad.

[246] Epictetus in Arrian, *Discourses*, III.9.2. I use "principles of correct judgment" for *dogmata* and *dogma* here. Often translators simply use "judgment," but that suggests *krisis* (judgment), or the act of judging (*diakrino*), where here it is more the sense of reliance on sound principles of judgment to make a decision. Such principles are beliefs (another way *dogma* can be translated).

A Stoic embraces Stoic *dogmata* but doing so is a matter of supposition (*hupolēpsis*)—taking up a position—and so a *dogma* is also a kind of *hupolēpsis*.[247] Like *doxa*, *dogmata* are rooted in the rational faculty, and also like *doxa* when emotions are involved, *dogmata* can afflict the individual with chaos, confusion, distress.[248] The importance of *dogma* lies in its bridging theory to *praxis*. Any *dogma* can itself be judged by how well it translates Stoic knowledge into the practice of virtue; it is subordinate to *epistēmē*.

The essence of *dogma* is the principle actually used. For Epictetus the decisive principle is *control*. A person must understand what is and what is not within one's own power. He presents instances of people in extreme instances where control of their body's fate was in the hands of others. Epictetus then engages in an imagined dialog:

> "What, then, should one have ready at hand for such circumstances?"
> What other than this?—what is mine or not mine, what is within my power and what is not. I must die; must I die moaning? I must be fettered; must I also wail? I must go into exile; is there, then, anyone to prevent me from doing so with a smile, a cheerful countenance, and a sense of well-being?[249]

I can choose how I live—virtuously or in emotional distress.

Epictetus sums it up well enough when he comments:

> Of all that is, some belongs to us and some does not. What belongs to us includes 'taking something to be the case' (*hupolēpsis*), how we set ourselves in motion, turning toward a thing, or turning away from it—in short, all of our acts. What does not belong to us includes the body, property, reputation, public office—in short, all that is not our acts.[250]

In all things, epistemological or moral, the external thing is subordinate to the internal thinking made about it.[251] As Epictetus puts it, "The hypothetical proposition is an indifferent matter. The judgment (*krisis*) about it is not an indifferent matter; that judgment is either knowledge (*epistēmē*), or belief (*doxa*), or delusion."[252]

---

247 In the *Discourses*, the terms appear together at II.9.13-15.

248 Epictetus in Arrian, *Discourses*, IV.5.29; cf. *Manual* (*Enchiridion*), 20.

249 Epictetus in Arrian, *Discourses*, I.1.21-22.

250 Epictetus, *Manual*, 1.1. Cf. ch. 20. I have employed the phrase "taking something to be the case" for ὑπόληψις (*hupolēpsis*), "how we set ourselves in motion" for ὁρμή (*hormê*)—trying to capture the Stoic sense of internal movements in the choices we make. I use "turning toward a thing" for ὄρεξις (*orexis*), still trying to capture the Stoic sense of a choice to move in a certain way; the word is usually rendered "desire." That then leads to "turning away from a thing" for ἔκκλισις (*ekklisis*), usually rendered "aversion."

251 See, for example, Epictetus in Arrian, *Discourses*, III.20.1: "With respect to our ability to perceive *phantasia* nearly everyone agrees that 'the good' and 'the bad' reside in us, and not in external things."

252 Epictetus in Arrian, *Discourses*, II.6.1.

10

The Skeptics

Where Stoics strive to follow Socrates and resist belief in favor of the attainment of knowledge through reason, the Skeptics find in Socrates' disavowal of certain success in achieving knowledge a guide to skeptical caution. When we began the discussion of Epicureanism we noted that in the latter part of the 4th century B.C.E. there appeared to be a shifting of the fundamental question about knowledge from assuming that it exists and asking what it is to a more radical query: 'Is there any knowledge?' Answers to this query sparked sustained controversy among our ancient Hellenistic thinkers. The positions of Stoicism, Epicureanism, and Skepticism arrange themselves along a continuum reflecting three major alternatives to the question of whether there is any knowledge:

Who knows? (Skepticism)

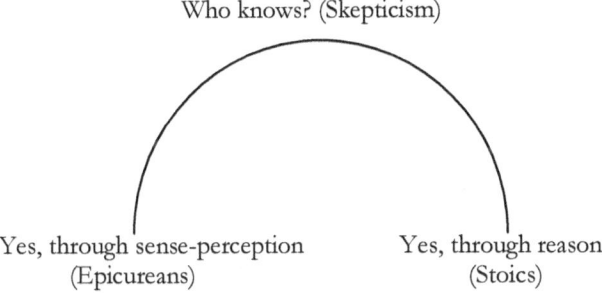

Yes, through sense-perception   Yes, through reason
(Epicureans)   (Stoics)

Of course, we must qualify this by noting that the question of whether knowledge is possible has in mind its *certainty*.

The Syrian satirist Lucian of Samosata (125-180 C.E.), in a dialog titled *Hermotimus*, captures well the essential spirit of Skepticism. In the dialog the character Lycinus, speaking for Lucian, encounters his friend Hermotimus, who is a dedicated student of Stoicism. During the course of their discussion Lycinus raises the difficulty he personally has in committing to a particular school of philosophy. He uses the example of wanting to get to Corinth and seeking direction to do so. He points out that when other travelers offer directions that vary from one another he knows not whom to trust. They may each provide good directions, but whether they be to Corinth or to some other city they have mistaken for Corinth is hard to determine. The dilemma is this: only one road leads to Corinth, but which guide with certainty knows the correct road?

Hermotimus agrees with him that different roads lead different directions to different destinations.[253] Lycinus then remarks:

> Well then, dear Hermotimus, we stand in need of no little amount of counsel in choosing roads and guides. We can hardly act according to the saying, "Wherever our feet lead, there we shall go." Doing so, we would find ourselves on the road to Babylon or Bactra rather than Corinth and not even know it. We cannot simply trust to good luck that we should stumble on the correct path by starting out in some direction without closer examination of it.[254]

The essence of the Skeptic's task and process is this "closer examination."

The term "Skeptic," from σκέψις (*skepsis*), means "examination" (among other things), and those who devote themselves to careful inquiry and deliberative thought are "Skeptics" (οἱ σκεπτικὸς, *hoi skeptikos*), "those who reflect." However, the word *skepsis* also acquired the sense of "hesitation," for those who reflect in the manner of the Skeptics are hesitant to make commitments to the conclusions being drawn by others, and given their penchant for raising questions the word also, inevitably, came to mean "doubt." Thus, while the original impetus for the way of Skepticism is careful inquiry and examination, the consequence of hesitation makes them popularly perceived as doubters—an association still so large for many that other elements of meaning are often lost.

Ancient Greek Skepticism broadly divides into two groups: Pyrrhonists and Academicians. The latter group includes members of Plato's Academy in two of its historical periods, most notably the Academy leaders Arcesilaus of Pitane and Carneades of Cyrene. Among the Pyrrhonists, in addition to Pyrrho of Elis himself, the most noted are Sextus Empiricus and Aenesidemus.

Though these two ways of practicing Skepticism were at odds with one another, and ought not to be regarded as merely variant branches of a single philosophical school, they do share some important commonalities. For our purposes it is sufficient to name two: their doubt over whether knowledge as true and certain information is possible for one to know that one has it, and their practice of thus suspending judgment because of doubt on the first matter.

In practice, the Skeptics—whether Pyrrhonists or Academic philosophers—leave a lopsided perspective, one heavy on the criticism of other philosophies but lean in setting out anything positive themselves. This was the case from the beginning. Diogenes Laertius, in writing of the early Skeptic philosophers under Pyrrho, comments, "The Skeptics zealously pursued a course of overthrowing the dogmas of everyone else, but themselves set out no dogmas of their own. They continued presenting those of others, and describing them in detail, without doing the same for themselves."[255]

---

[253] Lucian, *Hermotimus*, 27. The dialog is also sometimes known by other, more descriptive titles, such as *On Rival Philosophies* or *Concerning Different Sects*.

[254] Lucian, *Hermotimus*, 28.

[255] Diogenes Laertius, *Lives of Eminent Philosophers: Pyrrho*, IX.74 [*Pyrrho*, IX.8].

Pyrrho & Timon: The Basic Pyrrhonist Position

Some skeptical thinking by philosophers in epistemology has been around from the start. Skeptics can claim a precursor in Protagoras, of whom Diogenes Laertius says, "Protagoras was the first to say that concerning every matter there are two arguments (*logous*), each opposed to the other; and he was the first to show this in practice."[256] We noted above the Skeptics' appeal to Socrates, and there were other thinkers noted for that philosophical bent—the Sophist Gorgias of Leontini, for instance[257]—long before a formal Skeptic philosophy arose. However, the first expression of philosophical skepticism as a well-articulated and distinctive approach emerged in the 4th century B.C.E. and later became known as Pyrrhonism after the name of its founder.

Pyrrho of Elis (c. 360-275 B.C.E.) is reckoned as the father of Greek Skepticism as a distinct philosophical approach. With Pyrrho and his student Timon of Phlius (c. 315-225 B.C.E.) there developed a more formal and elaborated philosophy of Skepticism.[258] Pyrrho himself left nothing in the way of writings. Of the writings of his chief pupil, Timon, only fragments remain. The most important of these, regarded today as the best summary of early Pyrrhonism, comes from the 4th century Christian historian Eusebius, drawing on the 2nd century Peripatetic philosopher Aristocles of Messene, who reports Timon as follows:

> But his (Pyrrho's) disciple Timon says one who intends to live happily must look at three matters: first, what things are by nature; second, how we should be disposed toward them; and finally, what results from having such a disposition. He says Pyrrho shows that things are equally without difference, without consistency, and without determination—and therefore neither our sense-perceptions (*aisthēseis*) nor our beliefs (*doxas*) can be shown to be true (*alētheuein*) or to be false (*pseudesthai*). Accordingly, for this very reason we ought not to rely (*pisteuein*) on them, but rather to be without belief (*adoxastous*), without inclination, and unmoved, saying about each and every thing that it is no more *is* than *is not*, or is both *is* and *is not*, or neither *is* nor *is not*. At any rate, Timon says that those disposed as Pyrrho recommends first will be without speech, but then tranquil (*ataraxia*); but Aenesidemus says pleasure.[259]

---

[256] Diogenes Laertius, *Lives of Eminent Philosophers: Protagoras*, IX.51 [*Protagoras*, 3].

[257] See Sextus Empiricus, *Adversus Mathematicos: Against the Logicians*, I.65-86.

[258] This is the line of explanation adopted by Sextus Empiricus in explaining the name 'Pyrrhonism' (*Outlines of Pyrrhonism*, I.3.7.)

[259] Timon in Aristocles, *On Philosophy*, VII, quoted in Eusebius, *Preparation for the Gospel* (*Praeparatio Evangelica*), XIV.18.2-3. With respect to this text, the string of descriptors—*adiaphora, astathmēta*, and *anepikrita*–has occasioned much comment with translators often trying to decide based on whether the text should be read in reference to metaphysics or epistemology. The word ἀφασίαν (*aphasian*) in the final sentence is puzzling; it nowhere else is known to attach to Pyrrho and the suggestion has been the word is a copyist error for Aristocles' original choice ἀπαθίαν (*apathian*), "without passion," which certainly fits Skeptic thinking and expression.

117

Thus metaphysics meets epistemology and all one knows, says the Skeptic, is that one does not know how things really *are* or *are not*.

The Skeptics vigorously refrained from setting out a body of positive doctrines—'dogma'—and left us instead a number of pithy statements reflecting their epistemological attitude. For example, as Diogenes Laertius records, the kind of thing they would say is, "Not one thing do we determine."[260] He records that another kind of saying they employ is, "Every assertion has a corresponding assertion set against it."[261] Now this situation in itself would not be a significant problem if the contrary assertions, or propositions, were manifestly uneven so that a clear choice existed between them. However, Timon points out that this saying reflects a different reality: "But truly, matters disagree, while the assertions are equally strong, so as a consequence one remains ignorant of the truth."[262] So they frame a recommendation:

Arguments in favor of A

Arguments in favor of B

The arguments balance.
Therefore, *suspend judgment*

In any situation of uncertainty—which is the norm—one should suspend judgment; if one cannot have truth, at least avoid displaying ignorance by pretending to a certainty that does not exist.

From the Skeptics' point of view, we can't avoid forming statements to talk about things we have concepts for even if we don't know the empirical reality those concepts refer to. But simply because we can't avoid using words to talk to one another does not mean we actually know the thing we are talking about! So, Diogenes Laertius writes,

> They set out this kind of precept of interpretation: while things appear (*phainetai*) to be this or that, things *are* in actuality not as they only *appear to be* (*phainesthai*); they said both that they do not seek what one thinks—for thinking is obvious to itself—but that they seek what sense-perceptions (*aisthēsesi*) participate in.[263]

In other words, the Skeptic has no doubt about what he or she is *thinking*, but does have plenty of doubts about what sense-perception is reporting. Skeptics would like to know the reality of the thing the senses report about, but that reality is much harder to get at than one's thoughts (and subsequent assertions).

[260] Diogenes Laertius, *Lives of Eminent Philosophers: Pyrrho*, IX.74 [*Pyrrho*, IX.8].
[261] Diogenes Laertius, *Lives of Eminent Philosophers: Pyrrho*, IX.74 (end) [*Pyrrho*, IX.8].
[262] Diogenes Laertius, *Lives of Eminent Philosophers: Pyrrho*, IX.76 [*Pyrrho*, IX.8].
[263] Diogenes Laertius, *Lives of Eminent Philosophers: Pyrrho*, IX.77 [*Pyrrho*, IX.8].

It is important to see in this the Skeptics' desire to affirm a genuine and continuing interest in seeking knowledge of things as they really *are*. But the inconvenient facts are that neither the Epicureans' sense-perception nor the Stoics' reason is sufficient to provide the kind of certainty that secures a genuine, trustworthy claim to "knowledge." A Skeptic, then, sees him- or herself as a realist who does not flinch away from hard truths. But despite the obstacles, the Skeptic continues to search for truth and to test claims made about it. The Skeptic claims to be clear about a matter others are not—that there is a profound difference between what is clear and self-evident *to me, in the moment,* and what is the continuing, objective reality of a thing.

We might illustrate the whole matter this way:

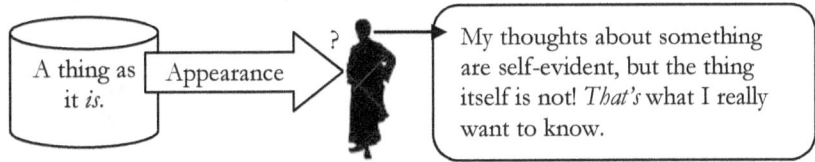

The Skeptic's interpretive rule is simply not to assume that what you see is what is really there; the reality may be different from its appearance.

Therefore the Skeptics oppose any argument—"demonstration" (ἀπόδειξις, *apodeixis*)—meant to establish some truth, because, writes Diogenes Laertius, "Every demonstration, they say, is either made from things needing proof, or depends on things that cannot be proved." If the former, then each constituent part also needs demonstration—and this requires an endless reductive process. If the latter, then it is self-evidently a waste of time; all that is required to show something to be indemonstrable is for a single part to be so. As for the appeal commonly made to the power of reason to discover so-called 'first principles' that need no demonstration, "If anyone thinks, they say, that there are some things needing no demonstration—what a marvelous mind!—such a one does not see that first one must offer demonstration that what is being asserted has its proof (*pistin*) in itself."[264]

The bottom line, Skeptics argue, is that there is no sound argument to substantiate assertions about what can be truly known about how things really are. So, Diogenes Laertius writes, they ask, "How, then, is anyone to conclude anything about uncertain things, about hidden things, when we know no demonstration for them? What they are searching for is not what things appear (*phainetai*) to be, but rather what they really *are*."[265] Thus, as 9th century Christian Patriarch of Constantinople, Photius, writes, "Pyrrhonists allow themselves to remain puzzled by things and oppose all dogma (*dogmatos*)."[266]

[264] Diogenes Laertius, *Lives of Eminent Philosophers: Pyrrho,* IX.90 [*Pyrrho,* IX.11].
[265] Diogenes Laertius, *Lives of Eminent Philosophers: Pyrrho,* IX.91 [*Pyrrho,* IX.11]. "What they really are" translates καθ᾽ ὑπόστασιν οὕτως ἔχει (*kath' hupostasin houtōs echei*), more literally, "what is according to the underlying essence they have."
[266] Photius, *List of Books,* 212.169b.

Aenesidemus

In the 1st century before the Common Era, Aenesidemus (c. 100-40 B.C.E.), who apparently began as a member of the Academy,[267] rejected both Arcesilaus and Carneades as too tepid in their so-called 'skepticism' to merit the name. Aenesidemus takes square aim at the idea of there being any self-evident comprehension. The later scholar Photius summarizes Aenesidemus' work as, "The whole purpose of the book is to confirm that there is no confirmation concerning comprehension (*katalēpsin*), either by means of sense-perception (*aisthēseōs*), or by any kind of 'understanding' (*noēseōs*)."[268] His position looks like this:

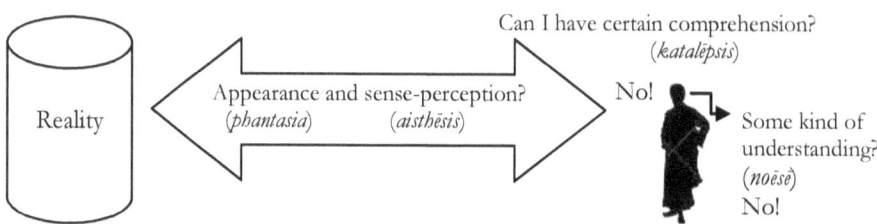

Like Timon, Aenesidemus sees the relation of tranquility (*ataraxia*) to suspension of judgment (*epochē*) as like a shadow—tranquility follows naturally along and behind suspension of judgment. Although this suspension of judgment might seem to rule out any kind of "comprehension" (*katalēpsis*), Photius' presentation offers Aenesidemus' allowance of a practical comprehension that is both subjective and temporary.[269] What Skeptics disavow is not some in-the-moment and to-the-point comprehension, but a comprehension like the Stoics mean—one self-evident and secure, that brings the certainty of knowledge.

Sextus Empiricus

Sextus Empiricus (c. 160-210 C.E.) provides us the most extensive record of Greek Skepticism and is the source most commonly looked to for understanding it. His work survives through two chief sources: the *Outlines of Pyrrhonism* (*Pyrrhoniae Hypotyposes*) which sets forth the Skeptical system and the so-called *Against the Professors* (*Adversus Mathematicos*), which brings together what remains of two works, the first of which is titled *Against the Schoolmasters* (*Adversus Grammatikos*), and the second titled *Against the Dogmatists* (*Adversus Dogmaticos*), aimed at any positive philosophical approach that presents and defends a particular view espousing how reality might with certainty be known.[270]

---

[267] This conclusion being based on Photius, *List of Books* (*Bibliotheca*, aka *Myriobiblion*), codex 212.169b, where in his report on having read Aenesidemus' *Arguments* notes the work was dedicated to Lucius Tubero, "one of his colleagues from the Academy."

[268] Photius, *List of Books*, 212.169b, 19-21.

[269] Photius, *List of Books*, 212.170a, 1-3.

[270] I cite the specific work that is part of *Adversus mathematicos*. Thus *Against the Logicians* is books VII-VIII of the whole, but often included with books IX-XI as part of *Against the Dogmatists*, where it is books I-II, and it is this latter way *Against the Logicians* is cited here.

Sextus Empiricus begins his *Outlines of Pyrrhonism* with what seems to him the fundamental difference among philosophies:

> The naturally expected result when looking into any matter is that the ones looking either find something, or deny finding it and confess that it is beyond comprehension (*akatalēpsias*), or they keep looking for it. Similarly, when it comes to philosophical investigations, some claim to have found the truth (*alēthes*), others that it is beyond grasp, and others are still looking for it.
>
> Those who think they have discovered it are called 'Dogmatists' and include the schools who follow Aristotle and Epicurus and the Stoics, and some others. Those who think it beyond the power of comprehension (*katalēphthenai*) include those who follow Clitomachus and Carneades, and some of the other Academic philosophers. The Skeptics are still looking for it.[271]

These three groups—the Dogmatists, Academic philosophers, and Skeptics—constitute the main divisions among philosophers, and what separates them is their level of confidence in whether truth can be found—i.e., known.

The proposed reasonableness of the Skeptic is the avowed willingness to accept as true and as knowledge anything that is genuinely self-evident, such as the Dogmatists think they have found but which to the Skeptics' eyes fails to have been satisfactorily proven. The problem that opponents to Skepticism find with this seeming reasonableness is that its initial premise—that something may be self-evident—is itself *not* self-evident. Logically, then, the Skeptic should not agree to it. This situation, say critics, leads to Skepticism being self-contradictory. But, the Skeptic views the matter differently, plausibly arguing that, in fact, they are being consistent in suspending judgment since, at least implicitly, they also recognize that the initial premise is debatable. Sextus would remind us that the Skeptic is undogmatic about his or her own judgments.

The definition he offers for Skepticism is as follows:

> Now Skepticism (*skeptikē*) is an ability to contrast appearances (*phaino-menōn*) of things with mental operations of any kind about them, the result of which—because of the equal validity and force of both the things and the reasons (*logois*) thought about them—brings us to first 'a suspension of judgment' (*epochēn*), and then alongside this, tranquility (*ataraxia*). We do not term it an 'ability' (*dunamin*) in any special way, but merely with reference to the plain sense of 'being able.' By 'appearances' (*phainomena*), in this present instance, we carry the sense of 'objects of sense-perceptions' (*ta aisthēta*), which explains why we contrast them with things of the mind (*ta noēta*).[272]

Sextus immediately clarifies what he means by two of the key terms in Skepticism: "Now *epochē* is a state of mind through which we neither deny nor affirm

---

[271] Sextus Empiricus, *Outlines of Pyrrhonism*, I.1.1-3.
[272] Sextus Empiricus, *Outlines of Pyrrhonism*, I.4.8-9.

anything. And *ataraxia* is a state of *psyche* both undisturbed and calm."[273] Put most simply, Skepticism means an ability to hold apart the things of sense-perception from our thoughts about them in order to suspend judgments that lead away from truth and by so doing they achieve a peace of mind while they continue searching for the truth.

The goal of "tranquility" (*ataraxia*), or "calmness"—an equanimity of the mind—is tied by Sextus to the reason philosophical Skepticism has come about:

> Now the original cause of Skepticism we say to be the hope of attaining tranquility. For very bright people, disturbed by anomalies in the things before them, and unsure as to which of these merit assent, then sought to uncover what in them is true (*alēthes*) and what is false (*pseudos*), so that such a determination would bring about tranquility (*ataraktēsontes*). And so the basic principle since the beginning of Skepticism has been that of opposing to each proposition an equal counterpart; for we think that by doing so we stop any dogmatizing.[274]

The tranquility the Skeptic achieves, or aims to attain, is a kind of peace of mind that permits continuing to search for truth, undaunted by the problems such searching encounters.

Like other philosophers—and, indeed, everyone—Skeptic philosophers have to wrestle with the appearances we encounter in sense-perception. Sextus argues that the Skeptic acknowledgment of *phainomena* ("appearances") is evident in their own use of the word "criterion" (*criterion*).

> The criterion (*kriterion*) we have in mind, of those who follow the Skeptic way, is the 'appearance' (*phainomenon*)—giving this label to what is called *phantasia*. For since this lies in feeling, and involuntary passion at that, it is beyond questioning. Therefore, no one, I imagine, argues that an underlying object appears this way or that way; the debate is over whether the object *is* such as it *appears to be.*[275]

The "appearances" (*phainomena*) the Skeptic appeals to as a criterion are what are commonly called "appearances" (*phantasia*): how objects *appear* to the senses.[276] These are involuntary—and there is no need to question that such occur. The debate is not about appearances as such, but rather about how well they may represent reality. The Skeptic rejects the idea of appearances as a criterion for establishing the truth of any alleged correspondence between an appearance and an object.

---

[273] Sextus Empiricus, *Outlines of Pyrrhonism,* I.4.10. The term ἐποχή (*epochē*) is used in a technical sense by the Skeptics—"suspension (of judgment)"; the common use refers to the cessation of some action. The word "calm" might also be rendered by "tranquility' or some similar word; the Greek ἀταραξία (*ataraxia*) refers to the kind of impassivity one might find in illness or, when in good health, of a mind at peace with itself.

[274] Sextus Empiricus, *Outlines of Pyrrhonism,* I.6.12.

[275] Sextus Empiricus, *Outlines of Pyrrhonism,* I.11.22.

[276] Before going further we should note that Sextus uses the term "appearances" loosely.

If appearance (*phantasian*) is set as the criterion (*kritērion*), then, we must say as Protagoras did that *every* appearance (*phantasian*) is true (*alēthē*), or as Xeniades of Corinth said, that all are false (*pseudē*), or as the Stoics and Academic philosophers and Aristotle's Peripatetics said, that some are true and some are false. But since, as we shall demonstrate, it cannot be said that every appearance is true, or every false, or some true and some false, thereby appearance cannot be asserted to be a criterion.[277]

To use *phantasia* as a criterion is to pick a side among the debaters. It abandons any suspension of judgment and peace of mind by entering the interminable and irresolvable fray of philosophical debate. In short, it is to become a dogmatist.

The range of unsatisfactory positions on "appearances" looks like this:

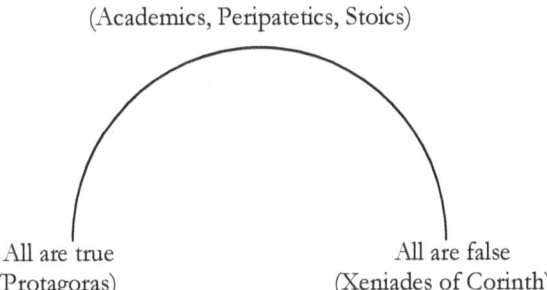

Some are true; some are false
(Academics, Peripatetics, Stoics)

All are true   All are false
(Protagoras)   (Xeniades of Corinth)

The Skeptic's own position differs from others like this:

| Judge Sense-perception as able to provide the truth. (Epicureans) | Suspend judgment as to what the truth is. (Skeptics) | Judge Reason as able to provide the truth. (Academics, Peripatetics, et al.) |

For simply living day-to-day, the Skeptic applies as his or her standard (i.e., 'criterion') the actual appearance, regardless of how well it may or may not represent reality. This is a *criterion of action*: it affords a practical, common sense basis for moment-by-moment action. Like anyone else, a Skeptic lives according to four regulating principles. First Nature itself guides simply by providing us the ability to form sense-perceptions. Second, there is the urgency imposed by feelings, which motivate such behaviors as eating. Third, is the guiding hand of Culture, with its laws and customs. Finally, there is education.[278] These forces inform and guide practical action.

[277] Sextus Empiricus, *Adversus Mathematicos, Against the Logicians,* I.388-390.
[278] Sextus Empiricus, *Outlines of Pyrrhonism,* I.11.23.

The Pyrrhonian Skeptics were not the only philosophers practicing a dedicated skepticism. The other notable Skeptics were part of Plato's school of philosophy, commonly referred to as 'the Academy.' Arcesilaus of Pitane (c. 316-c.241 B.C.E.), was the *Scholarch* ("Head Scholar") who first led the Academy into a focus on critiquing the positions of other philosophical schools and initiated the changes later known as the 'Middle' Academy.[279] In his time Academic philosophers, though still practicing the dialectical method developed by Socrates, increasingly left aside the positive presentation of a position to concentrate on the negative side, i.e., the side that raised questions and objections about a position. In this way 'Skepticism' became what was most associated with the school, though the Academicians themselves did not apply this label to their endeavors.

Cicero traces Arcesilaus' skepticism to roots in Socrates and Plato themselves.[280] Diogenes Laertius credits Arcesilaus with being the first to formally practice a "withholding" (*epischōn*) of judgment because of the contradictions found in the assertions of opposing arguments. Arcesilaus is said by his contemporary, Pyrrho's student Timon, to have been influenced by Pyrrho.[281]

Arcesilaus' basic stance is the same as the basic Pyrrhonist position:

Arguments *pro*   Arguments *con*

The arguments balance;
withhold judgment.

Arcesilaus' criticism of the Stoic position, the matter for which he is most remembered,[282] revolves around his contesting their ideas of suitable epistemological criteria, especially the notion of *katalēpsis*–the direct and certain apprehension, or "comprehension," of a self-evident appearance.[283] According to the Stoics, the "wise" are those who prove themselves disciplined enough to avoid giving assent to anything other than what is self-evidently true and thereby avoid the ignorance of belief. Cicero depicts Arcesilaus as reasoning as follows:

---

[279] Diogenes Laertius, *Lives of Eminent Philosophers: Arcesilaus,* IV.28 [*Arcesilaus,* 2]: "with him is the commencement of the Middle Academy."

[280] Cicero, *On the Orator* (*De oratore*), III.67 [ch. 19]. Cf. Plutarch, *Moralia: Reply to Colotes,* 1121f-1122a.

[281] Diogenes Laertius, *Lives of Eminent Philosophers: Arcesilaus,* IV.32-33 [*Arcesilaus,* 9].

[282] The 2nd century Platonist philosopher Numenius, *On the Dissension of the Academics from Plato,* as preserved in Eusebius, *Preparation for the Gospel,* XIV.6.11, claims Arcesilaus viewed the Stoic founder Zeno as a rival professionally and thus bent himself to overthrowing Zeno's arguments. See that place on claims about their rivalry.

[283] The critique of the Stoic position by Arcesilaus, especially with respect to *katalēpsis,* can be found in Sextus Empiricus, *Adversus Mathematicos: Against the Logicians,* I.150-158.

> If a wise person assents to anything, then he is forming beliefs.
> But a wise person does not form beliefs.
> Therefore the wise person does not assent to anything.[284]

In so doing Arcesilaus sought to employ the Stoics' own logic against them.

The 'New Academy' Skepticism: Carneades & Clitomachus

Carneades of Cyrene (214-129 B.C.E.), sometime before 155 B.C.E., became *Scholarch* of the Academy. Carneades set out to contest the Stoic position developed by Chrysippus, the noted Stoic defender against Arcesilaus. In so doing Carneades became well-known as perhaps Stoicism's chief critic.[285] Carneades continued pursuing the path established by Arcesilaus, but with some important modifications.[286] The changes under Carneades' leadership brought about the designation 'New Academy' by scholars to distinguish this later approach from the 'Old Academy' of Plato and the 'Middle Academy' of Arcesilaus.[287]

Carneades' examination of Stoic epistemology led him to conclude that *no* 'appearance (*phantasia*) is truly a *katalēpsis*—"self-evident." Cicero reports, "Carneades believes there are two ways to classify appearances, one way dividing them into those that can be perceived and those we cannot perceive, and the other way distinguishing those that are probable from those that are not."[288] Obviously, most attention must be directed to what we can perceive in order to judge whether they are likely true of not. With respect to this latter group, "those that can be perceived," Carneades has in mind the self-evident perceptions touted by the Stoics. We can draw out Carneades' view like this:

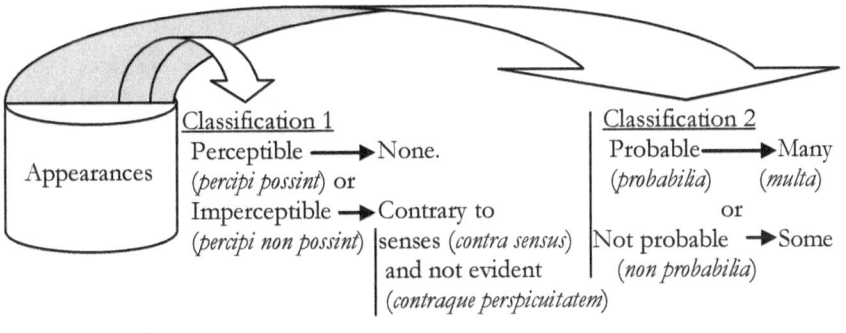

Appearances	Classification 1		Classification 2	
	Perceptible ⟶ None.		Probable ⟶ Many	
	(*percipi possint*) or		(*probabilia*) (*multa*)	
	Imperceptible ⟶ Contrary to		or	
	(*percipi non possint*)	senses (*contra sensus*)	Not probable ⟶ Some	
		and not evident	(*non probabilia*)	
		(*contraque perspicuitatem*)		

---

[284] Cicero, *Academics*, II.67 [ch. XXI]. Note also the remarks on Carneades (cf. II.78 [ch. XXIV]). Sometimes the alternate title *Lucullus* is used for book II of the *Academics*.

[285] Famously, Carneades is said to have wondered aloud where he would have been had it not been for having Chrysippus as a foil. See Diogenes Laertius, *Lives of Eminent Philosophers: Carneades*, IV.62 [*Carneades*, 2].

[286] See Numenius, *On the Dissension of the Academics from Plato*, in Eusebius, *Preparation for the Gospel*, XIV.7.15, who notes the similarity in method but modification of basic principles.

[287] But note Cicero, *Academics*, I.46 [ch. XII], where it is argued that the 'New' Academy is like the 'Old' and that Carneades was a faithful follower of Arcesilaus.

[288] Cicero, *Academics*, II.99 [ch. XXXI]. Cf. II.111 [ch. XXXIV]. The Latin *visorum*—"appearances"—embraces both things of sense-perception and mental images.

Carneades' conclusion that no appearance is self-evident also means no proposition concerning perception can be *certain* to be true. However, that does not mean that such propositions must be false. Instead, starting from the idea that a statement is neither necessarily true (i.e., 'self-evident') nor necessarily false, the goal is to discern which are more *probably* true. This leads him to set forth a criterion for truth designed to distinguish propositions that are more likely to be true from those less likely to be so.[289]

Carneades' Criterion of the Probably True Persuasive Appearance

Carneades develops a notion that a "probably true" *phantasia* is a "persuasive appearance" (*pithanēn phantasian*). He distinguishes between the appearance (*phantasia*) arising from an external object and the appearance in the person. This means there is a double aspect—or two states—for a *phantasia*. One is objective (i.e., relating to the external object) and the other is subjective (i.e., relating to the person's internal state). With respect to the first state, arising from the object, if the appearance agrees with the object it is true; otherwise it is a false appearance. With respect to the second state, arising within the person, if the appearance persuades that it is true, this 'emphasis' is a 'persuasion' and thus a 'persuasive appearance.'[290] We may picture this as follows:

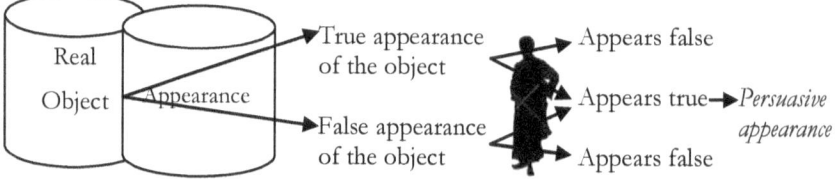

A chain of events must occur to create a persuasive appearance, but such still does not ensure that it is true. Some apparently true appearances are not as clear; their obscurity may be due to something applicable to the object itself, such as its size (e.g., very small), or distance (e.g., far away), but it may also be due to something in the observer, such as some sensory defect. Others are not merely apparently true but strongly so. Only the latter constitute a criterion for Carneades.[291] So we must slightly amend our above illustration as follows:

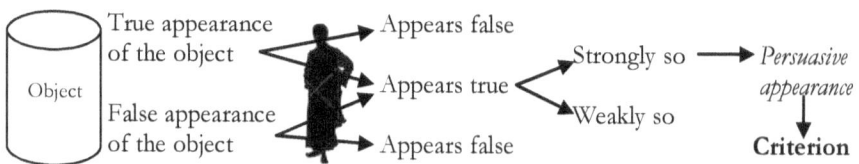

---

[289] On Carneades' "probable impressions" (probabilism), see Sextus Empiricus, *Outlines of Pyrrhonism*, I.227-230; also *Adversus Mathematicos, Against the Logicians*, I.166-189.

[290] Sextus Empiricus, *Adversus Mathematicos, Against the Logicians*, I.166-169. "Persuasive appearance" is πιθανὴν φαντασίαν (*pithanēn phantasian*). The 'apparently true' is termed ἔμφασις (*emphasis*), "emphasis," a term used frequently in Greek with references to appearances.

[291] Sextus Empiricus, *Adversus Mathematicos, Against the Logicians*, I.171-174. "Apparently true" here translates φαινομένης ἀληθοῦς (*phainomenēs alēthous*).

But note that an objectively false appearance can appear subjectively true, and if strong, be a persuasive appearance. This situation is why Carneades is only willing to speak of what is *probably* true. What the person possesses with a persuasive experience is, at best, true *belief* (i.e., something probable, not certain). Knowledge requires certainty, and that is lacking because there remains the possibility that the observer has incorrectly been persuaded.

Carneades uses the notion of "probable" to refer to three distinct situations:

1. what is both apparently true objectively and subjectively;
2. what is false objectively but appears true subjectively; and
3. what is common to both.[292]

The summation of the matter is thus: "Therefore the criterion (*kritērion*) is 'the apparently true appearance' (*phainomenē alēthēs phantasia*), which the Academic philosophers term 'persuasive' (*pithanēn*)."[293] This is just the first criterion.

Carneades then must add a second criterion because appearances are complex. The first criterion is probability; the second is "continuity"[294]—i.e., a *phantasia* continues to appear as probable. So, for example, the appearance of another person includes various physical characteristics and habits of presentation such as dress, gait while walking, and so forth. To these are added the environmental factors at hand, both physical (time of day, weather, etc.), and social (groups present, etc.). *If* everything is congruent so that no factor strikes one as false but instead everything appears correct, *then* belief is strengthened.[295] Accordingly, "an Academic philosopher makes a judgment (*krisin*) of the truth (*alētheias*) by the converging of appearances (*phantasiōn*), and when no one of these converging appearances turns him aside as false, he says that it strikes him as true (*alēthes*)."[296]

Finally, a third criterion is added: a "regularizing" of an appearance by its having been "tested thoroughly."[297] This means that each and every part of the appearance being judged is tested—closely examined—much like candidates for a judgeship are before being deemed fit for office.[298] This third criterion is the most decisive in Carneades' position. But even with all three criteria harmoniously converging to render a persuasive appearance probably true, the judgment

---

[292] Sextus Empiricus, *Adversus Mathematicos, Against the Logicians*, I.174. I have retained the ambiguity in the third point, which in the Greek manuscripts is uncertain: κατὰ δὲ τρίτον τὸ <ἀληθές> κοινὸν ἀμφοτέρων (*kata de triton to <alēthes> koinon amphoterōn*): "But according to the third the <true> common to both."

[293] Sextus Empiricus, *Adversus Mathematicos, Against the Logicians*, I.174.

[294] The Greek word is ἀπερίσπαστος (*aperispastos*)—something that continues without interruption.

[295] Sextus Empiricus, *Adversus Mathematicos, Against the Logicians*, I.177-178: "But when all harmoniously appear true, then there is greater belief (or trust)."

[296] Sextus Empiricus, *Adversus Mathematicos, Against the Logicians*, I.179.

[297] The Greek term is διεξωδευμένην (*diexōdeumenen*, fr. διεξοδεύω), "tested thoroughly" or "regularized," i.e., officially or correctly established. See Sextus Empiricus, *Adversus Mathematicos, Against the Logicians*, I.166.

[298] Sextus Empiricus, *Adversus Mathematicos, Against the Logicians*, I.181-183.

remains an assertion of *belief* rather than one of *knowledge*. (For the Pyrrhonist this still constitutes an unacceptable capitulation epistemologically and qualifies as dogmatism.) At any rate, Carneades' view may be illustrated as follows:

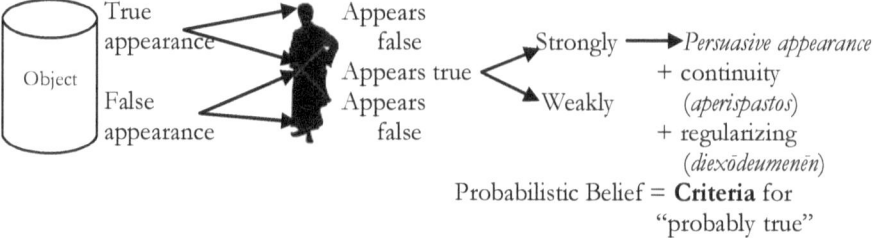

Carneades' three criteria support probabilistic belief, that is, the persuasion that undergirds a position that something is more-likely-than-not true.

Cicero, who in the late Roman Republic identified with Carneades' New Academy, summarizes attractively its appeal for himself and many others:

> Though all knowledge (*cognitio*) is obstructed by many difficulties—in things themselves there is darkness, and there is weakness in our own judgments (*iudiciis*)—such that it is not without reason that the most venerable and learned of folk have found themselves distrusting their ability to discover what they long for, yet neither did they grow weak, nor will our zeal to keep searching be abandoned from fatigue, nor are our discussions driven by any other end than that by our asserting (*dicendo*) each side to coax out and express something that either is true (*verum*) or may come closest to it.[299]

Carneades and the New Academy philosophers retain real confidence they can make progress toward knowledge.

Clitomachus

Much of what we presume to be the teaching of Carneades comes from his pupil Clitomachus (c. 187- c. 110 B.C.E.), who also served as *Scholarch* of the Academy. In substantial ways the presentation of Carneades that became dominant is the *interpretation* of his thinking set forth by Clitomachus. Cicero cites Clitomachus as presenting the Academy's position as follows:

> Academics are satisfied that there are differences among things of such a kind that some can appear probable, but others do not. But this is not sufficient grounds for saying that some things can be perceived (*percipi*) while others cannot be, because many things that are false are also 'probable,' yet nothing that is false can be either perceived (*perceptum*) or known (*cognitum*).[300]

In other words, Clitomachus denies there is any simplistic equation between what is probably true and perception, because many things judged as probable are actually false—and nothing false can be either perceived or known.

Cicero then writes:

---

[299] Cicero, *Academics*, II.7 (end) [ch. III].
[300] Cicero, *Academics*, II.103 [ch. XXXII].

After explaining this, he adds that there are two ways to assert that a wise person withholds assent: one way is that it is understood as meaning he entirely assents to nothing; the other way is that he holds back from approving or disapproving of something so that he neither denies nor affirms some particular thing; this being so, he holds that the one way is a *rule* to never assent, but the other way is the *practice* of following what is probable so that when such is the case that it seems present or lacking he can answer 'yes' or 'no' as fits the case.[301]

Cicero thus credits Clitomachus with developing a distinction between two kinds of withholding of assent: refusal to give assent as a general rule, and a practice of actually offering a tentative affirmation of something probable.

The resulting Academic position is as follows:

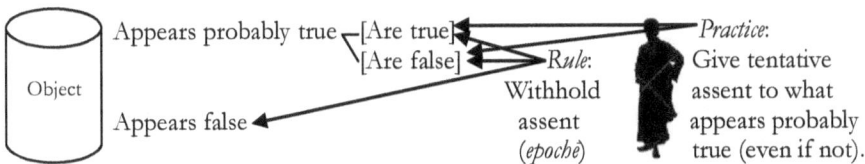

This upholds the practice of *epochē* (suspension of judgment) as a firm rule while allowing what is going to happen in ordinary experience anyway—assent to some things as probably true (i.e., actually the case). What makes both possible together is that the latter still obeys the general rule in that assent remains tentative, conditioned on the possibility that the matter might yet prove false though it now appears true. In theory, any dogmatic assent is still withheld.

Philo of Larissa & Modifications of Academic Skepticism

Philo of Larissa (c. 154-c. 84 B.C.E.), student of Clitomachus, was *Scholarch* from 110 B.C.E. until his death. His period of leadership marks a time of significant transition in the Academy's thinking and his passing marks the end of Academic Skepticism as an institutional entity (although its influence continues to live on in such individuals as Cicero). In the roughly quarter-century of his leadership, he appears to have undergone shifts in epistemological thinking.[302] Classicist Charles Brittain sees Philo's Academic epistemology as progressing through three stages:

1. an initial embracing of his predecessor's upholding of *akatalēpsia* (no self-evident comprehension) and *epochē* (suspension of judgment) [Clitomachian view];
2. retention of *akatalēpsia*, but rejection of *epochē* [Philonian/Metrodorian view]; and,
3. rejection of both [Roman view].[303]

---

[301] Cicero, *Academics*, II.104 [ch. XXXII].
[302] Sextus Empiricus, *Outlines of Pyrrhonism*, I.33.220, makes passing mention that some regard Philo (together with Charmidas) as being a "fourth school" of the Academy.
[303] Brittain, *Philo of Larissa*, 73.

The first stage shows continuity with Clitomachus.[304] The second is so named because Philo switched allegiance to Metrodorus of Stratonicea (late 2nd–early 1st cent. B.C.E.),[305] who also had firsthand acquaintance with Carneades.[306] According to Philodemus, "Metrodorus said Carneades had been misrepresented by all, for he had not judged that all things are incomprehensible (*akatalēpta*)."[307] Late in Philo's career, he relocated to Rome. His writings there seem to offer a third position. Not only is *epochē* rejected, but also *akatalēpsia*.

Sextus Empiricus offers this summary: "According to those who follow him, Philo says that insofar as the Stoic criterion (*kritērio*) applies, that is, with respect to 'self-evident appearances' (*kataleptikē phantasia*), things are not self-evidently comprehensible (*akatalēpta*), but with respect to the nature of these things they are comprehensible (*katalēpta*)."[308] The way that seems to make the best sense of his meaning is to see this in the familiar context of the difference between "things" (*ta pragmata*) "as they actually *are*" and "things as they *appear to be*" (the *kataleptikē phantasia*). Such knowledge is the kind obtained and appealed to in ordinary experience. It cannot be claimed to be infallibly certain, but it is reliable enough.[309] Philo's final position can be pictured like this:

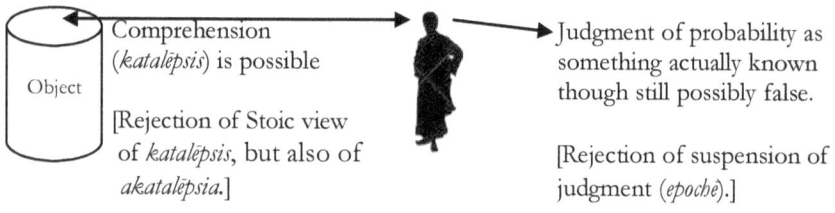

Object

Comprehension (*katalēpsis*) is possible

[Rejection of Stoic view of *katalēpsis*, but also of *akatalēpsia*.]

Judgment of probability as something actually known though still possibly false.

[Rejection of suspension of judgment (*epochē*).]

So Philo argues against the necessity of certainty for knowledge. His view, sometimes called 'Fallibilism,' defends the notion *there is fallible but reliable knowing*. Only *epistēmē*—so-called 'theoretical' or 'philosophical' knowledge, which is a body of true and certain propositions about the nature of things—remains outside general attainment.

---

[304] Numenius, in Eusebius, *Preparation for the Gospel*, XIV.9.1 [739b = fragment 28 in *Numenius*], writes, "And this Philo, when he received it in turn, was beside himself with joy and, with thanks to him, rendered service and extolled the doctrines of Clitomachus. . . ."

[305] Metrodorus, says Diogenes Laertius, *Lives of Eminent Philosophers: Epicurus*, X.9 [*Epicurus*, 5], mentioned as unusual among the Epicureans in having deserted their doctrine to give his allegiance to Carneades. Similarly, Philodemus, *Lives of Academic Philosophers*, in Mekler, *Index*, column XXIV, lines 9-12: "Metrodorus of Stratonicea, who previously had been a follower of the Epicureans." See Brittain, *Philo of Larissa*, 73-128.

[306] Cicero, *On the Orator*, I.45 [ch. 11], tells us, "Likewise there was Metrodorus, who with the others carefully listened to the famous Carneades himself." Cicero, *Academics*, II.78, alludes to the differences in interpretation of Carneades.

[307] Philodemus, *Lives of Academic Philosophers*, in Mekler, *Index*, column XXVI, lines 4-10. Others use "misunderstood" rather than "misrepresented," but the idea seems to me more the latter than the former in Metrodorus' charge.

[308] Sextus Empiricus, *Outines of Pyrrhonism*, I.235.

[309] Brittain, *Philo of Larissa*, 3, 129-168.

The Skeptics' position on belief is neither simple nor straightforward. To get at how the different Skeptic approaches regard belief we must first start with their shared conviction that assertions about reality as such and so, and certainly known, are not statements of knowledge but of belief. To avoid such assertions the Skeptic merely *describes* an appearance rather than *asserts* its truth or falsity.

Pyrrhonism vs. Academic Skepticism: The Problem of 'Dogma'

Sextus Empiricus contrasts Pyrrhonian Skeptics with Academic Skeptics.[310] A chief complaint is that New Academic Skeptics actually are dogmatists—they, in fact, have beliefs! Now we should pause and reflect a bit more on words like "dogma," "dogmatizing," and "dogmatists." The Greek term *dogma* (δόγμα) is closely enough associated with our English conception of "belief" that even today it surfaces most notably in theological discussions where it refers to those principles (or set of principles) set down as authoritative for members of a Church. A *dogma* is a "belief," but not quite like *doxa* is a belief.

Early in *Outlines of Pyrrhonism* Sextus Empiricus writes, "When we say, 'Skeptics do not dogmatize,' our sense of 'dogma' is not the same as some mean when using its common meaning of 'to be pleased to go along with something' (for the Skeptic does assent to the strong feelings (*pathesi*) forcibly pressed upon him by an appearance (*phantasian*))."[311] In other words, this common sense use is unobjectionable. He elaborates on what a Skeptic can accept by giving the example of a person remarking whether he or she feels hot or cold; the person is simply describing what is being felt, and not saying its opposite. In this manner they are "assenting" to the sensory impact of an appearance—and this assertion is a belief statement. Skeptics make such statements like anyone else.

But, he continues, what the Pyrrhonist Skeptic usually has in mind by the terms "dogma" and "dogmatize" is not this kind of casual, everyday assent where a person simply reports their experience. Rather, they are referring to what other philosophers are doing in making authoritative pronouncements of belief about things they cannot possibly know—things behind the appearances—the very 'non-evident' things that the endeavor of "knowing" professes to be about.[312] These other philosophers are truncating the search for truth and genuine knowledge when they trumpet some triumph of knowing (of hidden

---

[310] Sextus Empiricus, *Outlines of Pyrrhonism*, I.33.232-234, finds Arcesilaus not so much different from Pyrrhonian Skepticism. Sextus' criticism is largely directed at the 'New Academy' under Carneades.

[311] Sextus Empiricus, *Outlines of Pyrrhonism*, I.7.13 (beginning). The phrase "to be pleased to go along with" translates εὐδοκεῖν (*eudokein*), and the one word "acquiesce" or, a little less desirably, "approve" or "agree to" could be used as well. One could in this instance replace "dogmatize" with "believe," and "dogma" with "belief"—and such actually has been done by some translators.

[312] Sextus Empiricus, *Outlines of Pyrrhonism*, I.7.13-14: "But we are not talking about 'dogmatizing' according to the way some say 'dogma' is 'assent to something that is not evident,' which is the very thing knowledge (*epistēmas*) seeks."

things as they really *are*) which turns out to be nothing more than an assertion of believing (of visible things as they *appear to be*).

We may illustrate the differences between Pyrrhonists and others this way:

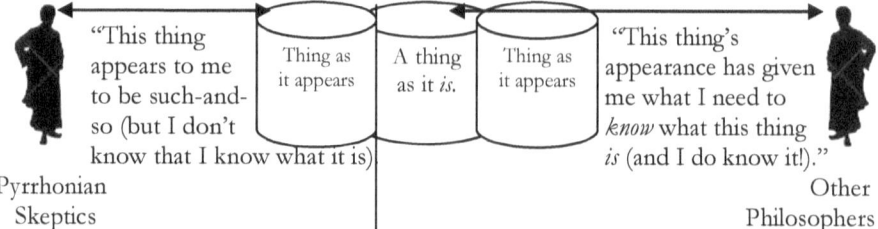

The Pyrrhonist draws a line beyond which he or she regards any statement as being one of belief rather than knowledge. All one can *know* is what one immediately experiences, which can be factually described (e.g., "I feel cold."). Anything else is *belief* and when other philosophers confidently assert their beliefs as being knowledge, they are being *dogmatic*.

Sextus turns specifically to the matter of "belief" in the basic sense of "being persuaded" of something. He writes:

> Now even though the Academics and the Skeptics both speak of being persuaded (*peithesthai*) of some things, the difference between these philosophies is plain here, too. For 'being persuaded' (*peithesthai*) has different meanings—it can mean not to brace in an opposite direction but instead, without either much partiality or strong feeling, simply to follow, as when we say 'the child is being persuaded (*peithesthai*) by the teacher.' But it can also mean, with a type of sympathy stirred by much desire, to give assent (*sugkatatithesthai*) to something, as when a dissolute fellow is 'persuaded' (*peithetai*) by the approval of another for living beyond his means.[313]

The sense in which the Pyrrhonian Skeptic means 'being persuaded' is the former (which is like not objecting to the way 'dogma' is used for the kind of 'belief' where people simply go along with a feeling something right now is this way and not that). In contrast, the Academic philosopher is persuaded in a different sense, with *conviction*. The Academic allows himself to be strongly persuaded, while the Pyrrhonian Skeptic is only mildly—or better, 'indifferently'—persuaded; in Sextus' words, "without strong feeling."[314]

Suspension of Judgment, Tranquility, and Belief

The avoidance of strong feeling is why the Pyrrhonian Skeptic can achieve tranquility (*ataraxia*) following suspension of judgment (*epochē*). Early in his *Outlines of Pyrrhonism*, in explaining the goal (*telos*) of Skepticism, Sextus writes that the Skeptics' *telos* is "tranquility in matters of belief (*doxan*), and in things that compel us a moderate degree of feeling."[315]

[313] Sextus Empiricus, *Outlines of Pyrrhonism*, I.33.229-230.
[314] Sextus Empiricus, *Outlines of Pyrrhonism*, I.33.230.
[315] Sextus Empiricus, *Outlines of Pyrrhonism*, I.12.25.

He then adds:

> For when beginning to philosophize for the purpose of passing judgment upon (*epikrinai*) appearances (*phantasias*), which are true (*alētheis*) and which false (*pseudeis*), in order to attain tranquility (*ataraktēsai*), the Skeptic discovered himself among differences of equal strength and unable to pass judgment upon (*epikrinai*) them he suspended judgment (*epeschen*). But in suspending judgment (*epischonti*), as it happened, there was a fortuitous occurrence of tranquility (*ataraxia*) with respect to matters of belief (*en tois doxastois*).[316]

Fortuitous indeed! Sextus Empiricus' claim is that the very process of balancing the scales with regard to judging appearances, which resulted in suspension of judgment and brought tranquility, proved to hold true in matters of *doxa*.

Tranquility (*ataraxia*) includes an absence of strong feelings (*pathē*) and Sextus associates this with the Skeptic practice of reporting what seems to him or her to be true, but doing so "without belief" (*adoxastōs*), in the sense of 'without persuasion.' Sextus writes, "But most importantly, in the offering of his slogans he is speaking of the appearances (*phainomenon*) as they are to himself and announcing their emotional affect on himself without belief (*adoxastōs*), thereby avoiding any strong affirmations concerning things as they really are."[317]

The word for "belief" associated with persuasion is not *doxa*, but *pistis*. To what exact degree *doxa* and *pistis* might be related in Sextus' thinking is debatable. But it seems that "belief"—whether *doxa* or *pistis*—with respect to knowing things as they *are* is rejected. The Skeptic reports how things *seem to be* personally, but does so without the strong feeling or intellectual commitment associated with "belief" as *dogma*.

Early in *Outlines of Pyrrhonism* when Sextus offers definitions of some key terms he employs *pistis* and its opposite. They occur in his explanation of what *isostheneia* (ἰσοσθένεια)—"equipollence" or "equal in force"—means for the Skeptic: "By 'equal in force' (*isostheneian*) we mean an equality (*isotēta*) with respect to belief (*pistin*) and disbelief (*apistian*), by which we mean nothing proposed among opposing arguments is more believable (*pistoteron*) than another."[318]

Later in the *Outlines* he provides an example of his reasoning. He presents the argument that a person should simply believe one who is deemed especially wise—a Sage—indeed, *the* Sage, or wisest person of all. But who is that? First, people, including philosophers, argue over who that person is. But, Sextus says, even if everyone unanimously agrees on who it is—the wisest person past and present—what about the future? It is possible someone yet to come will be the

---

[316] Sextus Empiricus, *Outlines of Pyrrhonism*, I.12.25-27.

[317] Sextus Empiricus, *Outlines of Pyrrhonism*, I.7.15.

[318] Sextus Empiricus, *Outlines of Pyrrhonism*, I.4.10. Cf. Diogenes Laertius, *Lives of Eminent Philosophers: Pyrrho*, IX:73 (end) [*Pyrrho*, 8], where he refers to the belief some held that Homer was the founder of Skepticism because he speaks of the equipollence of opposite sayings. Here the forms of *pistis* carry the sense of belief as something "credible" or "persuasive," or "convincing," and a good translation choice here would be an English word like "credibility."

wisest of all people. "So then," he remarks, "just as we are told to believe (*pisteuein*) the person who is said to be more sagacious than anyone else past or present, we ought even more so to believe (*pisteuein*) the one who in the future is even more sagacious."[319] Obviously such an argument can go on *ad infinitum*. Therefore, the prudent course of action is to suspend judgment.

In the *Outlines* he argues that if one accepts the premise that all appearances are to be believed (*pisteusomen*), then that means also accepting the contention of Xeniades that all *phantasia* are *not* to be believed (*apistous*). The problem is just as acute if one decides, like the Stoic, to believe only *some* appearances. "And if only some, how shall we judge that it is these *phantasia* we are to believe (*pisteuein*) and those we are to disbelieve (*apistein*)?"[320] If the argument is made to judge some *phantasia* by another, which *phantasia* will be used? Once more, very soon an argument *ad infinitum* results: every *phantasia* needs another one to establish it, with no end in sight. Since it is impossible to continue on in such a process forever, the only sensible conclusion, say Sextus, is the following:

> Accordingly, since even if we grant that we ought to judge (*krinein*) external things according to *phantasia*, whether we decide to believe (*pisteuein*) all *phantasia*, or only to believe (*pisteuein*) some, or to disbelieve (*apistein*) all, with respect to being criteria (*kriterioi*), in any case the argument (*ho logos*) is overthrown, and we are made to conclude *phantasia* are not to be drawn upon as criteria (*kriteria*) for judgment (*krisin*).[321]

In *Against the Logicians*, Sextus remarks:

> It is the Skeptic habit, with things believed truly (*pepisteumenois*), not to be an advocate, but with such things find it is enough first to be satisfied with the common notion itself, yet also to be an advocate for the things *not* believed (*apistois*), and thus to bring them both into a place of equal weight (*isostheneian*), the opposite alongside the belief (*pistis*).[322]

Given the association of tranquility with a lack of strong, disturbing feeling, *pistis* is an appropriate "belief" term because belief can and often is associated with *emotional conviction*. The very thing a member of the New Academy finds so convincing is the sort of thing a Skeptic wants to avoid: strong *pathē*. When the Skeptic weighs things such that belief and disbelief are equal, it means neither position under consideration carries more emotionally convincing power than the other.

---

[319] Sextus Empiricus, *Outlines of Pyrrhonism,* II.40. He uses *pisteuein* again in II.42 to press the point that even if one agrees someone is the wisest person who ever was, is, or will be, one should still not believe him because precisely such a person may be prone to promoting incorrect dogmas and persuading others to believe him. The sense of *pisteuein* here can also be understood as "to rely upon."

[320] Sextus Empiricus, *Outlines of Pyrrhonism,* II.76-77 (quoted material from start of 77). Xeniades was a philosopher at about the same time as Democritus.

[321] Sextus Empiricus, *Outlines of Pyrrhonism,* II.78.

[322] Sextus Empiricus, *Against the Dogmatists: Against the Logicians,* I.443.

Sextus Empiricus observes that philosophers—supposedly the wisest among people—cannot agree among themselves on any criterion. He remarks, "whether a person adopts as a criterion the mind (*dianoian*), or sense-perception (*aisthēsin*), or the two as working together, it still remains necessary for either something evident or not evident to be adopted in order to judge (*krisin*) who is right."[323] In *Against the Logicians*, he discusses the search for some criterion to distinguish among the philosophical schools which one is to be trusted. He examines a wide range of possible criteria, demolishing each in turn. He then turns to the claim that the philosopher should be trusted who enjoys the support of 'the majority.' He points out that those who follow Epicurus seem to be equal in number to those who follow Aristotle. He makes the counter-argument that it may be philosophers are like other folk in that one might be sensible and the majority like geese who simply follow the leader; their 'majority' is of no real merit. Sextus also points out that those who disagree with any position will always be more than the number adhering to it. Even when a great number agree they are only voicing one position that remains counterbalanced by those holding a different view.[324]

Summary Picture of Pyrrhonian Position on Belief

The common (or majority or expert) belief weighs a matter in one direction only. It is imbalanced, but

The scales are balanced by the Skeptic (*isosthenia*) in a suspension of

But . . . *Thus . . .*

accompanied by strong feeling (*pathē*)

The Skeptic sees the proverbial 'other side' (a contrary belief or disbelief (*apistian*) of the common belief) drawing attention to it, but dispassionately.

judgment (*epochē*), which leads to desired tranquility (*ataraxia*).

At the same time . . .

The Skeptic is guided by the appearance at hand (the criterion for action), taking it at face value, as it seems in the moment, but without any investment of feeling or dogmatic belief. Thus the Skeptic remains unperturbed.

323 Sextus Empiricus, *Against the Dogmatists: Against the Logicians*, I.369.
324 Sextus Empiricus, *Against the Dogmatists: Against the Logicians*, I.317–35.

The Pyrrhonian Sextus Empiricus views the Academic Arcesilaus as a kindred Skeptic spirit,[325] so we should not be surprised to find substantial agreement between the 'Middle Academy' Skepticism and Pyrrhonian Skepticism when it comes to the matter of belief. Arcesilaus' position on the question of belief, like much of what we know of his views, is framed in the context of his opposition to Stoic philosophy. In his desire to accomplish what he thought the Stoics did not, Arcesilaus was the first to articulate the notion that it is possible to *not* believe (*nihil opinari*)—and essential to not do so in order to be wise.[326]

Arcesilaus offers no epistemological criterion of his own. He does, however, respond to the need to set forward some criterion with respect to ethics, i.e., concerning the conduct of life. Sextus Empiricus says in this regard Arcesilaus proposes "the reasonable" (*to eulogon*). Exactly what this means, especially in conjunction with his remarks on knowledge and belief, has provoked debate. But it seems plausible that what Arcesilaus has in mind is a person acting reasonably by responding in a natural manner to sensory input without also forming beliefs, giving assent, or pretending to knowledge.

Plutarch, in his work against the Epicurean writer Colotes, says that Arcesilaus envisions the *psyche* regularly experiencing three movements. The first is the involuntary movement occasioned by sense-perception. The second is an internal impulse aroused by this sense-perception that generates goal-directed behavior. The third movement is the formation of belief. This last movement can be avoided. Thus a person can act in a reasonable, natural fashion by following an internal impulse in the direction of an ethical goal.[327]

On this decisive second movement, Plutarch writes of Arcesilaus' position as follows:

> Now the impulse awakened by the appearance (*phantastikou*) sets a person in motion toward a suitable goal, acting like a weight tipping the scale and inclining us to act. So, quite clearly, this impulse is not shut out by those who withhold judgment on all things. Rather, they follow this impulse which in a natural manner leads them to what is suitable in response to the appearance (*phainonemon*).[328]

All of this can be pictured as follows:

---

[325] Sextus Empiricus, *Outlines of Pyrrhonism*, I.33.232-234. In I.232 Sextus proclaims, "Nevertheless, Arcesilaus, whom we have mentioned as the *Scholarch* and founder of the 'Middle' Academy, seems to me to follow Pyrrho with shared reasoning such that his way certainly looks like ours." Similarly, Numenius, *On the Dissension of the Academics from Plato,* as recorded by Eusebius, *Preparation for the Gospel,* XIV.6.6, says Arcesilaus was a Pyrrhonian Skeptic in all but name and an Academic philosopher in name only!

[326] Cicero, *Academics,* II.77 [ch. XXIV]: "No one, I say, before him expressed things this way—that is possible for a person not to believe, and not only possible, but necessary to be wise."

[327] Plutarch, *Moralia: Reply to Colotes,* 1122b-c.

[328] Plutarch, *Moralia: Reply to Colotes,* 1122c.

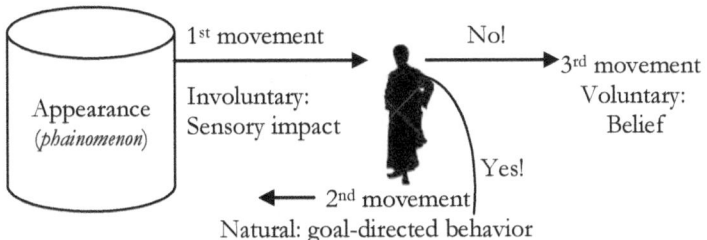

1st movement — No! — 3rd movement

Appearance (*phainomenon*) | Involuntary: Sensory impact | Voluntary: Belief

Yes!

← 2nd movement

Natural: goal-directed behavior

Only the first movement is beyond the individual's control. The person can choose to exercise belief, but the Skeptic is opposed to doing such. Instead, they advocate a "natural" acting in suitable (i.e., appropriate) accord with the impulse aroused by sense-perception.

It is not too difficult to see how Arcesilaus' position on belief is like the Pyrrhonist notion that one can—and should—"without either much partiality or strong feeling, simply to follow"[329] as a way of being persuaded without being dogmatic. In this sense, the Pyrrhonist is 'without belief' in the same way that Arcesilaus meant when one simply follows along a natural way of response.

As we saw earlier, Carneades introduces the idea of 'persuasive' experience that makes possible saying that something is 'probably' true. As pointed out when looking at this notion, what a person possesses with a persuasive experience is, at best, true belief. Thus Carneades opens the door for a substantive place for belief that remains lacking in Arcesilaus and the Pyrrhonists.

Perhaps we can picture his position like this:

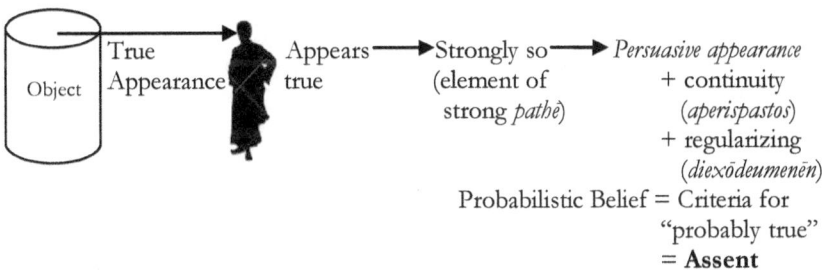

Object | True Appearance | Appears true | Strongly so → Persuasive appearance
(element of + continuity
strong *pathē*) (*aperispastos*)
+ regularizing
(*diexōdeumenēn*)
Probabilistic Belief = Criteria for
"probably true"
= **Assent**

Cicero in his *Academics* offers the opinion that Carneades' occasional allowance of belief by even the wise may be simply for the sake of argument rather than any personal conviction on his own part.[330] He then adds, "It is certain that it logically follows that when belief (*opinatione*) and perception (*perceptione*) are both removed, then all assent (*adsensionum*) is withheld; therefore, if I show it is not possible to perceive (*percipi*), then you must concede nothing is to be given assent (*adsensurum*)."[331] Later he cites Carneades' disciple Clitomachus with re-

---

[329] Sextus Empiricus, *Outlines of Pyrrhonism*, I.33.229-230, quoted and cited earlier.
[330] Cicero, *Academics*, II.78 [ch. XXIV].
[331] Cicero, *Academics*, II.78 [ch. XXIV].

spect to his teacher having "rescued our rational souls (*animis*) from assent (*adsensionem*), that is, from belief (*opinationem*) and rashness."[332]

Under Philo the Academy's Skepticism is modified still further. It retains doubt about knowledge in the sense of *epistēmē*, but ordinary "knowing," which is really just "believing," is accepted as reliable enough to make a casual, ordinary equation of belief with knowledge. Such belief/knowledge does not require a suspension of judgment (*epochē*), and can even give acceptance to the kind of comprehension (*katalēpsis*) people achieve in ordinary experience.

Concluding Reflection: The Skeptic's Dilemma

In the dialog *Hermotimus*, Lucian writes, "For I do not say we should not seek philosophy, but that since we must, and there are many ways, each asserting that it leads to virtue, and yet the true (*alēthēs*) way among them uncertain, we must make the most careful decision."[333] Prudent advice—yet, it is hard not to have some sympathy for poor Hermotimus. The imposing task set by the Skeptic to achieve "knowledge" in the sense of *epistēmē* as a full-bodied and secure repository of true and dependable information requires a degree of certainty that is *absolute completeness*. In other words, everything relevant must be fully available and understood to qualify as the certainty needed to call something knowledge in this sense. Since such a condition is rarely if ever met, there are seldom if any times when one can say he or she has "knowledge" apart from the mundane knowing of everyday matters of experience.

In effect, while the Skeptic may assert that "knowledge" is possible, the bar is typically set so high that in practice it is never surmounted. All that is left is belief. Even that may be denied by the Skeptic; some argue that true Skepticism means disavowal of belief as well. In sum, what we are left with is largely a collection of arguments *against* the positions of others who are more optimistic about the possibility of knowledge. When it comes to setting out their own positive agenda the Skeptic position is limited. The Skeptic task is a daunting one and while some degree of skepticism has remained a feature of good, rational thinking, the degree to which a Pyrrhonist insists has generally been resisted. This is not a philosophical path for the faint-hearted or the lazy. That is why professional philosophers are so often amused—or bemused—by the common claim to be a 'Skeptic' that is voiced by many students and others. It is one thing to practice a general skepticism characterized by an open mind, questioning, awareness of alternatives, and reluctance to embrace hasty judgments, and quite another to practice the rigorous Skepticism advocated by the Skeptical philosophers we have discussed in this chapter.

---

[332] Cicero, *Academics*, II.108 [ch. XXXIV].
[333] Lucian, *Hermotimus*, 52.

11

The Puzzle of Knowledge, I: Heart Pieces

We began this volume with Aristotle's conviction that "All people by nature stretch themselves toward knowledge." That is the metaphorical sun that every philosophical tree extends its limbs toward—even the Skeptics, who as Sextus Empiricus reminds us, are still searching, still reaching. He also has a clear realization of the stakes involved:

> With respect to the search for the criterion—not only because human beings are by nature lovers of truth (*philalēthes*), but also because those belonging to the most authoritative schools of philosophy are serving as judges on the weightiest matters—everything is contested. Either the great and serious claims of the Dogmatists' boasts will be completely thrown away because no guiding rule (*kanonos*) has been discovered concerning the truth (*alēthian*) of things that really *are*, or contra wise, Skeptics will be convicted as reckless and insolent with respect to common belief (*tēs koinēs pisteōs*) because something has appeared (*phanētai*) capable of showing us the way to the comprehension (*katalēpsin*) of the truth (*alēthias*).[334]

Nothing has changed. The dogmatists among us—of whatever creed and canon—still boast of having discovered the one criterion (or set of criteria) that secures the truth of their knowledge that *this* is the way things truly *are*. And the skeptics among us still enjoy showing everyone else why their claims are not as secure as they believe, offering in response disbelief and counter beliefs.

While we have examined various figures and schools individually, we have made only relatively minor remarks on their interactions, save for Plato's Socrates in his examination of Protagoras' proposal. In this chapter we shall undertake a comparison of the positions we have studied organized around the basic pieces to the puzzle of knowledge set out at the beginning of the book.

We shall presume that epistemology arises from metaphysical reflections and takes as its starting point the desire to understand reality—to know what *is*, and to know it with *certainty*. Looked at from this initial perspective, the question of knowing is largely one of *how* we know. When, like Socrates, we want to know *what* knowledge is we must begin with how we know. Since what we want to know—the object of our knowledge—is reality, the question of how we know becomes one of how we interface with reality. Inescapably, human beings

---

[334] Sextus Empiricus, *Adversus Mathematicos: Against the Logicians*, I.27.

must reckon with their own abilities and limitations and with them in mind form some judgment as to whether our abilities suffice or, instead, our limitations prevail. Thus, in seeking to know reality we cannot content ourselves with the external objects of reality alone but must instead begin with the question of what we bring to the task of knowing.

From the beginning, thinkers have identified two human attributes related to knowledge: *body* and *mind*. Roughly speaking, these two attributes can be matched to two presumed paths to knowledge (i.e., ways of knowing). To the body belongs sense-perception; to the mind belongs reason. Over the long course of history the prioritizing of one or the other has led to identifying two distinct camps labeled *empiricism* and *rationalism*. Both labels have been avoided in this volume because what we associate with each owes its identity substantially to ideas developed later than our thinkers.

While many thinkers prioritize either body or mind, most tend not to put all their epistemological eggs in one basket. Most thinkers prefer to see one as more fundamental but both as being involved. For example, a thinker like Aristotle starts with sense-perception but regards reason as the higher, more dependable path to knowledge—without sacrificing either mind or body. On the other hand, Epicurus distrusts reason to the same degree that the Stoics trust it.

Now many, both then and now, might wonder about other alleged ways of knowing, such as authority, revelation, intuition and the like. Yet time and again our thinkers return to their primary conviction that human bodies and minds are the natural, fitting, and sufficient sphere within which to wrestle with questions about knowledge and belief. These basic ideas must be kept in mind as we consider the puzzle of knowledge.

In chapter 1, I offered three 'heart pieces' to the puzzle of knowledge. We perhaps can see better these pieces now than when we began. Let me suggest that we may reasonably add some further detail:

> ➤ *Information*—'data'—comes through *appearances* (primarily sense-perceptions, but secondarily through ideas as well).
> ➤ *Reality* concerns the way things really *are*, which information purports to represent.
> ➤ *Judgment* relies on some *criterion* of truth by which information can be established as accurate and thus reality comprehended.

In their vigorous disputations, our Greek thinkers pretty much agree these are the pieces they are fighting over. It is not so much a question of arguing, for example, *if* information is important as it is a question about *what* information is most important, *how* it contributes to knowing, and *why* it can be trusted or must be doubted. It is true that depending on time, place, and thinker the attention given to each of these may vary—and none of them present the matter quite so starkly as is done here. Yet these are elements clearly discernible in the long debate over the nature of knowledge.

Knowledge is founded on information. The goal may be conceived either as understanding, or as the securing of a sense of certainty sufficient to claim more than mere belief. Either way, though, information is the stock from which the soup of knowledge is brewed. We have seen that the concept of "appearances" is fundamental in Greek epistemology and now we can posit that appearances provide information, the raw data around which knowledge forms.

The primary way in which appearances are talked about is with respect to sense-perception. Soon enough the notion of concepts (or ideas) attached itself, too. This connection may seem puzzling to us today. The Greek philosophical notion of a *concept* is rooted in the notion of an *image*. Classical philologist Olga Freidenberg explains:

> The classical languages had many terms for "image" but not one for "concept." The "external appearance" without the "essence" of the object is called εἰκών, εἶδος, or ἰδέα (*imago, forma, figura, species*). All of these meant "image", but ἰδέα, εἶδος, *species* were used when one wanted to refer to a "concept." Thus ἰδέα and *forma* ("idea" and "form") were used alike to signify "image," "idea," and "outer form," "external appearance"—in other words "idea" originally corresponded to a formal feature of the object.[335]

In short, the sense of what a concept is develops in Greek epistemological thinking from consideration of what *appearances* are. Three terms—appearance, image, concept—are inextricably linked. We might picture it like this initially:

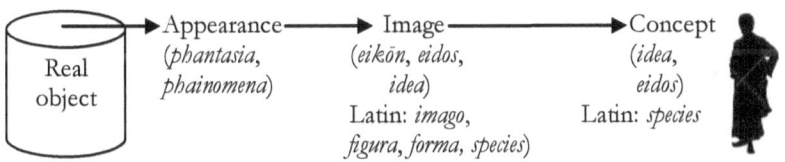

That is, all three—appearance, image, and concept—belong to the object.

As philosophers turned more attention to what is going on in the *psyche* and the role it plays in knowing, shifts in conception of these three matters occurred. Thus in Epicurean representation, the image still belongs to the object, but the appearance (*phantasia*), whether sense-perception or idea, belongs to the mind.[336] We can picture it in this manner:

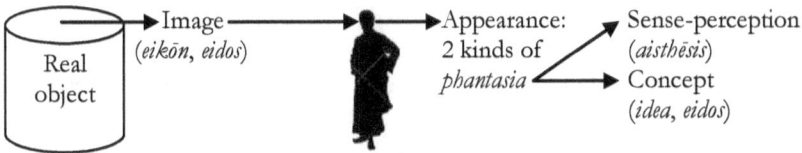

---

[335] Freidenberg, *Image and Concept*, 99-100 (see 99-107). The illustration incorporates some of her work but is not intended to convey her presentation.

[336] The Epicurean Philedomus, *On Methods of Inference*, VI, says that an image (*idōla*), however it comes about (i.e., from an external object or 'of itself'), cannot be false.

The Epicurean conception varies from their Stoic rivals:[337]

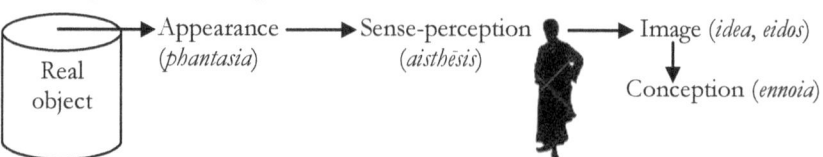

Yet another way to envision the relations among these things is Plato's, where the real object is known only through reason. The image is the faintest, weakest representation of it. The appearance in sense-perception is more vivid, and joined with *doxa*. It requires the concept to reach beyond mere belief:

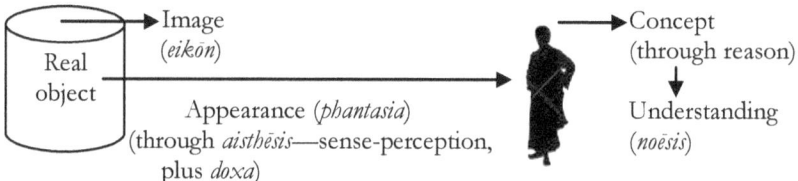

The point should be clear: over time discussions of how these terms relate to each other and how they should be understood *changes* to reflect particular nuances of thought, or to wax and wane in importance.

Let us imagine how the figures and schools settle into various positions.

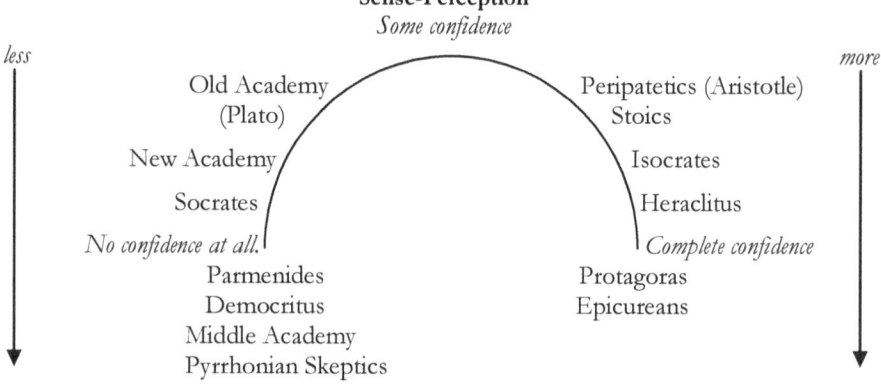

Note that I have presented this as a continuum of *confidence* rather than of dogmatic certainty. This is an important distinction because, for example, the Skeptics of the Middle Academy (e.g., Arcesilaus) or of Pyrrhonism (e.g., Aenesidemus or Sextus Empiricus) carefully avoid dogmatic certainty, holding out the possibility that sense-perceptions *might* provide what Stoics and Epicu-

[337] Aëtius, *Opinions of the Philosophers,* IV.11 [=*Stoicorum Veterum Fragmenta* [*SVF*], II.83 (p. 28), uses the term φάντασμα (*phantasma*). The word Aëtius uses for "conception" is ἔννοια (*ennoia*) [=ἐννόημα (*ennoēma*)]. He writes that "a concept is a *phantasma* in the thoughts of reasoning beings." Aëtius explains that the very term "concept" (*ennoēma*) derives from its connection to νοῦς (*nous*), "mind" or "thought."

reans hold true of them. But they find no grounds for confidence that this is the case. Also remember that the positions on the spectrum are not meant to represent absolute ones but only relative to the other schools of thought or figures.

The figures and schools represented as showing some confidence in sense-perception do so not only in varying degrees but also in different ways. For example, Plato's approach to sense-perception is different from that of the Stoics. For Plato, sense-perception belongs to the Sensible world where the best we can achieve is *doxa* because nothing is certain—things are always coming into existence, changing, and passing from existence. The Stoics reserve for *some* sense-perceptions the possibility of their being true and producing knowledge. So, in the above illustration, I have placed the Stoics further along the scale of confidence. Aristotle is situated between Plato and the Stoics, but relatively closer to the Stoics because he gives greater weight to the value of sense-perception information as related to knowledge than does Plato.[338] But, where a figure or school is placed is subject to different perspectives and the real point is to encourage further reflection to aid one's own thinking on the matter.

Now the above is only part of the picture. Appearances involve not merely sense-perception but thinking. That leads to a different picture.

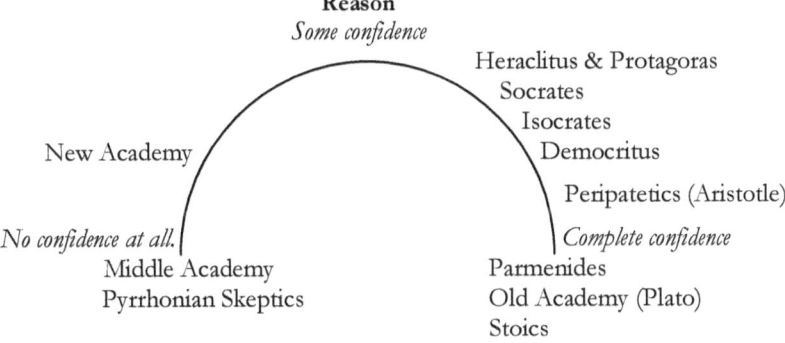

Reason
Some confidence

Heraclitus & Protagoras
Socrates
Isocrates
Democritus

New Academy

Peripatetics (Aristotle)

No confidence at all.
Complete confidence

Middle Academy
Pyrrhonian Skeptics

Parmenides
Old Academy (Plato)
Stoics

Once again the figures and schools represented are with respect to a continuum of confidence, this time in reason. Though one pole states "no confidence at all," we have to add the caveat that the Skeptics of the Middle Academy and those of Pyrrhonian persuasion may lack confidence in reason, but do stay open to the possibility that reason might, after all, prove it can do what some of its advocates claim. So their positioning at this extreme is like that in the illustration for sense-perception. Formally the Skeptics accept the possibility that either sense-perception or reason may provide sufficient information for knowledge— but they are yet to be convinced. Thus, from the perspective of dogmatists the Skeptics appear to have no real confidence in either.

---

[338] Cf. Theophrastus, *On First Principles (Peri Archōn)*, 9b [=Usener, 25].

Information from appearances—whether sense-perceptions or concepts—is about *reality*. This does not mean we cannot imagine non-existent things. What it does mean is that reality, as about things that *are* and *are not*, includes everything. Thus appearances, which include things judged as actually existing or as imaginary, encompass *all* things, from dogs to gods.

The piece that is reality in the puzzle of knowledge requires that epistemology remain bound to metaphysics. For our ancient thinkers the matter of metaphysics is about what *is*, and thus to some extent also what *is not*. The 'what is' concern is about that which is fixed and abiding—a conception of reality as having some eternal, universal essence that makes it possible to declare, "At the heart of the universe, *this* is the way things *are*." Metaphysics is a science—i.e., a search for *knowing*—aiming at describing the nature of existing things and where they come from. They want *both* certainty *and* understanding—to see things with depth and clarity, confident they will not change.

Early in this book, when discussing Protagoras, the observation was made that he reacts to early metaphysical positions, effectively choosing a side in the debate between Parmenides and Heraclitus. Since those two provide a stark contrast in terms of their answers as to what does not change, we might profit from considering our thinkers with respect to these two early figures. Along this continuum both the metaphysics of Democritus and of Aristotle sit consciously between the extremes. For Democritus, the atoms and the void are an unchanging constant, but atoms (literally, an indivisible substance) are constantly in motion and are combining, dissolving, and recombining to form all that exists. Thus there is both an eternal essence and constant change. For Aristotle, who opposes Democritus' solution, there is both permanence and change because reality is comprised of "matter" and "form." The eternal forms reflect themselves in changeable matter, obeying Aristotle's four causes.

We might venture a picture like this one:

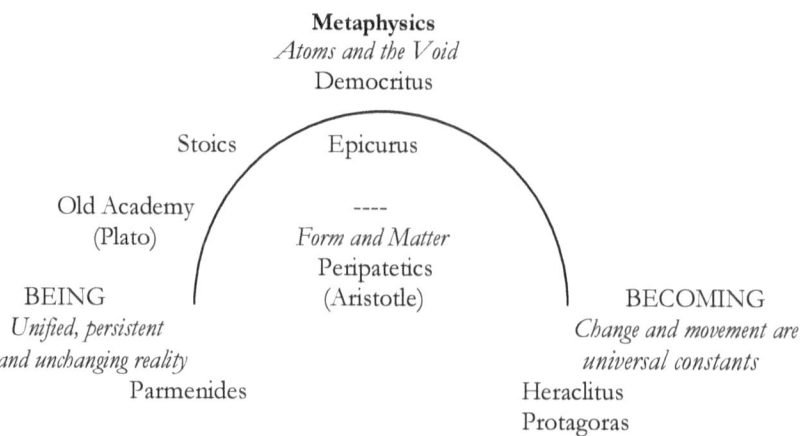

Metaphysics
Atoms and the Void
Democritus

Stoics Epicurus

Old Academy
(Plato) ----
Form and Matter
Peripatetics
BEING (Aristotle) BECOMING
Unified, persistent *Change and movement are*
and unchanging reality *universal constants*
Parmenides Heraclitus
Protagoras

Judgment: Epistemological Method

The fields of metaphysics and epistemology intersect at the point where the idea of truth resides. Truth is central to the enterprise of judgment, and the question of whether our judgment applies to a part or the whole of knowledge is critical. A key part of epistemological debate is whether one can have knowledge of particulars yet never have knowledge as a whole and full body. The matter is somewhat akin to distinguishing between 'truth' and 'Truth.' Perhaps we should speak of 'knowledge' and 'Knowledge.'

For the metaphysician, truth is what is real; for the epistemologist, truth is what is unchanging. They can agree that what is real is also epistemologically true. The intersection of metaphysics and epistemology at truth leads us to this final heart piece. Information and judgment are like the slices of bread in a sandwich: between them lies the meat of reality—the object and point of knowledge, its *telos*.

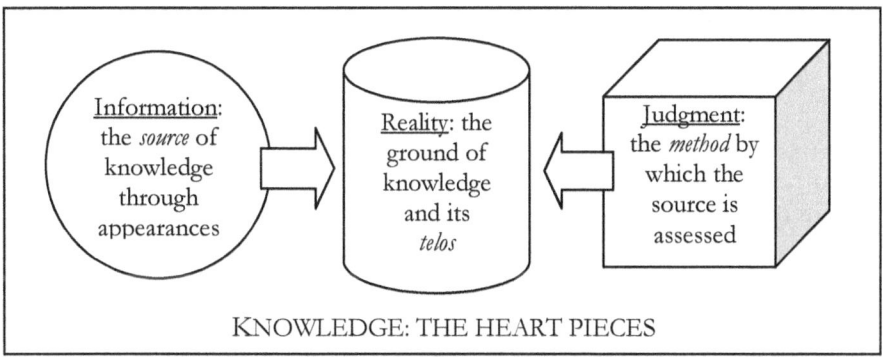

KNOWLEDGE: THE HEART PIECES

While the above is accurate enough, it is also fruitful to see these three elements as coordinated pieces in the process we call "knowing." Information functions as the *source* from which knowledge derives, while judgment is the *method* by which it is assessed as having been reached (or not); both drive toward knowing the *object* of knowledge—reality. We may picture the matter like this:

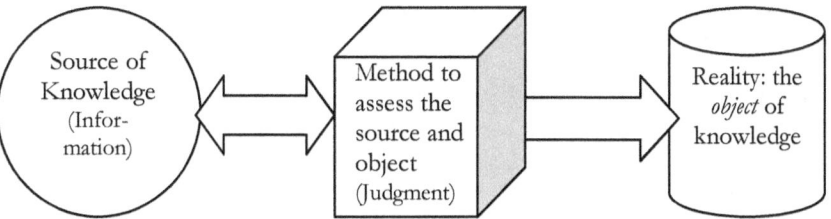

Again, with metaphysics in mind, this is more like an endless circle than a line. Reality is the ground in which all information resides: the source of the source.

So reality (metaphysically) offers appearances/sources that the method of judgment assesses to know reality (epistemologically).

There is in all information—whether from sense-perception or reason—an element of judging, just as all judgment requires some information. But whereas information can at least pretend to some degree of objectivity, no matter how objective one intends to be in judgment there is always subjectivity. Epistemology always has wrestled with the issues of objectivity and subjectivity. Ultimately such wrestling produces another continuum of possibilities:

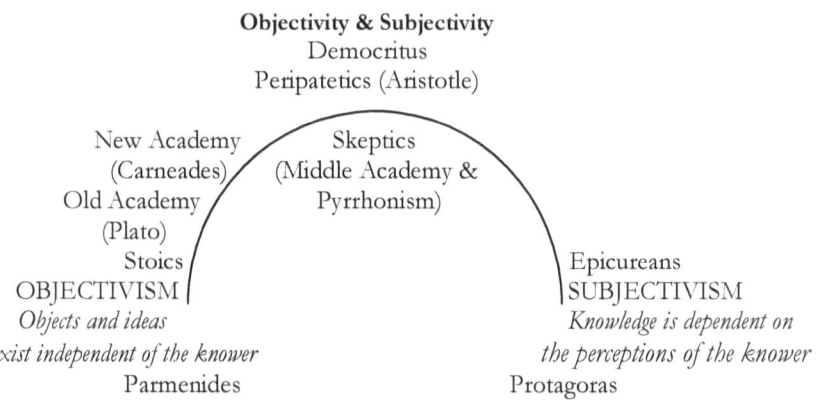

Objectivity & Subjectivity
Democritus
Peripatetics (Aristotle)

New Academy   Skeptics
(Carneades)   (Middle Academy &
Old Academy   Pyrrhonism)
(Plato)
Stoics   Epicureans
OBJECTIVISM   SUBJECTIVISM
Objects and ideas   *Knowledge is dependent on*
exist independent of the knower   *the perceptions of the knower*
Parmenides   Protagoras

As before, the Skeptics try to maintain neutrality and balance both sides in order to suspend judgment. So I have placed the more conservative Skeptics at the top of the continuum. The New Academy of Carneades seeks a balance of the objective and subjective but, in my estimation, leans toward objectivity. A figure like Isocrates simply repudiates the whole metaphysical enterprise.

Information, to use a metaphor, is the cloth which judgment measures to determine the pattern that constitutes knowledge and then cuts out that material to produce the desired pattern. Judgment measures information as a yardstick does the cloth, and with the aim of fitting some pattern, then takes from the cloth what is needed to create the body, or pattern, we call knowledge. Let us picture it this way:

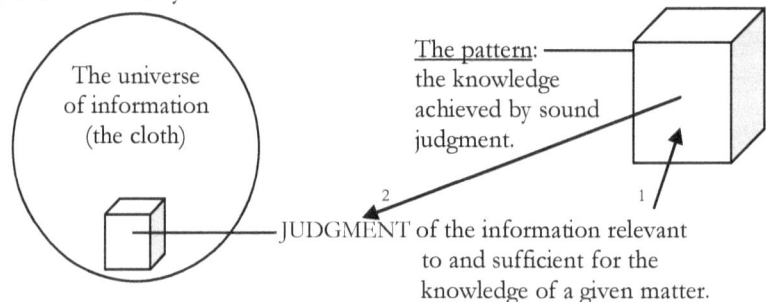

The universe
of information
(the cloth)

The pattern:
the knowledge
achieved by sound
judgment.

JUDGMENT of the information relevant
to and sufficient for the
knowledge of a given matter.

[1] and [2] reflect the reciprocal relationship between the method
of judgment and the 'pattern' of knowledge (explained below).

The *method* of knowledge assesses and determines what information from the vast store that exists is relevant and adequate. Sound judgment leads to the specific pattern we recognize as knowledge for that matter. That pattern can be conceived of as either related to just a particular or as itself the grand pattern we label Knowledge. So even when dealing with judgment of 'knowledge' we may still entertain the possibility of 'Knowledge.'

Judgment & the Criterion

The quest to discover an indisputable criterion for judgment has been one of the chief preoccupations of epistemologists. At one level, an answer comes readily to mind and enjoys a consensus of agreement: *the criterion for judgment must be truth.* A true judgment leads to a true pattern and is knowledge. Put most simply, without truth there is no knowledge and all knowledge requires true judgments. At the most basic level of agreement the situation looks like this:

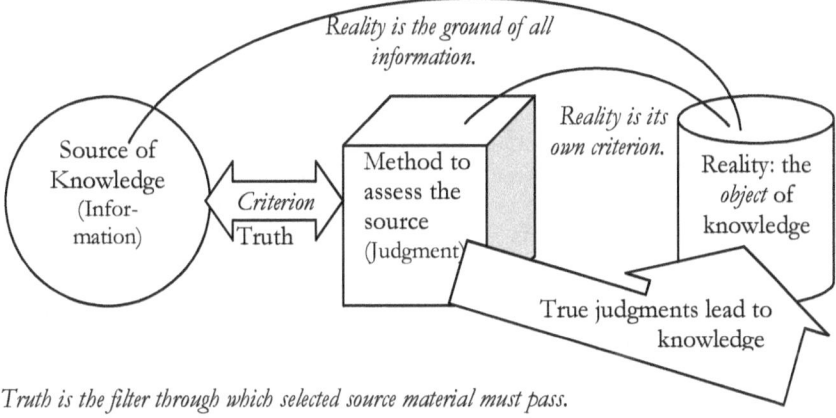

Truth is the filter through which selected source material must pass.

Simply put, the whole process of knowing reduces to the following steps:

1. Appearances (sense-perceptions and concepts) present themselves.
2. Judgment selects (true) appearances using the criterion of truth.
3. True judgments lead to knowledge, i.e., a correct and sufficient pattern in the *psyche* that truly represents the actual object in reality.

All of our 'dogmatists,' each in their own way, think they have mastered this process and have thus achieved knowledge.

Truth provides the criterion for judgment by which knowledge is measured as existing or not existing; that is uncontroversial. But how truth itself is established is *very* controversial. Our method's criterion itself needs a criterion! As the criterion of epistemological method, truth is the yardstick by which information is assessed with respect to its accuracy, suitability, and so forth, for knowing reality. But one must know what truth is to be confident one has it. How can we know we have the truth? What is the criterion (or criteria) for truth?

The dogmatists of every stripe agree there is a criterion of truth. But from that initial agreement they descend into a number of significant disagreements. The Skeptics suspend judgment on whether there is such a criterion or not because the arguments of Dogmatist A can be counterbalanced by the arguments of Dogmatist B. Who is to know which is correct when both are equally plausible? Since the answers our schools and figures offer correspond to convictions about other matters, we can present our continuum using confidence in the two kinds of appearances as an ostensible criterion of truth.

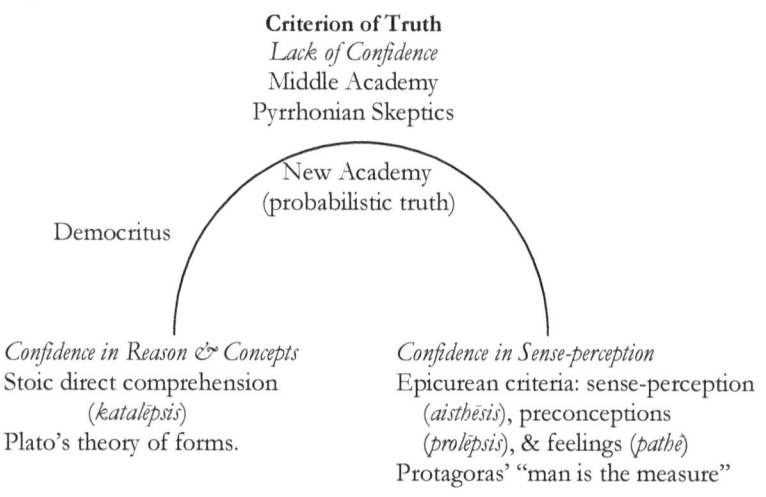

Criterion of Truth
Lack of Confidence
Middle Academy
Pyrrhonian Skeptics

New Academy
(probabilistic truth)

Democritus

Confidence in Reason & Concepts
Stoic direct comprehension
(*katalēpsis*)
Plato's theory of forms.

Confidence in Sense-perception
Epicurean criteria: sense-perception
(*aisthēsis*), preconceptions
(*prolēpsis*), & feelings (*pathē*)
Protagoras' "man is the measure"

Although predating the period of intense interest in the criterion of truth, Protagoras is included because his "measure" (*metron*) is understood by Plato's Socrates as a "criterion" (*kritērion*). Democritus, according to Sextus Empiricus, "calls knowing through the mind 'authentic,' testifying that it is trustworthy (*piston*) in the judgment (*krisin*) of truth (*alēthēias*)."[339] Similarly, it seems at least some of the Stoics (including Posidonius) add "correct reason" (*orthon logon*) as a criterion alongside self-evident appearances (*kataleptike phantasia*).[340] Plato himself is included too, though he did not use the word "criterion" (*kritērion*) in such a phrase;[341] his "judgment of truth" (*iudicium veritatis*) is paralleled by Cicero with the views of Protagoras and Epicurus, among others, so that the Latin *iudicium* ("judgment") can reasonably be translated "criterion" in the sense of a judgment using a 'test' or 'standard' as, for example, both Protagoras and Epicurus do.[342]

---

[339] Sextus Empiricus, *Adversus Mathematicos: Against the Logicians,* I.138-139 (quoted more fully in the chapter on Epicurus).

[340] Diogenes Laertius, *Lives of Eminent Philosophers: Zeno,* VII:54 [*Zeno,* 37].

[341] Plato's two uses of it in the *Theatetus* (178b-c) are with reference to Protagoras.

[342] Cicero, *Academics,* II.142 [ch. XLVI]: "One alternative on judgment (*iudicium*) is that of Protagoras, who thinks that for each person what is true is what seems true to the person; another alternative is that of the Cyrenaics, who say there cannot be any judgment (*iudicii*) except that of emotions; another position is that of Epicurus, who sets all judgment (*omne iudicium*) in the senses

Aristotle is absent because while he offers a definition of truth, he does not address the issue of a criterion of truth *per se*. It should be noted that while Democritus is skeptical about knowing, he nevertheless is a 'dogmatist' convinced that reason requires the existence of atoms and the void in which they move. Sextus Empiricus treats him as an adherent to *logos* as the criterion of truth and so he can be positioned at the left side of the continuum. However, given the nature of Sextus' presentation, which entertains the possible links between Democritus and Epicurus on appearances and feelings as criteria, it seems sensible to place him only a little to the left.[343]

Judgment & Belief: Two Arguments

One might argue that as judgment is taking up a position and so is belief, then all judgment expresses belief. On the other hand, one might argue that belief is a subspecies of judgment and thus some judgments need not express belief even though they share with belief the taking up of a position. In this latter argument stress is placed on the elements differing between judgment and belief, while in the first argument the two are equated.

The argument that judgment and belief are the same can run this way:

1. Decision-making is the taking up of a position; it is *belief*.
2. Since it uses the criterion of truth, it yields *true belief*.
3. Since the information thus filtered must be relevant and adequate—or warranted—it provides *justified, true belief*.

In this manner an epistemologist can arrive at the conclusion that knowledge is justified, true belief.

This argument seems to say, in effect, a difference that makes no difference is no difference. Since both belief and judgment are defined as taking up a position, they are two words that say the same thing. Why bother with two words, then? The answer is immediate: because each calls attention to particular aspects of what it means to take up a position. The notion of taking up a position is complex enough to warrant different words used together to convey a more holistic sense of what is involved. We can picture it like this:

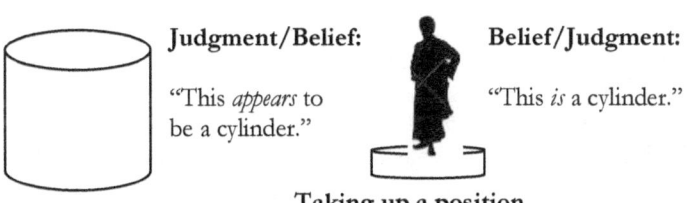

Judgment/Belief:

"This *appears* to be a cylinder."

Belief/Judgment:

"This *is* a cylinder."

Taking up a position

(*sensibus*) and in the general notion of things (*rerum notitiis*), and in pleasure; Plato, on the other hand, held that all judgment (*omne iudicium*) of the truth and truth itself (*veritatis veritatemque*) is separated from belief (*opinibus*) and from the senses (*a sensibus*), instead belonging to thinking (*cogitationis*) and to the mind (*mentis*)."

[343] Sextus Empiricus, *Adversus Mathematicos: Against the Logicians,* I.135-140.

The above illustration makes a simple point. The judgment that an object appears to be something is the taking up of a position about it, but not identical with the belief that it *is* the object it appears to be (which is also the taking up of a position). It is a different sort of taking up of a position and not merely a different belief of the same kind. The nature of the taking up looks different depending on how it is expressed, which itself reflects two different aspects of the same process. The criterion of truth—the second point above—says that when taking up a position the belief expressed can be a true belief. It perhaps does not have to be, as Protagoras maintains, but it can be. That is why truth as a criterion matters so much. It is the hinge.

Truth does not depend on having adequate and relevant information; we may make a lucky guess based on little, none, or irrelevant information and still be right. But having adequate and relevant information makes for a compelling case that one also has truth. Thus, a true belief (step 2) may not depend upon adequate and relevant information (step 3), but having the latter helps secure our confidence in the former.

A counterargument begins by observing there must be some significance in the fact we use different words—knowledge, judgment, belief—and each intends different meanings. An argument that knowledge and belief are not the same because not all judgment is belief might run like this:

1. All knowledge entails judgment, the taking up a position as decisions are made about the relevance and adequacy of information. But that is not all there is to knowledge. It is just one element.
2. All belief entails judgment, which is taking up a position as decisions are made about the approval of a person, thing, or idea as valuable, important, meaningful, and trustworthy, but that is not all there is to belief. It is just one element.
3. A shared element links items but does not equate them. Knowledge and belief can entail judgments of different kinds.

In this line of reasoning the focus is not upon the similarity or difference between the words "judgment" and "belief," but rather on the words "knowledge" and "belief." Instead of arguing that all judgment is belief because all judgment is the taking up of a position, this line of thought argues that there is a fundamental difference between the judgment of knowledge (that a thing *is* or *is not*) and belief (that thing *appears* to be or not to be). A proponent might seize upon the idea raised by the other side that there is indeed a different sort of taking up of a position—but that this is not a difference in kinds of belief, but a fundamental difference in the judgment of knowledge from that of belief.

So an abiding debate remains about the nature of taking up of a judgment. We shall return to the matter when we look at the core elements of belief. But next we must complete our picture of the puzzle of knowledge.

12

The Puzzle of Knowledge, II: Border Pieces

After setting out the'heart' pieces, we earlier added four other elements I termed the 'border pieces,' more specifically the cornerstone border pieces, characterized as the elements that delimit and qualify the heart pieces. Once more I suggest that our time with our Greek friends now offers us a way to see these with more fullness.

> ➤ *Certainty* is achieved when information and propositions based on it offer an accurate and enduringly stable demonstration of the truth.
> ➤ *Clarity* is established when a matter is so vivid or distinct that it is unmistakable as this and only this.
> ➤ *Recognition* occurs subjectively, which means varying standards are appealed to (e.g., that a thing is self-evident, or seems more likely to be the case, or seems so to the individual or group).
> ➤ *Sufficiency* is related to *logos*, an adequacy of reason that presupposes a matter is rational and reasonable.

Each of these has in its own way helped shape an understanding of what knowledge is. But they have not done so equally. As is the nature of long and complex discussions of important matters, emphasis and focus have shifted from time to time from one to another element. Yet, given a long enough perspective, these four emerge as significant and merit our attention.

Certainty

Perhaps more than any other quality ordinary people associate certainty with knowledge. Often when people say they "know" something what they are saying is that they are certain their statements about it are accurate—that their propositions actually mirror the reality of the matter—and will continue to do so. Consider the wording above: Certainty is achieved when information and a proposition based on it offer an accurate demonstration of the truth. This statement qualifies certainty as something related to all three heart pieces. The information must be what is needed for the reality to be known and the proposition must methodologically demonstrate that situation so that the reality can be assessed as truly known. It looks like this:

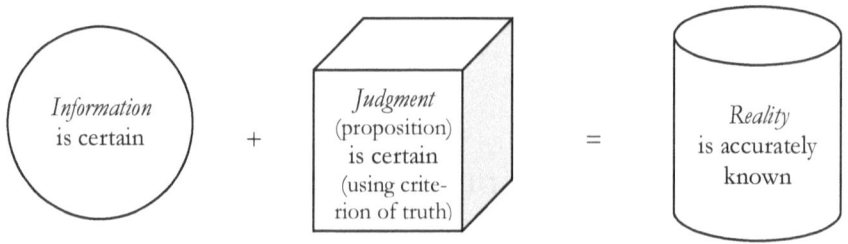

Information is certain + Judgment (proposition) is certain (using criterion of truth) = Reality is accurately known

Epistemic certainty (i.e., certainty with respect to knowledge) requires that the source and method accurately reflect the object of knowledge.

Certainty epistemologically is not "complete confidence"—a psychological certainty—but an aspect of propositional assertions of knowledge. But in popular use certainty entails two dimensions—a subjective one and an objective one. It means, at least ideally, that a person offering a proposition has complete confidence that something is known because the proposition accurately mirrors the reality of the object or idea about which it is said, or to put it even more simply, *certainty means that the person's subjective certitude has objective warrant.*

Again a continuum can display the different philosophical positions:

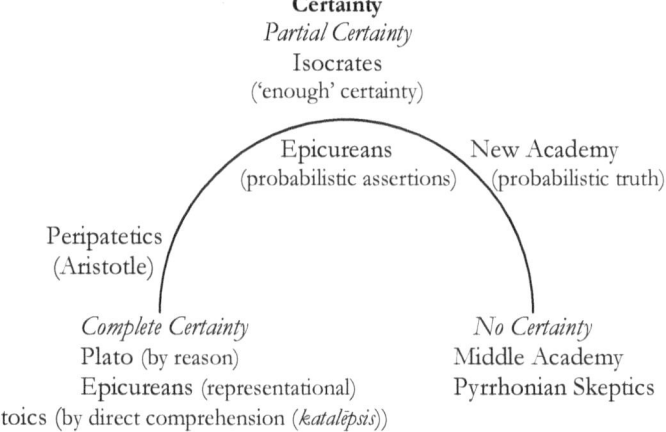

Certainty
Partial Certainty
Isocrates
('enough' certainty)

Epicureans
(probabilistic assertions)

New Academy
(probabilistic truth)

Peripatetics
(Aristotle)

Complete Certainty
Plato (by reason)
Epicureans (representational)
Stoics (by direct comprehension (*katalēpsis*))

No Certainty
Middle Academy
Pyrrhonian Skeptics

The Greek word best associated with our sense of "certainty" is βεβαιότης (*bebaiotēs*), a sense of certainty rooted in stability, i.e., something constant and unchanging so that it can be firmly relied upon.[344] But is certainty an absolute quality—you have it or you don't—or is it something existing in degrees? For Plato it is an absolute quality of *epistēmē*. The Stoics think not only that certainty is possible but that it can be stated propositionally. The Epicureans, on the other hand, agree that certainty is possible in sense experience, if not always in propositions about it. But for Aristotle and Carneades it is an *ideal*, rather than a *necessity*. Isocrates is convinced that all stochastic problems must settle for 'enough' certainty—belief adequate to get one by well-enough in living.

---

[344] The word is closely related to βέβαιος (*bebaios*) and to the verb βεβαιόω (*bebaioō*).

Clarity

Our second border piece is clarity and is especially associated with the Greek term ἐνάργεια (*enargeia*, whose Latin cognates include *illustratio, evidentia,* and *demonstratio*). Clarity means a vividness and/or distinctness that says that something can only be *this* and not *that*. The clarity is of such a nature that the identity or nature of a thing is not disputable. The essential idea is that *an object is only known when it discloses itself with such vivid distinctness that it is evident that the object and it alone is present.* A continuum shows the relative positions:

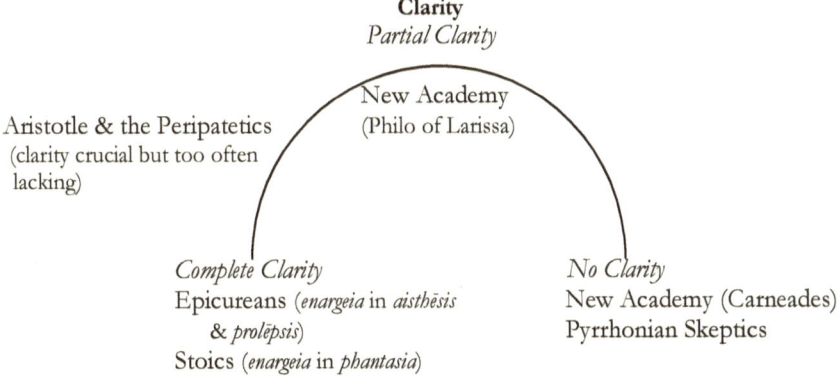

Clarity
Partial Clarity

New Academy
(Philo of Larissa)

Aristotle & the Peripatetics
(clarity crucial but too often lacking)

Complete Clarity
Epicureans (*enargeia* in *aisthēsis* & *prolēpsis*)
Stoics (*enargeia* in *phantasia*)

No Clarity
New Academy (Carneades)
Pyrrhonian Skeptics

Plato, in his consideration of Protagoras' position, considers the notion that immediate experiences of sense-perception are true because they are clear—and thus knowledge.[345] In the *Phaedrus* he uses the idea in connection to the senses; they at best perceive dimly, though vision offers the clearest perception, aided by the clarity of the object it perceives.[346] Aristotle uses instead forms of the term σαφής (*saphēs*), which in addition to the ideas of "clarity" and "distinctness" can mean "plain," as in speech or perception. Clarity is associated with assertions of truth and relevant to knowing a matter.[347] But the concept of clarity is more prominent in Hellenistic and Roman times. The Epicureans relate *enargeia* to sense-perception as the guarantee of its validity. The Stoics describe the clarity or distinctness of an appearance by more than just *enargeia* such as by the words *plēktikos* (πληκτικός), *tranē* (τρανῆ), or *ektypos* (ἔκτυπος)—a "striking," "piercing," or "distinctly formed" quality to an appearance. Carneades and the New Academy are quick to grant that if a criterion of truth exists, it relies on *enargeia*, but then argue that no such criterion of truth can be shown.

---

[345] Plato, *Theaetetus*, 179c: "and those who assert that these (sense-perceptions (*aisthēseis*)) are clear (*enargeis*) and thus knowledge (*epistēmas*) may be right in what they say."
[346] Plato, *Phaedrus*, 250d. Plato uses the phrase "through our clearest sense-perception the clearest brightness."
[347] See Aristotle, *Physics*, 184a [I.1]. The writer Asclepius of Tralles (6th cent. C.E.), in his *On Nicomachus' Introduction to Arithmetic*, Ia, associates clarity (*saphia*) with wisdom (*sophia*), and argues that *saphia* is derived from *phaos* (light), appealing to Aristotle's association of what is lighted to what is most evident. See Aristocles, *Aristocles*, 2-3 [Testimony 3]; cf. Testimony 5, pp. 4-7.

Recognition

Recognition is a term by which one might mean:

1. *Awareness.* An object is perceived as *there*, the generator of sensory data, and with no further differentiation.
2. *Acknowledgement.* The English term itself hints at a connection to knowledge and emphasizes a cognitive action with respect to what is recognized, thus being a step above mere awareness.
3. *Recollection.* The connection of recognition to memory is sometimes highlighted so that recognition is almost equated with recollection.
4. *Identification.* Differentiation is key; recognition as identification sees uniqueness, or individuality.

Among our thinkers the notion of recognition largely remains implicit. A particular word—αναγνώρισις (*anagnōrisis*)—is associated with it. Plato differentiates between those with knowledge and those without based on whether they recognize an eternal Form stands behind an appearance or merely recognize the appearance itself. Aristotle declares, "Recognition (*anagnōrisis*), as its very name indicates, is a change from ignorance (*agnoias*) to knowledge (*gnōsin*)."[348] The idea becomes more important in Hellenistic philosophy. In Epicurus, sense-perception (*aisthēsis*) is itself the recognition of a sensible object or observable fact and is a basic building block for knowledge. In Stoic epistemology recognition can serve as a fundamental step. But recognition serves a higher purpose, too, in that it is used to *distinguish* one thing or person from another based on uniqueness. Recognition is an *absolute* quality suited to infallible identification. Cicero, using the example of a person who sees one fellow but thinks he sees another, applies the Skeptic idea that no sign exists to mark off a true appearance from a false one. If the distinguishing mark is not to be had, what else is left as possible to use to recognize someone?[349] Our figures line up like this:

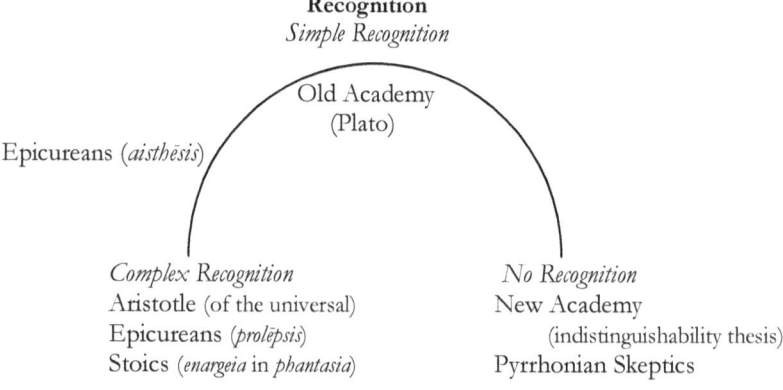

Recognition
Simple Recognition

Old Academy
(Plato)

Epicureans (*aisthēsis*)

Complex Recognition
Aristotle (of the universal)
Epicureans (*prolēpsis*)
Stoics (*enargeia* in *phantasia*)

No Recognition
New Academy
(indistinguishability thesis)
Pyrrhonian Skeptics

---

[348] Aristotle, *Poetics,* 1452a [XI.3-4].
[349] Cicero, *Academics,* II.84 [ch. XXVI].

Sufficiency

Our fourth corner border piece to the puzzle of knowledge is "sufficiency," a concept associated with more than one word. There is the verb ἐπαρκέω (*eparkeō*) and the adjective ἐπαρκής (*eparkēs*), both of which carry a more qualitative sense ("adequate" or "enough"). More prominent is the Greek term ἱκανός (*hikanos*), "sufficiency," which can carry either a qualitative (subjective) or quantitative (objective) sense, or both. A person, for example, might have sufficiency in medicine, referring to either ability or training, or both. With this in mind, it is not difficult to see that it sometimes conveys a sense of "completeness"—an absolute sufficiency in which nothing is lacking. Both "relevant" and "adequate" are terms referring to sufficiency. To assess something as *relevant* is to make a qualitative judgment that it is sufficient to the purpose at hand. To call something *adequate* might be used in a similar manner (qualitatively), but also that it can be measured quantitatively, that it is sufficient in possessing enough evidence or magnitude to warrant the assertion made.

Our thinkers, if asked to reflect on the matter, would all agree that sufficiency is an idea relevant to knowledge. There must be some bar reached in order to say, "I have knowledge." The issue is not whether sufficiency matters, but whether the bar set to meet it is low, moderate or high. A continuum might look like this:

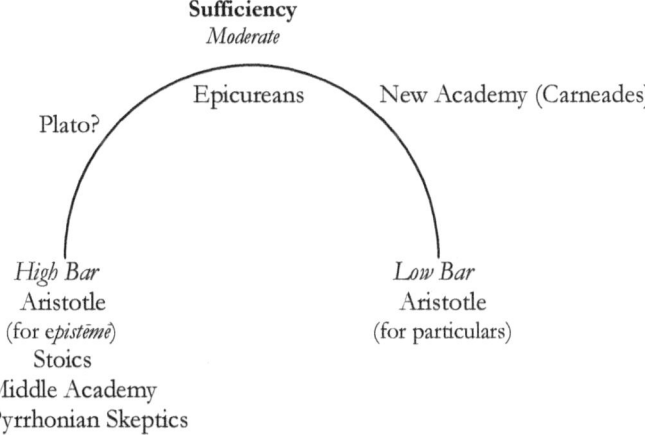

As the continuum shows, this subject of sufficiency leads to some strange bedfellows. The Stoics and the Skeptics both set a high bar; the difference is in their varying confidence as to whether it can be reached or not.

Plato's Socrates, in the *Phaedo*, makes use of the idea of sufficiency in the context of explaining a method that he has developed for inquiry about things. He explains that he begins with whatever hypothesis he thinks strongest and then assesses as true those propositions agreeing with it while judging as false those that disagree with it. We can picture his argument this way:

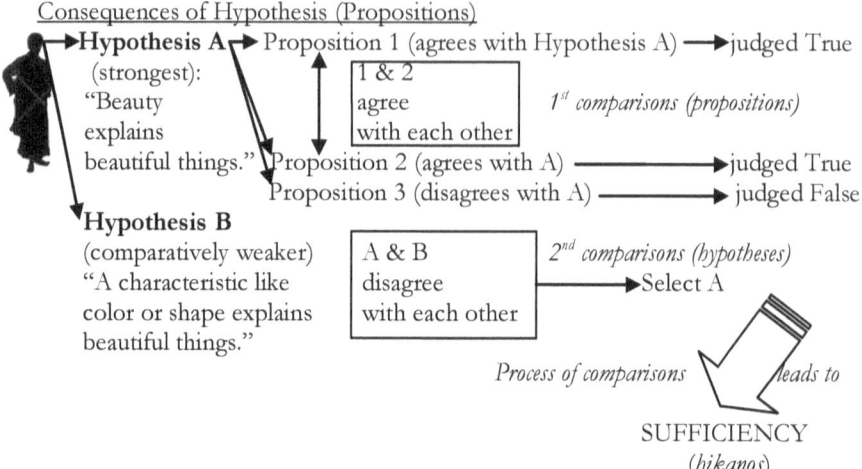

Consequences of Hypothesis (Propositions)

Hypothesis A → Proposition 1 (agrees with Hypothesis A) → judged True
(strongest):
"Beauty
explains
beautiful things." Proposition 2 (agrees with A) → judged True
Proposition 3 (disagrees with A) → judged False

1 & 2 agree with each other   *1ˢᵗ comparisons (propositions)*

Hypothesis B
(comparatively weaker)
"A characteristic like
color or shape explains
beautiful things."

A & B disagree with each other   *2ⁿᵈ comparisons (hypotheses)* → Select A

Process of comparisons   *leads to*

SUFFICIENCY
(*hikanos*)

For Plato the Forms explain the origin and cause of things (e.g., the eternal form of Beauty explains the existence of beautiful things).[350] By a comparison of hypotheses one rationally arrives at "that which is sufficient (*hikanon*)"—the highest hypothesis.[351]

Aristotle, too, uses *hikanos*. In the *Posterior Analytics*, where he sets forth distinctions between kinds, or degrees of knowledge, the concept of sufficiency is at least implicitly involved. Philosopher Vasilis Politis, an expert on Aristotle, draws on both the *Metaphysics* and the *Posterior Analytics* to form a view of Aristotle's presentation on different kinds of knowledge using the language of sufficiency.[352] If we put Politis' depiction into illustrated form, it looks like this:

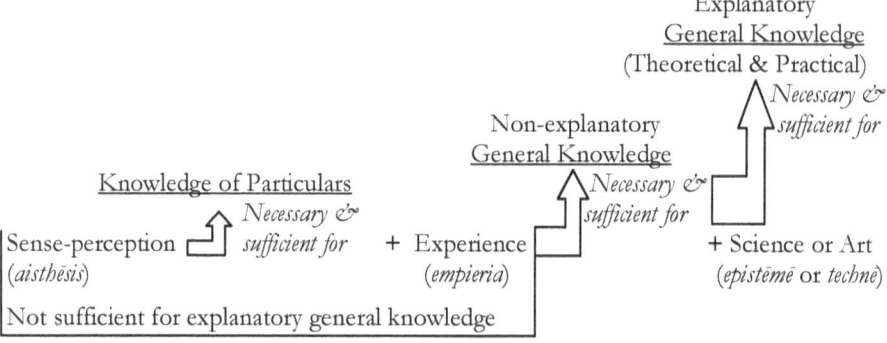

Explanatory
General Knowledge
(Theoretical & Practical)

Necessary &
sufficient for

Non-explanatory
General Knowledge

Necessary &
sufficient for

Knowledge of Particulars
Necessary &
Sense-perception   *sufficient for*   + Experience   + Science or Art
(*aisthēsis*)   (*empieria*)   (*epistēmē* or *technē*)

Not sufficient for explanatory general knowledge

Consistent with his epistemological spectrum, there are varying levels of sufficiency as one pursues knowing all the way to *epistēmē*.

---

350 Plato, *Phaedo*, 100a-e.

351 Plato, *Phaedo*, 101d-e; the quoted phrase is ἕως ἐπί τι ἱκανὸν ἔλθοις (*heōs epi to hikanon elthois*).

352 Politis, *Guidebook to Aristotle*, 31-36. The illustration based on p. 36. Politis has in view *Metaphysics*, 980a-981a [I.1].

Epicurus argues for the modest goal of achieving enough knowledge of such things as to promote a calm mind and happiness.[353] Philodemus argues for the sufficiency of experience based on repeated sense-perceptions rather than the Stoic appeal to certainty by reason. He writes, "[I]t will be sufficient (*eparkesei*) for us to be persuaded, as we are with other things, according to experimental experience, that is, according to what is reasonable"—and offers the example of previous experience teaching a person that summer sailing will be safe.[354] Past experience is sufficient for making current decisions.

With respect to the idea of sufficiency, the Stoics are most famous for their relating the concept to virtue, wisdom, and the pursuit of happiness. Their logic:

➢ Virtue is sufficient for happiness.
➢ Virtue is equal to wisdom.
➢ Therefore, wisdom is sufficient for happiness.

In a fragment attributed to Epictetus, he tells an anecdote about Socrates, whose response to the invitation to be made rich sums up the general attitude of the Stoics about one who is wise: "For if the things I presently have are not sufficient (*hikana*) for me, nevertheless I am sufficient (*hikanos*) for them and so they are for me as well."[355] The self-sufficient person is a Stoic ideal; they mean it in the manner expressed in the story about Socrates: a self-sufficient wise person acquires for his- or herself what is needed for happiness, and that is virtue, which is itself wisdom. We can picture this whole matter this way:

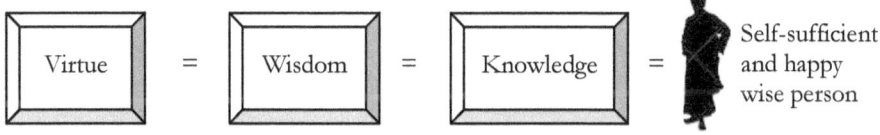

Among the Skeptics, Carneades and the New Academy argue that no one relies on direct comprehension of an appearance beforehand, but instead considers the apparent factors at hand and forms a belief based on how likely true the considered factors are. What is sufficient for action is just enough probable truth—and "knowledge," which eludes our grasp, can take care of itself.

[353] Diogenes Laertius, *Lives of Eminent Philosophers: Epicurus*, X.80 [*Epicurus*, 24]: "Do not suppose that our consideration of such matters has not reached the desired precision; it is as much sufficient as needed to contribute to our peace of mind and happiness." The phrase "it is as much sufficient as" renders ὅση (*hosē*, fr. ὅσος), which has the sense of 'just as much as needed to be enough.'

[354] Philodemus, *On Methods of Inference*, VII.32-38. The word rendered "sufficient" here is ἐπαρκέσει (*eparkesei*). I have rendered πείρας (*peiras*) as "experimental experience" rather than "trial." The Greek text is from De Lacy and De Lacy, *Philodemus*, 38; they read this (p. 39) as the *Epicurean* position in response to the Stoic Dionysius of Cyrene (see n. 21); Long and Sedley, *Hellenistic Philosophy*, 263, attribute it to the *Stoic* position—and to that of Diogenes of Babylon (Dionysius' teacher).

[355] Epictetus, *Fragments*, 174 [= Stobaeus, *Anthology*, IV.33, 28]. This passage is alluded to by Seneca, *Moral Letters to Lucilius*, 9.1.

Arcesilaus and the Middle Academy set a high bar for reaching epistemological sufficiency. Because they judge that Stoics and Epicureans (and everyone else) do not achieve it—their contrary positions cancelling one another—they suspend judgment on the matter. The Pyrrhonian Skeptics are like them on this matter. Skepticism, then, in general does not dispute the notion of sufficiency but rather questions if it can be reached.

Much as is the case for Socrates, Plato, and Aristotle, for the Hellenistic schools it would be pressing the matter to say that the notion of sufficiency becomes a technical aspect in determining whether knowledge has been achieved. At the same time, we can hardly dismiss the impression that our thinkers valued the idea and had it in mind at various times as they sought to articulate their understanding of knowing and knowledge. It is a common sense notion that some bar must be reached, either qualitatively or quantitatively (or both) in order to say one has knowledge, and the idea of sufficiency expresses that however a particular person or school might imagine it.

13

The Elements of Belief, I:
Core Elements

We have noticed that with large ideas like "knowledge" a number of words (e.g., *gnosis* and *epistēmē*) are needed to capture various nuances of the concept. This situation holds true for "belief" as well, where a variety of words (e.g., *doxa* and *pistis*) capture different important senses. But the vocabulary for belief is not as cleanly delineated as is the vocabulary for knowledge. Belief's nature makes for more imprecision in trying to distinguish the separate elements from one another. The Greek belief vocabulary overlaps significantly with the English words used to describe belief and with each other. This complicates things in a way we did not encounter with the vocabulary for knowledge.

Our three core elements can be briefly elaborated:

> ➢ *Trust* is the source of belief, being the relational ground upon which belief is founded.
> ➢ *Assertion* is the object of belief and is a volitional *act* that may take the form of a statement, feeling, or behavior.
> ➢ *Judgment* is the method by which belief forms and tests itself.

As with knowledge, these elements are closely coordinated. But unlike knowledge, where the terms related to each element are more clearly separate, with belief the vocabulary, as indicated above, is more homogenous.

Trust: The Source of Belief

Our English word "trust" can be either a noun or verb. The idea of trust encompasses both notions of 'confidence' and 'belief'—the latter in the sense of assenting to someone or something as credible and worthy of personal investment. These last two words perhaps best capture the sense of trust. As the source of belief, *trust is a personal investment in someone or something (e.g., an idea) as being, literally, "trustworthy."* When we discuss the element of trust in belief for each of our thinkers what we are most interested in is what each invests in as being trustworthy. Of the primary words associated in Greek with belief, the noun "trust" aligns most closely with *pistis* and the verb "to trust" aligns most closely with *pisteuō*; the related term *pistos* conveys "trustworthy."

Just as *pistis* can carry the sense of different English words, so can other Greek terms important to our sense of "belief." With respect to the element of trust, the Greek verb *peithō*, which we have seen conveys the basic sense of "to persuade," can on occasion be used to convey the kind of 'being persuaded' that yields trust (or confidence).[356] Similar to what the Greek noun *pepoithēsis* (see below) does for the English nouns trust and confidence, the verb πεποιθέναι (*pepoithenai*) can reflect the English "to trust," in the sense of placing confidence in someone or something.[357] The impression one gains is that trust is the kind of personal investment in which one truly puts oneself on the line—an act that expresses belief in the self, or others, or something, and one that expresses confidence, or even courage.

If trust is the source of belief, all belief has an object toward which its trust is directed. This indicates one way of seeing the variation among our thinkers in the object of trust.

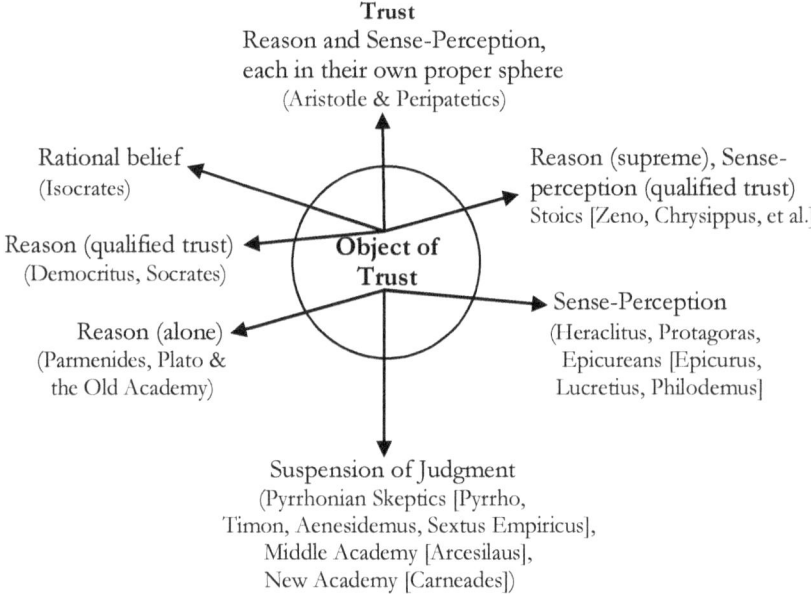

Trust
Reason and Sense-Perception,
each in their own proper sphere
(Aristotle & Peripatetics)

Rational belief
(Isocrates)

Reason (supreme), Sense-
perception (qualified trust)
Stoics [Zeno, Chrysippus, et al.]

Reason (qualified trust)
(Democritus, Socrates)

Object of Trust

Reason (alone)
(Parmenides, Plato &
the Old Academy)

Sense-Perception
(Heraclitus, Protagoras,
Epicureans [Epicurus,
Lucretius, Philodemus]

Suspension of Judgment
(Pyrrhonian Skeptics [Pyrrho,
Timon, Aenesidemus, Sextus Empiricus],
Middle Academy [Arcesilaus],
New Academy [Carneades])

Not surprisingly, reason and sense-perception, whether separately or together, are the objects of trust specified by our thinkers.

Parmenides, who influences the tradition of Socrates and Plato, puts his trust in reason (with the poetic wisdom provided from the goddess). He articulates a 'way of conviction' that has truth as its companion.[358] He calls his words

---

[356] See, in the New Testament, Philippians 2:24, "And I trust/place confidence in the Lord."
[357] See, in the New Testament, Philippians 3:4, "If anyone else thinks he has cause to trust/put confidence in the flesh, I have more."
[358] Parmenides, *On Nature*, fragment 2 (translated in the next chapter).

and thinking about truth "trustworthy" (*piston*).[359] Democritus, who influences the thinking of Epicurus but also is seen by many Skeptics as like themselves in outlook, is linked by Sextus Empiricus with Plato as putting his trust in the perceiving mind (*noētos*) as alone true (*alēthē*).[360] Protagoras, that provocateur who so arouses Plato's Socrates in the *Theaetetus*, trusts human experience completely, calling humanity "the measure of all things." Specifically, he trusts both sense-perception as adequate for experiencing real things and human reason as adequate to then say what this experience means.

Plato regards the trust associated with belief to be relegated to the Sensible world and far less dependable or useful than reason. His own trust is in reason, with its power to peer behind the curtain to see the Eternal Forms. In the *Timaeus* Plato says succinctly, "what Being is to Becoming, truth (*alētheia*) is to belief (*pistin*)."[361] In short, *pistis* can only be an imperfect copy of the truth.

Isocrates places his trust in well-considered, goal-driven belief as sufficient to guide a person through life while being a responsible citizen. Isocrates places trust solidly in the realm of relationships, which is the context in which uses of belief-vocabulary with the sense of trust occur. Trust is a virtue shown in acts that reveal personal character and when this virtue is betrayed it is not easily restored.[362] There is a responsibility implicit in trust; if one upholds it as a virtue, one must both be trustworthy and offer trust.[363] In a world where boundaries are fuzzy and knowing uncertain, it is wise to cultivate a virtuous character around sensible beliefs that will more often than not keep one safe and healthy in relationships.

Aristotle's trust, epistemologically speaking, is robust in that he can place it in both sense-perception and reason, though the latter is the most trustworthy. Like Plato he agrees that rhetoric is about producing belief. He points to the powerful persuasive effect of trusted witnesses used as convincing evidence.[364] In his *Rhetoric*, when speaking of epideictic speeches (i.e., those of praise and blame), he points out that the 'facts' appealed to "must be taken on faith"[365]— trusted because they are not proved. Belief, then, always takes an act of trust (a leap of faith?), whereas knowledge needs no trust, but generates it.

Epicureans trust sense-perception completely. Lucretius employs *fides*, the Latin counterpart to *pistis*, to express in his poem *On the Nature of Things* the Epicurean faith in the senses and sense-perception as that which can be trusted most. He writes, "For that is most trustworthy (*fide*) which is able to discover, at

---

359 Parmenides, *On Nature*, fragment 8 (lines 50-52; the translated quote begins with δόξας (*doxas*)). The Greek μάνθανε (*manthane*), "learn," is imperative.
360 Sextus Empiricus, *Against the Dogmatists: Against the Logicians*, II.6.
361 Plato, *Timaeus*, 29c. Cf. 37c.
362 Isocrates, *Against Callimachus*, 56.
363 Isocrates, *Against the Sophists*, 6.
364 See Aristotle, *Rhetoric*, 1394a [II.20.9], discussed and quoted in our next chapter in considering the element of persuasion/conviction.
365 Aristotle, *Rhetoric*, 1417b [III.17.3].

once and by itself, what are true (*veris*) things and then is able to overcome what are false (*falsa*) things. Therefore, what can be supported as more trustworthy (*fide*) than sense-perception (*sensus*)?" Furthermore, because what sense-perception yields is true, and the senses cannot contradict one another, all the senses must be accorded "equal trust" (*aequa fides*). He acknowledges that reason may fail to live up to what sense-perceptions present, but argues it is better to put up with faulty reason than in dismissing it also throw out clear sense-perceptions. He accuses those who suggest such a thing of—in our modern parlance—throwing the baby out with the bathwater. He writes that such a course is "to do violence to the foundation of belief and to tear away the very basis upon which depends life and health."[366]

The Stoics have as much trust in reason as the Epicureans do in sense-perception. They place their greatest trust in "self-evident comprehension" (*katalēpsis*). Although himself aligned with the New Academy, Cicero remarks accurately about the Stoics, "But between *scientiam* and *inscientiam* Zeno arranged that kind of perception of which I have spoken, and he counted it neither virtue nor vice, but taught that it alone is to be trusted (*credendum*)."[367] They, too, draw on *pistis*/*pisteuō* vocabulary. The infinitive form of *pisteuō*—*pisteuein*—often lends itself to the sense of belief as either "to trust" or "to rely upon."

The Skeptics trust the process of questioning and balancing arguments most, but even that is a qualified trust. For them, nothing warrants itself as so trustworthy as to be awarded complete trust. With respect to the New Academy Skepticism inaugurated by Carneades, Cicero remarks that Skeptics of this stripe see themselves standing in a long tradition of thinkers dissatisfied by human abilities; as he puts it, "it is not without reason that the most venerable and learned of folk have found themselves distrusting (*diffisi*) their ability to discover what they long for . . . ."[368] In fact, Cicero then goes on to favorably contrast Skeptics with the Dogmatists by arguing that the Skeptic is more free because he or she retains the power of judging for oneself the claims made by others whereas the Dogmatist must trust (or "rely upon," *credere*) what has been received from some reputed sage. He points out that such a wise person presumably became so from listening to and testing the claims of many, not just one person, yet most folk who are dogmatic make up their mind as soon as they hear one side of a matter—and then cling to it defiantly.[369]

---

[366] Lucretius, *On the Nature of Things,* IV.480-510. First quote (IV.480-483).

[367] Cicero, *Academics,* I.42 [ch. XI] (cf. II.145). The word "trusted" is *credendum* (fr. *credere*). On the contrast between knowledge and ignorance, see Galen, *The Doctrines of Hippocrates and Plato,* VII.2.4-8, on Chrysippus' view.

[368] Cicero, *Academics,* II.7 (end) [ch. III]. The verb *diffido/diffidere* (root of *diffisi*) belongs to belief vocabulary as it is formed from *dis-* and *fido* ("to trust," "to rely upon," or (with the dative) "to have confidence in"), and is a cognate to our chief Latin belief word *fides* ("belief," "trust," "confidence," "faith"), cognate to the Greek *pistis.*

[369] Cicero, *Academics,* II.8-9 [ch. III]. The part in which *credere* occurs is: "For, they say they put all their trust in one who they judge to have been wise."—This is referring, for example, to the founder of a school, like Epicurus.

Assertion: The Object of Trust

Philosophical discourse uses assertions ubiquitously. They are so commonplace we may remark that all of our thinkers use them. In formulating my depiction of belief I am using the word assertion in a broader, more comprehensive sense than it generally is in philosophy. Belief is a complex human action that we have seen our thinkers wrestle with as a matter involving cognition, feeling, and behavior. This is why the term "assertion," when considered broadly, seems peculiarly well-suited to express the central essence of belief. Assertion is always an *act*. This point matters in that assertion broadly considered is more than an utterance of speech. The particular kind of utterance that draws attention in the philosophic literature is that of affirmation—"assent." In epistemological debates the question of what gains our assent proves a pivotal concern. In short, *the very essence of assertion is an interest in recognizing and assenting to truth.*

The Greek term *doxa*, as the taking up of a position, is the principal belief word. But the word itself is not translated as "assertion" though it can convey that sense at times. Instead, taking a position entails the expression of it through assertion. With respect to thought, which especially takes us into the epistemological sphere, another Greek word, *logos*, deserves special note. *Logos* can convey the sense of our English "assertion." Broadly speaking, it encompasses both the reasoning thought and its expression, so it would not be unexpected to find it on occasion expressing an assertion as a reasoned statement set forth in speech. A number of ordinary terms also can be used in Greek to convey one or another sense of what we in English mean by "assertion." Over the course of time, as increasing attention was given to the mental act of affirming or denying the truth of things that can be expressed in utterance, special attention came to be given to the idea of assent. This focus is understandable; *by assent the mind expresses its trust and confidence that its perception of a thing is true, whether based on sense-perception or reason (or both).*

Though there came to be an emphasis on assent, to represent the range of our thinkers we do better with a broad continuum more like the following:

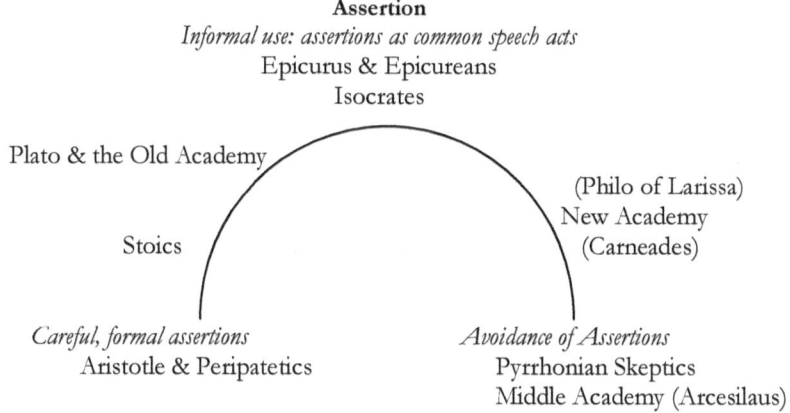

Assertion
Informal use: assertions as common speech acts
Epicurus & Epicureans
Isocrates

Plato & the Old Academy

(Philo of Larissa)
New Academy
(Carneades)

Stoics

Careful, formal assertions
Aristotle & Peripatetics

Avoidance of Assertions
Pyrrhonian Skeptics
Middle Academy (Arcesilaus)

It seems sensible to see Protagoras and other Presocratic thinkers as genuinely concerned with truth, but not as yet focused on the formal assessment of utterances. With Plato it may be that a new sensibility about assertion begins to emerge. He uses a number of different Greek words to convey aspects of assertion. But it is only with the association of assertions to *logos* that the stakes are raised. Plato attaches *logos* to the notion of assertion in the *Cratylus*, where Socrates engages in a dialog about names. His companion Cratylus thinks names should be appropriate to the things they name so that when a name is offered for something it presents a true statement. Of course, Socrates points out the difficulties that arise in such a position. Socrates argues one must think carefully at the start about the first principles of things.[370] Obviously, names—nouns—are basic to utterances and thus also to spoken or written assertions. However, a *logos* as an utterance is not just the constituent parts (e.g., subject and predicate, the thing spoken about and what is said concerning it), but their relation; it is how they combine that makes *logos* as an assertion possible. If thinking is entailed in naming, so also it is involved in forming assertions, and even more so. Though the concept of *logos* may sit quietly in the background—implicit rather than explicit—it provides a framework within which to understand.

The idea of assertion is prominent in Aristotle. Assertions are statements about what is true or false. They are not themselves beliefs, but an *expression* of belief. Aristotle—focused on assertions as *speech* utterances—distinguishes between beliefs and their utteranes. Aristotle does not need a specialized vocabulary; common words like φημί (*phēmi*), "to say," or "to declare," can easily be determined in context to mean what we mean in English when we say, "to assert."[371] He employs the term *phasis* in the *Metaphysics*, where it is used as something positive asserted, or affirmed, about reality.[372] A little later in the same text we find a well-known remark that it is illuminating to us for its bringing together a number of dimensions on belief: "Therefore, truly the most certain (*bebaiotatē*) belief (*doxan*) of all is that assertions (*phaseis*) and their opposite cannot both be true at the same time."[373] Here belief is thought of as the taking up of a position set forward in assertions that can be judged by how certain they are. The word *logos* also is important to Aristotle; it offers for his logic a rational standard. In his *Categories*, Aristotle makes the point that, "Certainly an affirmative saying (*kataphasis logos*) is an affirmation (*kataphatikos*), and a denying statement (*apophasis logos*) is a denial (*apophatikos*), but neither the things of which affirmation nor denial are spoken are themselves *logos*."[374] There exists a differ-

---

[370] Plato, *Cratylus*, 435d-436d.

[371] See, for instance, Aristotle, *Metaphysics*, 1012b [IV.8]: "And if to assert (*phanai*) something true is no more than to deny (*apophanai*) that it is false. . . ."

[372] Aristotle, *Metaphysics*, 1008a [IV.4.9-10]. The word *phasis* as an "affirmation" is counterbalanced by the Greek *apophasis* (ἀπόφασις), "denial."

[373] Aristotle, *Metaphysics*, 1011b [IV.6.10]. Other uses of *phasis* in the *Metaphysics* are at 1062a-b [XI.5-6] and 1063b [XI.6]. Cf. the use of εἰρημένον (*eirēmenon*) at 1005b.

[374] Aristotle, *Categories*, 12b [§10].

ence between one's utterances and the realities to which they point; affirmative sayings and those of denial are assertions *about* reality, not reality itself. To get closer to reality itself, assertions need something to complete them. Accompanying *logos* we often encounter another word, ἀπόδειξις (*apodeixis*)—literally, an exhibiting of something in order to make it known, and in philosophical discourse such as employed by Aristotle, a "demonstration" or "proof." In sum, assertions in Aristotle are an aspect of a package of ideas that communicate how what is known or believed is set forth to others to help understand reality.

Epicurus, in the literary remains we possess, is not shy about making assertions but seems not to have been overly concerned with setting out precise notions about logic. Diogenes Laertius says of Epicurus that, "In speech he expressed himself according to ordinary conventions"[375]—though the clarity of his utterances seem to have been variously appraised. Still, Epicurus does coin philosophical usage for some words and he does tell us that his *Canon* sets out principles and rules.[376] There and elsewhere we find his assertions. These are expressed by common words and used to affirm his convictions about the truthfulness and certainty of sense-perception.

The founder of Stoicism, Zeno, introduces the Greek term συγκατάθεσις (*sunkatathesis;* Latin *adsensionem*),[377] an important word in the ongoing development of thinking about assertions. His innovation in using the term to suggest the human mind casts votes like citizens in an election proved important not only to Stoics but to others as well. Zeno argues that the process of judgment that produces mental assent is natural—and decisive. The Stoics emphasize reason and the role of thinking. They see the human mind at work giving assent to this and that idea. But not all assent is the same in nature. Assent to that which is self-evident correlates to knowledge, but assent to that which is not self-evident is only belief, which may or may not be correct. But what we need to focus on here is that all belief involves assent, and that is a kind of assertion.

The Skeptics, who want no part in dogmatic belief, accordingly avoid making assertions, which they see (correctly) as expressing at least belief, and if those who make them are right, perhaps knowledge as well. Diogenes Laertius remarks on the Skeptics' willingness to set out and expound upon the dogmas of others while refraining from making any assertions of their own. They think that by setting out the dogmatic assertions of others they thus show them to 'balance' one another, by which they mean 'cancel each other out' so that nothing remains standing as certain. The Skeptic thinks any dogmatic assertions run the risk of confusing the utterance for the thing it describes.[378]

---

[375] Diogenes Laertius, *Lives of Eminent Philosophers: Epicurus,* X.13 [*Epicurus,* 8].

[376] See Epicurus, *Letter to Herodotus,* in Diogenes Laertius, *Lives of Eminent Philosophers: Epicurus,* X.36 [*Epicurus,* 24], cited in the chapter on the Epicureans.

[377] The form συγκατάθεσις is also found. The word derives from συγκατατίθημι (*sunkatatithēmi*).

[378] Diogenes Laertius, *Lives of Eminent Philosophers: Pyrrho,* IX.77 [*Pyrrho,* 8].

Let us return to an earlier portrayal of the core elements of knowledge and instead substitute the core elements of belief:

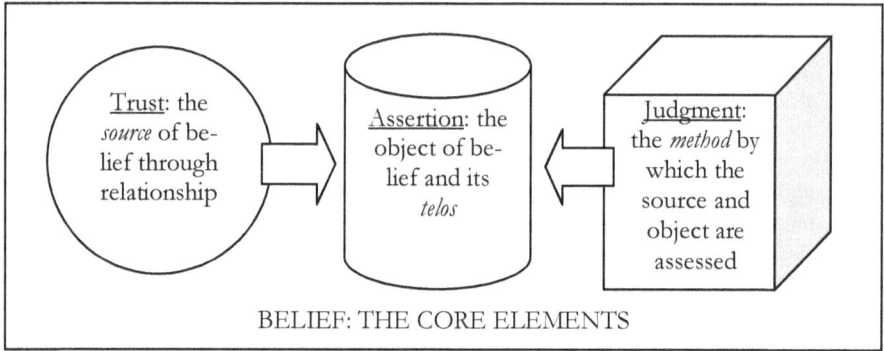

BELIEF: THE CORE ELEMENTS

The *method* of belief is also its *source*, though in a peculiarly specific way.

If *pistis* is the Greek term that represents the element of trust in belief, *doxa* is the Greek belief word that captures the element of judgment, because judgment entails rendering a decision and is only complete when a position is taken up. Yet, just as Plato embedded *pistis* within *doxa*, we can say that the judgment taken up in belief's position (*doxa*) is based on the *criterion of trust* (*pistis*), not the criterion of truth discussed earlier in relation to knowledge.

The element of judgment is reflected in more than one Greek word. A very basic one carrying the sense of judgment as 'distinguishing one thing from another' and making a 'decision' is κρίσις (*krisis*).[379] Plato uses it in the *Theaetetus* to contrast the judgment that is without authority from that of an expert.[380] It is something that assesses both sense-perception and reason, deciding how trustworthy each is. It triggers the assertion about an object of trust and thereby completes the core of belief. *Where knowledge seeks a criterion of truth to achieve partial or full certainty, belief seeks a criterion of trust to achieve enough confidence for assertion.*

Both knowledge and belief converge epistemologically in a concern for truth. But whereas knowledge tries to secure itself with some criterion of truth so as to judge whether knowledge has been achieved, belief is content to secure itself by some criterion of trust so as to judge whether a belief is secure. Belief *needs* trust, where knowledge does not. As the source of belief, trust precedes the core of assertion; in knowledge trust is a consequence of knowing. Belief would like to know the nature of things, the truth of the way things really are. But it does not *need* to know in order to act; it only requires sufficient trust. Our fundamental orientation to life is relational, operating on trust (belief) rather than truth (knowledge). *A criterion of trust is a standard by which one finds another per-*

---

[379] See, for example, Marcus Aurelius, *Meditations,* VIII.28: "For all judgment and impulse, and yearning and avoidance, are within us, and thus no one rises above such."
[380] Plato, *Theaetetus,* 178d.

son or something (e.g., an idea) trustworthy enough to act upon. It is, so to speak, how high the bar is set to warrant trust by assessing the trustworthiness of whatever is being trusted. The action resulting from a belief judgment represents the taking up of a position and is an assertion, broadly conceived. In the narrower sense, it is an affirmative utterance, an assent to someone or something in accord with the measure adopted as to whether it meets the bar as sufficiently trustworthy.

This leads us to another continuum:

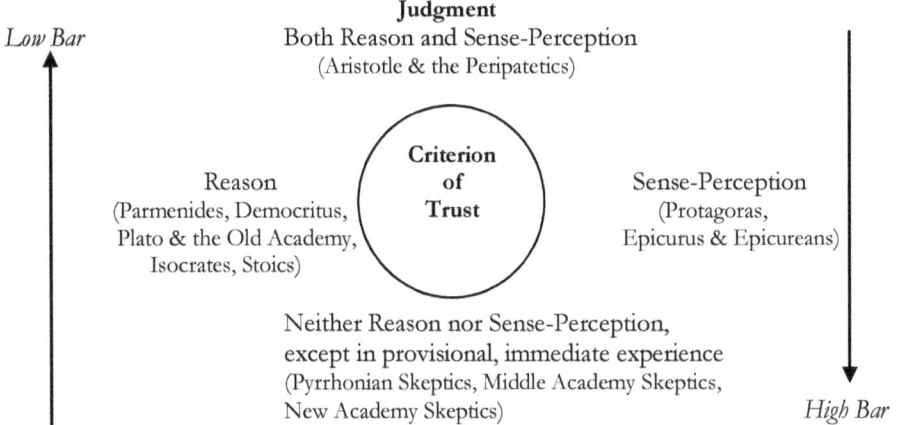

Judgment
Both Reason and Sense-Perception
(Aristotle & the Peripatetics)

Low Bar

Reason
(Parmenides, Democritus,
Plato & the Old Academy,
Isocrates, Stoics)

**Criterion
of
Trust**

Sense-Perception
(Protagoras,
Epicurus & Epicureans)

Neither Reason nor Sense-Perception,
except in provisional, immediate experience
(Pyrrhonian Skeptics, Middle Academy Skeptics,
New Academy Skeptics)

High Bar

Parmenides' trust is in reason so sublime that, surmounting the senses, it can only be depicted as divinely given.[381] Democritus provides a more puzzling situation. He seems at points to offer a grudging trust in sense-perception, and more in reason in general, all while maintaining that "truly we can know nothing, for truth is in a deep sea."[382] He is said to have judged knowing through the mind "authentic," testifying that it is trustworthy (*piston*) in the judgment (*krisin*) of truth (*alētheias*)."[383] Protagoras puts his trust in human perceptual judgments; his trust is in the human being, but we can call it also qualified in that he grants that the consequences of belief—the results of the trust people put in their perceptions—vary in their quality. Thus the standard for trust rests ultimately in the consequences belief generates.

Plato's criterion of trust is reason. He uses *doxa* in the *Sophist* such that it is the consequence of the kind of thinking involving affirmation or denial, i.e., a judging process.[384] Reason, employing its own dialectic, when guided by the

---

[381] Sextus Empiricus, *Adversus Mathematicos: Against the Logicians,* I.112. Sextus says of him that he presents his journey as an ascension wherein, "beholding by divine Reason, this same Reason like a divine guide leading to the knowledge (*gnōsin*) of all things."

[382] Diogenes Laertius, *Lives of Eminent Philosophers: Pyrrho,* IX.72 [*Pyrrho,* 8].

[383] Sextus Empiricus, *Against the Dogmatists: Against the Logicians,* I.138-139. More fully cited in the chapter on Epicurus.

[384] Plato, *Sophist,* 263d-264b. It is common in translating this passage to use the word "judgment" instead of "belief."

Eternal Forms it alone can apprehend, yields beliefs that are trustworthy—"true." Reason apart from such guidance is irrational and beliefs can also be false. What makes the decisive difference is whether the mind transcends mere thought to achieve understanding.[385]

Aristotle puts his faith in carefully established facts and theories, but these are most trustworthy when abundantly testified. Generally speaking, *multiple testifiers provide a more secure foundation.* A large part of the reason for this is probably the connection with persuasion. Aristotle says, "Every belief position (*doxē*) implicates a belief conviction (*pistis*), belief conviction likewise with persuasion, and persuasion with reason (*logos*)."[386] Persuasion is bolstered by *endoxa* as it also is by careful reasoning and a multitude of empirical data. In his *Topics*, he gives the following as an example of a correct statement: "It is a property of knowledge (*epistēmēs*) to be 'the most trustworthy (*pistotaton*) conception.'"[387]

Epicurus, who regards all sense-perceptions as true, makes of them his criterion—not of knowledge alone, but of belief, too. He argues, "If you want to fight against all sense-perceptions (*aisthēsin*), then you will not have anything by which to judge (*krinēs*) the very perceptions you declare are false."[388] To prefer a prematurely formed belief is to throw into confusion one's other sense-perceptions so that the individual's "baseless belief" (*mataiō doxē*) supplants the criterion for truth—and that means, inevitably, to make errors and thus introduce uncertainty "into every judgment of what is correct or incorrect."[389]

The Stoic Epictetus remarks, "The hypothetical proposition itself is neither good nor bad; the judgment (*krisis*) about it, however, is not an indifferent matter! It will be knowledge (*epistēmē*), or belief (*doxa*), or error (*apatē*)."[390] By 'hypothetical proposition' he has in mind things like the premise in a logical argument. The element of judgment pertains to both knowledge and belief.

When Skeptics claim to be "without belief" (*adoxastōs*) they are making a credible case because belief requires judgment. But when Sextus Empiricus speaks in this manner he has in mind belief with respect to epistemological claims about knowing the way things really are. Skeptics accept the little beliefs about ordinary experience in the moment. The real difference between Pyrrhonian and New Academy Skeptic is not so much *what* they trust—the immediacy of experience rather than dogmatic claims about reality—but the *degree* to which they trust it, with the New Academy Skeptic more trusting than either the Skeptic of the Middle Academy or the Pyrrhonist.

---

385 Plato, *Republic,* VI.510b-511d.

386 Aristotle, *On the Soul,* 428a [III.3]. Rather than render both the forms of *doxa* and *pistis* as 'belief,' I have used phrases: "belief position" for δόξη (*doxē*), and "belief conviction: for πίστις (*pistis*).

387 Aristotle, *Topics,* 131a [I.5.3].

388 Epicurus, *Maxim* 23, in Diogenes Laertius, *Lives of Eminent Philosophers: Epicurus,* X.146 [*Epicurus,* 31].

389 Epicurus, *Maxim* 24, in Diogenes Laertius, *Lives of Eminent Philosophers: Epicurus,* X.147 [*Epicurus,* 31]. The phrase "baseless belief" renders ματαίῳ δόξη (*mataiō doxe*).

390 Epictetus in Arrian, *Discourses,* II.6.1.

14

The Elements of Belief:
Other Defining Elements

As the four corner pieces to the puzzle of knowledge help form a border within which one may say knowledge exists, so the four defining elements of belief act to better define its nature. Now let us revisit and elaborate the defining elements of belief:

- ➢ *Confidence* is a psychological state of partial or complete certainty.
- ➢ *Persuasion* names an internal motion that tips the *psyche's* judging scales in one direction or another.
- ➢ *Reliance* refers to relational dependence aroused by need and completed by trust.
- ➢ *Malleability* expresses the fact that belief exists in adaptive beliefs of varying strength, with all beliefs subject to change.

Confidence

Confidence is an attitude of assurance that has a strong affective dimension and influences behavior. Cicero identifies confidence (*fidentia*) as an aspect of courage and describes it thus: "Confidence is that which sets about great and honorable affairs as the rational soul puts trust and a sure hope in itself."[391] In the same work, using a different Latin word, Cicero describes the effect confidence has as well as its supposed implicit link to reason: "For when a listener observes that the person they reckon must be confounded by an adversary's speech instead stands prepared to speak powerfully in reply, that listener most often concludes he has been rash in having assented to the adversary's speech rather than concluding that the new speaker is confident (*confidere*) without reason."[392] This shows confidence's persuasive effect; confidence does not merely affect the one who has it but exercises influence on others as well.

These two Latin words—*fidentia* and *confido*—capture aspects of our English term, though the latter more completely. *Fidentia* emphasizes, as one would expect of a word associated with courage, a sense of boldness. This is the kind of

---

[391] Cicero, *On Rhetorical Invention (De inventione)*, II.54 [§163].
[392] Cicero, *On Rhetorical Invention*, I.17 [§25].

confidence, though, that can also transform a virtue into the vice of impudence or recklessness—what we call overconfidence.[393] *Confido* expresses a sense captured by familiar belief words like "trust" and "reliance"—and even "belief" itself. *Confidence is that firm assurance that conveys a sense of being so certain that one stakes oneself on it, which is why it carries such persuasive power.*

It is no surprise our English word "confidence" likewise embraces various senses requiring different Greek words. An important one remains *pistis*. When forms of *pistis* are rendered in English by "confidence" they capture the sense of it as something counted as credible and trusted. This is also closely related to the idea of "reliance," since what we are confident about we also rely upon. But there are other words to consider as well. Both the verb πείθω (*peithō*) and the noun πεποίθησις (*pepoithēsis*) can convey confidence; the former relating confidence to persuasion and the latter linking it to trust and reliance. Also, there is the verb θαρρέω (*tharreō*), "to have confidence" in the sense of possessing courage or boldness, and the noun παρρησία (*parrēsia*), an assurance or confidence in speech that likewise highlights the courage of the speaker.

Though our thinkers often address confidence in matters apart from epistemology, their sense of it may still have relevance for ideas about knowledge and belief. Our thinkers and schools might be ranged along a continuum with respect to sense-perception and reason.

Confidence
Lack of Confidence
Middle Academy
Pyrrhonian Skeptics
[New Academy]

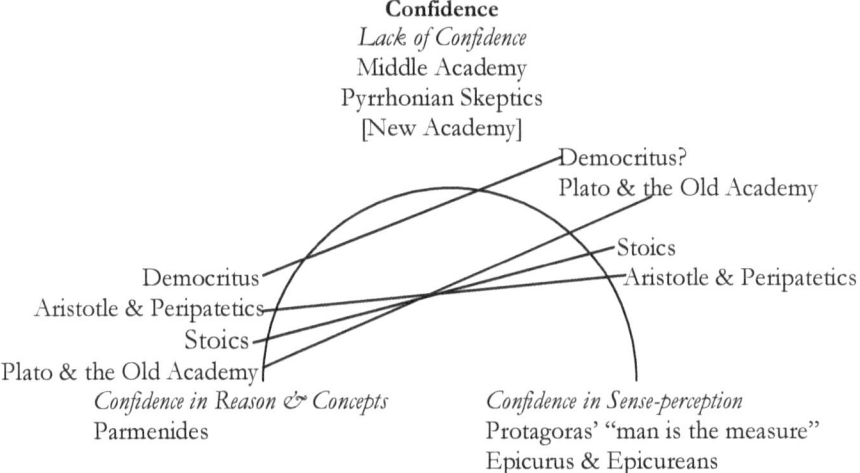

Democritus?
Plato & the Old Academy

Stoics
Aristotle & Peripatetics

Democritus
Aristotle & Peripatetics
Stoics
Plato & the Old Academy
Confidence in Reason & Concepts
Parmenides

Confidence in Sense-perception
Protagoras' "man is the measure"
Epicurus & Epicureans

While there is some uncertainty about how much confidence Democritus has in sense-perception, it is clear he has confidence in reason—especially his own.[394] Protagoras, who makes human beings the measure of all things, has un-

[393] See Cicero, *On Rhetorical Invention*, II.54 [§165], on those qualities that border on confidence but are vices rather than a virtue.

[394] Sextus Empiricus, *Against the Dogmatists: Against the Logicians*, I.236, writes: "In his *Confirmations*, despite promising to establish confidence (*pisteōs*) in the senses, he is found condemning them! For he says, 'But we in reality do not comprehend anything as it actually is, but only what shifts

equivocal confidence in sense-perception, the bedrock of belief and knowledge. In Plato's dialog bearing his name, Protagoras—in Plato's words—says, "Those who know how to do something are more confident ones (*tharraleōteroi*) than those who do not know how to do something; and the same, when they learn, are more confident than before they had learned." Knowing what one is doing builds confidence.[395]

Plato gives grudging consent to a limited confidence in sense-perception, but has enthusiastic confidence in reason. He employs the Greek infinitive *tharrein* in the *Phaedo*, where the context is clearly one where knowing and believing are relevant matters. This whole section is framed by a prominent role for persuasion. A dual sense about confidence is raised: confidence requires, ultimately, placing confidence (*pistis*) in the Forms accessible through reason to have confidence-as-courage (*tharrein*) when facing something like death.[396]

Aristotle has confidence in both, but expects higher returns from his confidence in reason. In his *Rhetoric* he offers attention to *tharrein* and writes of it:

> For confidence (*tharsos*) is the opposite of fear, just as what gives confidence (*thappaleon*) is the opposite of what causes fear. This being so, hope accompanies the appearance (*phantasia*) of that which makes us secure as being near at hand while the things that elicit fear seem far away, or not even to exist. Confidence (*tharralea*), then, is about fear-producing things being far from us and the things producing security being near."[397]

He proceeds to elaborate on the kinds of situations and experiences that build or deteriorate confidence. He remarks that there are two basic conditions in which confidence replaces fear. On the one hand, a person may have confidence from an ignorance or lack of experience of a fearful situation, or, on the other hand, because they have had such an experience and learned from it. Aristotle points out that confidence is built by observational learning,[398] such as when a person sees that others are not made fearful by something. Finally, con-

---

around according to the body's disposition and of things both entering it and resisting it.'" Cf. Galen, *On Medical Experience* (*De Experientia Medica*), XV.7 [= Diehls, *Die Fragmente der Vorsokratiker*, 408 (frag. 125)]: "He made sense-perception (*aisthēsis*) speak to the reasoning mind (*dianoian*) as follows: 'Miserable mind, do you take your evidence (*pisteis*) from us to overthrow us? Our overthrow is your defeat!'"

[395] Plato, *Protagoras*, 349e-351a; the quoted material is from 350a. This thinking is quite consistent with his basic position Plato, *Theaetetus*, 167a: "This is what education is about—change from a poorer condition to a better one. While a physician uses medicines for this purpose, a Sophist does it by reasoned persuasion." Persuasion is meant to be educational and yield better knowing.

[396] Plato, *Phaedo*, 87a-88c. *Phaedo*, 87a, "sufficiently demonstrated"—good epistemological language! The end, at 88c, "because from what we had heard before we had been very convinced, but now our thinking was upset and reversed so that we were catapulted into disbelief"—equally good belief talk! Also see *Phaedo*, 95c.

[397] Aristotle, *Rhetoric*, 1383a [II.5.16-17]. I have rendered τῶν σωτηρίων (*tōn sōtēriōn*) as "that which makes us secure"; a common translation is "salutary things," but the word "salutary" is not commonly used today. The adjective θαρραλέα is from θαρσαλέος (*tharsaleos*).

[398] Cf. the Epicurean, Philodemus, *Rhetorica*, II, §1.2.

fidence is built by rational belief, as when a person appraises her- or himself as possessing resources (e.g., financial, physical, or social) adequate to meet challenges, or as having not made enemies to fear (human or divine), or as being righteously justified to be angry (which pushes away fear and bolsters confidence), or as having reasonable grounds for hope in the future, or at least no grounds for being fearful.[399]

Epicurus, with his supreme confidence in sense-perception, stays customarily grounded in the world of lived experience. He desires people to have enough knowledge to live their lives in tranquility. In one of his sayings he cautions, "It is necessary to consider what end undergirds things and all the evidence (*enargeian*) that leads to what we believe (*doxazomena*); otherwise, everything will be full of bad judgment and confusion."[400] This requires discernment and the same discernment used in choosing friends also provides conviction about other things, with the result that "the same discerning judgment makes confidence (*tharrein*)."[401]

The Stoic Chrysippus reasons that knowledge and virtue are linked such that they constitute a single unity which has as its opposite the singular vice of ignorance, accompanied by false and evil acts. "Accordingly, by this reasoning, there is one virtue, which is knowledge (*epistēmē*), and there is likewise one vice—and this vice is sometimes called 'ignorance' and sometimes 'lack of knowledge'." If one views circumstances such as poverty, illness, or even death with fear rather than confidence (*tharrein*), it shows defective reasoning, "from a lack of knowledge, being ignorant of the truth."[402] Galen references both Chrysippus and Ariston as maintaining that the aforementioned fear is the vice of cowardice and its opposing virtue is courage, "which is knowledge (*epistēmēn*) of the things where confidence (*tharrein*) is needed and those where confidence (*tharrein*) is not needed"—and then explicitly links this to knowledge and belief: knowledge yields a true perception of what things really are good and bad, while "false belief" (*pseudē doxan*) merely makes assumptions about these things.[403]

The Skeptics of both the Middle Academy under Arcesilaus and of a Pyrrhonian orientation offer little confidence in either sense-perception or reason so long as these are dogmatically chained to assertions about the way things really *are*. All one can have confidence in is the judgment of what is being experienced in the moment—what *seems to be*. The New Academy is optimistic enough to think that some of what *seems to be* probably actually *is*. Their confidence is accordingly higher than other Skeptics.

---

[399] Aristotle, *Rhetoric*, 1383a-b [II.5.18-22].

[400] Epicurus, *Maxim* 22 in Diogenes Laertius, *Lives of Eminent Philosophers: Epicurus*, X.146 [*Epicurus*, 31].

[401] Epicurus, *Maxim* 28 in Diogenes Laertius, *Lives of Eminent Philosophers: Epicurus*, X.148 [*Epicurus*, 31]. The word *gnōmē* is commonly translated "conviction" but I have chosen "convincing judgment" as more closely communicating Epicurus' meaning.

[402] Galen, *On the Doctrines of Hippocrates and Plato*, VII.2.4-8.

[403] Galen, *On Hippocrates and Plato*, VII.2.6.

Persuasion (or Conviction)

Though the word "conviction" might be used instead, my preference is for "persuasion" as being the more robust choice; conviction is what results from persuasion and endures, but the notion attached to belief is more than just the result. Indeed, we sometimes use the word persuasion to itself mean a belief or an opinion, as in the phrasing, "I am of the persuasion that *x*." This element has important epistemological ramifications because it is the aspect of belief perhaps most associated with *evidence*. Persuasion does not just happen; it is based on an appeal to one or more kinds of evidence. As we saw earlier, the belief word *pistis* is related to the verb πείθω (*peithō*, "persuade"). The Greek form πεποίθησις (*pepoithēsis*) manages to blend belief and persuasion so that it is sometimes translated "religious persuasion" and sometimes "religious belief," in either instance referring to the kind of belief following convincing persuasion.[404]

Persuasion, or conviction, is typically viewed as a power to be taken seriously, but as the illustration shows our figures vary in how much they trust it.

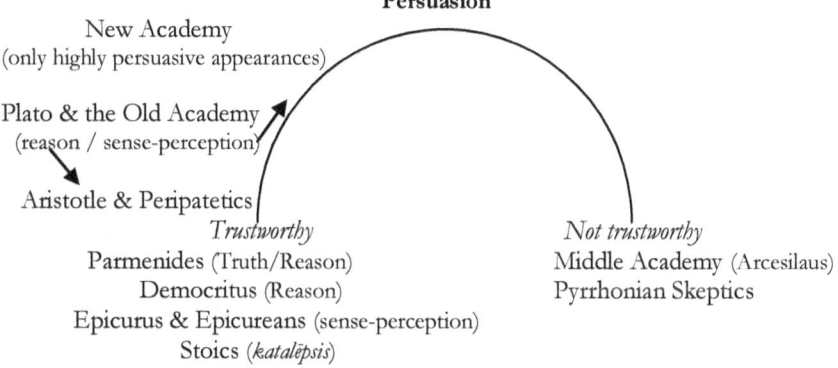

Persuasion

New Academy
(only highly persuasive appearances)

Plato & the Old Academy
(reason / sense-perception)

Aristotle & Peripatetics

Trustworthy
Parmenides (Truth/Reason)
Democritus (Reason)
Epicurus & Epicureans (sense-perception)
Stoics (*katalēpsis*)

Not trustworthy
Middle Academy (Arcesilaus)
Pyrrhonian Skeptics

The genitive form πειθοῦς (*peithous*, "persuasion") is derived from *peithō*. We find *peithous* attaching to thinking and truth in the surviving fragments of Parmenides' metaphysical poem. In his famous section on truth, he writes:

So come and I will tell you, and when you hear my account, attend
the only ways of seeking for thinking:
one way, 'how a thing *is*' and 'how a thing *is not*' that it is not,
is the path of Persuasion (*peithous*) (for truth (*alētheiê*) follows it);
the other way, 'how a thing *is not*' and 'how it *must not be*,'
is, I tell you, an inscrutable path yielding nothing.
For you cannot know (*gnoiēs*) what *is not* (for it is inaccessible)
nor speak of it.[405]

---

[404] In Hellenistic times a word like αἵρεσις (*hairesis*) was popularly used to label a "persuasion" to a group or system; it was eventually adapted by Christians to refer to minority views—"heresies"—that the orthodox Church rejected.

[405] Parmenides, *On Nature*, fragment 2 [= Diels, *Die Fragmente*, 116].

Truth and persuasion are pictured here as comrades-in-arms.

Democritus remarks that, "With respect to persuasion (*peithō*), it often happens that reason (*logos*) is stronger than gold."[406] The persuasive power of reason is such that he can say, "Many people live by reason (*logon*) even though they do not understand reason (*logos*)."[407] But Democritus does not possess abundant confidence in what human beings can know. For him, says Sextus Empiricus, "nothing appears in accord with truth (*alētheian*), but only in accord with belief (*doxan*)"[408]—and *doxa* is the kind of position-taking that may be rational, but also relies on persuasion (which may not depend absolutely on reason).

Talk of belief (*pistis*) is never far from the idea of the role played by persuasion (*peithō* or *peithous*). In the dialog *Gorgias* Socrates leads Gorgias to the conclusion that the kind of persuasion found in courts of law belongs not to knowledge but belief.[409] Similarly, we might understand the *Timaeus* to make a like point: "what Being is to Becoming, truth (*alētheia*) is to belief (*pistin*)"[410]—where *pistin* is a "conviction" or "persuasion" rather than actual knowledge. Plato conveys a sense of belief as being persuasive, and—like Parmenides—views this as a two-edged sword. On the one side, persuasive belief affirms our sensory experience of the Sensible world. On the other side, though, it can lead us astray and hinder our apprehending the truth behind sensory experiences.

Isocrates is also interested in persuasion; like many others, he makes his living by it. He links it to character, arguing that the more virtuous a person is the more persuasive his or her words will be.[411] In this respect, Isocrates anticipates Aristotle's use of *pistis*. At least one commentator has explicitly linked Isocrates' view of persuasion to his thinking about belief, arguing that the idea of virtuous character carrying persuasion is instrumental to governing by informed belief.

Aristotle attaches *pistis* to rhetoric and the sense of "persuasion" is a natural one.[412] Rhetoric, Aristotle declares, is about being persuasive (*pithanon*) and is so with respect to any subject—including knowledge (*epistēmōn*).[413] He shares with Plato's Socrates the idea that rhetoric aims at producing belief. Aristotle makes

---

[406] Democritus, Fragment 51 in Diehl, *Die Fragmente*, 400 [Stobaeus, *Anthology*, II.4.12, IV.8.11].

[407] Democritus, Fragment 53 in Diehl, *Die Fragmente*, 400 [Stobaeus, *Anthology*, II.15.33].

[408] Sextus Empiricus, *Against the Dogmatists: Against the Logicians*, I.135. The larger passage is translated in the chapter on Epicurus.

[409] Plato, *Gorgias*, 454e-455a. "Rhetoric, then, it so seems, is like a craftsman making persuasion (*peithous*) disposed to trust (*pisteutikēs*). . . ." For persuasion leading to conviction associated with knowledge, see just above this remark Socrates' question in 454e: "Do you wish, then, to set out two kinds of persuasion (*peithous*), one being a conviction (*pistin*) produced without knowledge (*aneu tou eidenai*), or with knowledge (*to d' epistēmēn*)?"

[410] Plato, *Timaeus*, 29c.

[411] Isocrates, *Antidosis*, 278: "And truly the one desiring to be persuasive will not be neglectful of virtue. . ."

[412] See, for example, Aristotle, *Rhetoric*, 1377b [II.1], where *pistis* is used in connection of the idea that Rhetoric's object is to lead to a judgment and thus to persuade so as to produce in the hearer a sense of conviction.

[413] Aristotle, *Rhetoric*, 1355b [I.2.1].

clear that in producing belief through persuasive utterances the element of truth is important. For instance, in presenting a demonstration (*apodeixis*) examples should be used because "from these come persuasion (*pistis*)." Examples serve as "witnesses" (*marturiois*, in the sense of "evidence"), and "a witness always is persuasive (*pithanos*)"; in fact, at the end of a persuasive presentation "a single good witness is adequate," or "sufficient" (*hikanon*).[414] Aristotle sometimes employs *pistis* itself in the sense of providing "evidence" or "proof."[415]

Epicurus, though he judges belief as belonging to reason, finds it thereby prone to error. The Epicureans, precisely because they think beliefs can be either true or false, with the distinction being whether they are adequately supported by evidence, thereby leave a place for persuasion. What makes persuasion a separable idea from belief as a whole is that it communicates a moving or being moved by evidence. In his judgment true persuasion generates action.[416] Like all other matters, persuasion is a matter of sense-perception and a true belief is persuasive because it rests on true perceptions that have been built up over time to yield a reliable general conception (*prolēpsis*).

In Stoic thinking the conviction wrought by belief can never have the persuasive certainty of knowledge. The Stoics, of course, regard belief *per se* as ignorance and equate knowledge with virtue; knowledge is always practiced by ethical behavior. As Zeno puts it, "The one who has been well-persuaded (*eu peisthenti*) also has added action."[417] Nothing is more persuasive than knowledge.

In Skepticism we find a link between persuasion and belief when Timon praises his master Pyrrho as one who has freed himself from "all the deceiving persuasion" (*peithous*) of the Sophists."[418] The Skeptic's outlook on the matter is neatly caught by Diogenes in his summary of their views:

> One must not suppose that just because he is being persuaded (*peithon*) it is to be taken as true (*alēthes*). For the same thing does not persuade (*peithei*) all people, nor even the people it does persuade does it do so all the time. But persuasiveness (*pithanotēs*) derives from outside, such as from a widely supported belief (*endoxon*) in the person who is speaking, or from his thoughtfulness, or his cunning words, or a familiarity with what he says, or the agreeableness of what he says.[419]

---

[414] Aristotle, *Rhetoric,* 1394a [II.20.9]. The choice "conviction" would work equally well for *pistis*; "belief" is an adequate, but more generalized choice that does not as well capture the sense here.

[415] See, for example, Aristotle, *On Rhetoric,* 1356a [I.2.3]: "Now the three kinds of evidence (*pisteōn*) provided by the speech are. . . ."

[416] Epicurus, *Letter to Meneoceus,* in Diogenes Laertius, *Lives of Eminent Philosophers: Epicurus,* X.127 [*Epicurus,* 27]. He asks of a fellow who has remarked that it would better not to have been born, but having been born to hasten to Hades, that, "If he truly says this from persuasion," why has he not killed himself?

[417] Diogenes Laertius, *Lives of Eminent Philosophers: Zeno,* VII.26 [*Zeno,* 21].

[418] Diogenes Laertius, *Lives of Eminent Philosophers: Pyrrho,* IX.65 [*Pyrrho,* 8].

[419] Diogenes Laertius, *Lives of Eminent Philosophers: Pyrrho,* IX.94 [*Pyrrho,* 11].

Reliance is a specific relational quality in belief most closely related to trust; reliability is the same with respect to trustworthiness. Like persuasion, reliance and reliability are often closely connected to *evidence*. As a separable idea "reliance" expresses *need*, as in *dependence*, so that often enough we find belief vocabulary tied to a need for, or dependence on, evidence. Because human beings have an innate need to know, when knowledge is out of reach and belief steps in to fill the gap it relies on someone or something reliable to meet that need.

What is trusted is what is relied upon, so our illustration looks familiar:

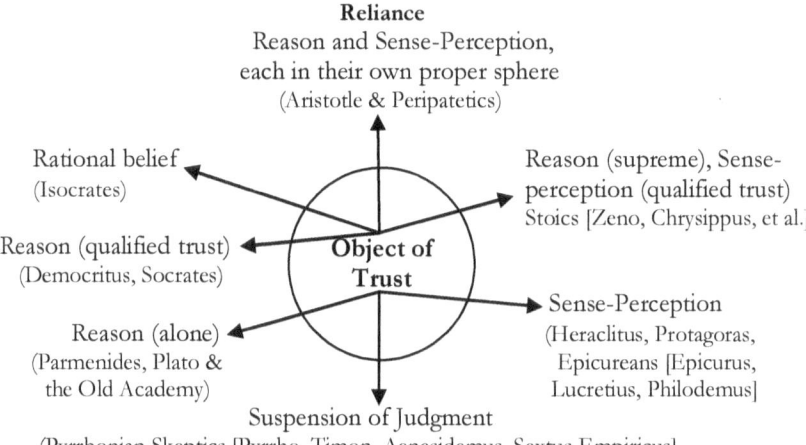

Reliance
Reason and Sense-Perception,
each in their own proper sphere
(Aristotle & Peripatetics)

Rational belief
(Isocrates)

Reason (supreme), Sense-perception (qualified trust)
Stoics [Zeno, Chrysippus, et al.]

Reason (qualified trust)
(Democritus, Socrates)

Object of Trust

Reason (alone)
(Parmenides, Plato &
the Old Academy)

Sense-Perception
(Heraclitus, Protagoras,
Epicureans [Epicurus,
Lucretius, Philodemus]

Suspension of Judgment
(Pyrrhonian Skeptics [Pyrrho, Timon, Aenesidemus, Sextus Empiricus],
Middle Academy [Arcesilaus], New Academy [Carneades, Clitomachus])

A general impression emerges that when the notion of reliance is intended it is expressed by the infinitive form of *pisteuō* and is in a context where the issue of evidence is being considered. In the Hellenistic writers whom we have considered *pistis* appears to enjoy relatively greater use in conversations about knowledge and belief than was the case in earlier times. The personal qualities inherent in *pistis* make it a term more important for understanding relational aspects of belief than *doxa* can convey, and just such qualities of belief were pivotal in the Hellenistic and Roman worlds.

A good example of conceptual overlapping is found in Parmenides' poem. Directly after speaking of the "unshaken heart of persuasive Truth" (*Alētheiēs eupeitheos*), he contrasts it with the lack of "true *pistis*" (*pistis alēthēs*) among mortals—and *pistis* here has been variously rendered as "reliance," "conviction," or "belief".[420] The truth provides a trustworthy foundation upon which to build so that reliance on the divine truth revealed through reason stands in stark contrast to the lack of conviction prevailing among double-minded mortals.

---

[420] Parmenides, *On Nature*, fragment 1, line 30.

Plato's sparing use of *pistis* may acknowledge a sense of reliance. In a passage in the *Republic*, where before I used "confident belief" for *pistis*, perhaps the sense is as well or better rendered by using the idea of "reliance":

> SOCRATES: The Good, then, is what every *psyche* chases after, and for its sake does all that it does, being driven by the intuition of what the Good *is*, yet simultaneously baffled by the Good's nature, unable to grab hold of it, or even rely (*pistei*) on it like the *psyche* can do with other things. . . .[421]

Because *pistis* is a verbal noun, when joined with χρήσασθαι (*chrēsasthai*) the two may provide a periphrastic sense of "to rely." The essential meaning remains the same: the *psyche* is unable to have the same reliance/confidence/belief it is accustomed to having with other things.

Isocrates uses the infinitive *pisteuein* to communicate "to rely." In his speech *Archidamus* he employs it in a manner quite in line with his view on belief: people argue against going to war by using a number of 'proofs,' especially experience, to conclude how problematic it is to rely (*pisteuein*) on war to solve matters.[422] In his *Busiris* he questions the credibility of Busiris' alleged fame because of not only a lack of evidence but, in fact, evidence against such claims, which makes it difficult "to rely on" (*pisteuein*), or "to give credence to," or "to trust" what is being said.[423]

Aristotle employs *pistis* far more often than did his teacher Plato. It is an important term in his *Rhetoric* where he uses it some 41 times, with distinctly different senses. But it is with the verb *pisteuō* we are more likely to encounter the sense of "to rely." On more than one occasion he ties the verb to discussion of belief/trust/confidence/reliance on evidence. For example, in the *Metaphysics* he uses it in reference to the study of his predecessors, arguing that either he will discover something different which he should know, or he will find his ability to rely (*pisteusomen*) on his own work increased.[424] In his *Rhetoric* he uses the verb in this manner in contending that in attacking slander one can show its great evil in that it alters judgment (*kriseis*) by refusing to rely (*pisteuei*) on actual facts.[425] In his *Politics* he argues, among other things, "therefore not to rely (*pisteuein*) on the clever contrivances cobbled together for the pleasure of the mob."[426] The infinitive is also used in the pseudo-Aristotelian work *Physiognomonica* (c. 3rd cent. B.C.E.), with respect to drawing inferences from sense perceptions in differentiating people: "Now surely to rely (*pisteuein*) on a single sign

---

[421] Plato, *Republic*, VI.505d-e.
[422] Isocrates, *Archidamus*, 49.
[423] Isocrates, *Busiris*, 7.
[424] Aristotle, *Metaphysics*, 983b [I.3].
[425] Aristotle, *Rhetoric*, 1416a (end) [III.15.9].
[426] Aristotle, *Politics* (*Politica*), 1307b (end) [V.2 (end)]. Rackham's translation of the *Politics*, 421, supplies "put faith in" for *pisteuein*, which has the same sense of "to rely on" or "to trust in." Jowett's translation of the same text uses "rely."

is simple-minded; but when you have more than one in agreement pointing one way, then it is more likely the sign is true."[427]

Despite a paucity of belief terms in what survives of Epicurus' writings that might be translated as "reliance," it is clear enough that Epicureans associate true belief with reliance on always true and oft-repeated sense-perceptions. The idea is absolutely intrinsic to their epistemology. Because of that they also relate reliance to the self—what we term "self-sufficiency." So Epicurus remarks, "Of self-sufficiency the greatest fruit is freedom."[428]

Preeminently, thought the Stoics, one must rely upon him- or herself. So Seneca writes that a wise person is neither elevated nor deflated by circumstances but rather "labors always to rely (*poneret*) upon himself in most things and in himself seek all joy." But, he immediately adds, still stinging from the exile that has been forced upon him, as he tries to build up his own self-reliance he continues to avail himself of a reliance on the Stoic sages who teach him how to handle fortune and misfortune alike.[429]

Skeptics find both reason and sense-perception notoriously unreliable. The early Pyrrhonian Timon says that because neither one's sense-perceptions nor beliefs can be proved indisputably true (or false), "for this very reason we ought not to rely (*pisteuein*) on them, but rather to be without belief (*adoxastous*), without inclination, and unmoved. . . ."[430] Similarly, Sextus Empiricus writes:

> Accordingly, since even if we grant that we ought to judge (*krinein*) external things according to *phantasia*, whether we decide to rely on (*pisteuein*) all *phantasia*, or only to rely on (*pisteuein*) some, or to not rely on (*apistein*) any, with respect to being criteria (*kriterioi*), in any case the argument (*ho logos*) is overthrown, and we are made to conclude *phantasia* are not to be drawn upon as criteria (*kriteria*) for judgment (*krisin*).[431]

This same logic occurs in the satirist Lucian, on the question of finding a trustworthy guide: "I must either rely (*pisteuein*) upon them all—which is a really hilarious notion!—or not rely (*apistein*) upon any of them." He ventures that the latter course is the safer one until the truth is discovered.[432]

---

[427] Pseudo-Aristotle, *Physiognomics* (*Physiognomonica*), 807a.

[428] Epicurus, *Fragment* 77 (Bailey, *Epicurus,* 118, for the Greek text). In Epicurus, *Maxim* 35, in Diogenes Laertius, *Lives of Eminent Philosophers: Epicurus,* X.151 [*Epicurus,* 31], we have a fragment in which the infinitive might be variously translated as "to rely on," or "to trust," or "to be confident about," when he says that a person who has done wrong in secret can never rest easy for no matter how often it seems he or she has gotten away with it, it is impossible "to rely (*pisteuein*) upon escaping notice."

[429] Seneca, *Consolation to Helvia,* 5 (quoted material in 5.1).

[430] Timon in Aristocles, quoted in Eusebius, *Preparation for the Gospel* (*Praeparatio Evangelica*), XIV.18.2-3.

[431] Sextus Empiricus, *Outlines of Pyrrhonism,* II.78. Our earlier choice of translating *pistuein* as "to believe" was to accent the fact that belief was at issue. But it seems clear in context that it is belief precisely as "reliance" that Sextus has in mind.

[432] Lucian, *Hermotimus,* 29.

Malleability

Malleability means belief is adaptive and variable. Belief is adaptive in that it changes in order to facilitate meeting relational needs, including to self, others, and Nature. Adaptiveness explains variability; the latter is needed for the former. Belief resides in *beliefs*, and these are variable. The personal, subjective requirement of being human in the world is to develop relationships with the world and its denizens, including the self. The adaptive malleability of belief in the service of relationships aimed to build and express trust means that belief changes in response to the environment. We all form beliefs about the nature of reality and these beliefs develop alongside our experience, whether we interpret that experience with more reliance upon sense-perception or on reason.

We stretch toward knowledge because of a fundamental instinct that knowledge is the most secure foundation for relationships. Yet we depend primarily on belief because of an equally fundamental uncertainty that we now possess or ever can achieve the knowledge we seek. *The constant inquiry as to whether belief is ever knowledge rests squarely in the hope that the belief we need might prove to also be the knowledge we crave.* This leads us to a crucial point. Adaptive malleability may be belief's chief attraction, but it is almost certainly what constitutes its chief danger. People believe what they *want* to believe, what they think they *need* to believe. From an objective viewpoint it is worrisome that beliefs about highly valued matters so strikingly correspond to what an individual desires.

Let us picture how adaptive our figures may imagine belief can be:

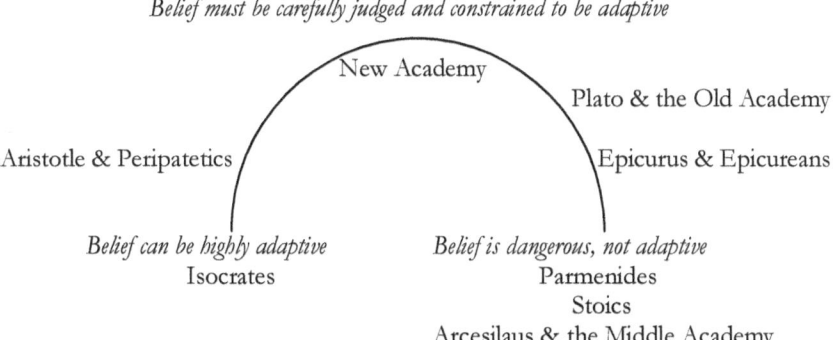

Malleability
Belief must be carefully judged and constrained to be adaptive

New Academy

Plato & the Old Academy

Aristotle & Peripatetics

Epicurus & Epicureans

Belief can be highly adaptive
Isocrates

Belief is dangerous, not adaptive
Parmenides
Stoics
Arcesilaus & the Middle Academy

Parmenides' poem is framed as a journey with the traveler offered guidance by divinity toward that which is certain and away from the deceptiveness of apparent variability. Parmenides, in the voice of the goddess, sets a stark contrast between divine truth and mortal belief: "You must learn all things, of Truth's persuasive heart and of mortal belief (*doxas*), which cannot be true persuasion (*pistis alēthēs*)."[433] The former is one, constant, and true; the latter is many, changeable, and undependable. To human beings, by nature, belongs belief, and

---

[433] Parmenides, *On Nature*, fragment 1, lines 28-30.

by it often keep themselves from knowledge. They are, says the goddess, "two-headed,"[434] or as we might say, of two minds. This leads to an unfortunate result: "For mortals have set down their judgment to name two forms, one of which is not right, and in this they go astray."[435]

Plato's Socrates presents belief (*doxa*) as something that remains an unsettled matter with respect to whether it can ever coincide with knowledge (*epistēmē*). In the light of all we have seen, it does not seem disingenuous that Socrates claims ignorance on the matter. The presentation in the *Republic* is an important one and if we do not press it too hard it seems to serve sufficiently as a broad depiction of some basic ideas Plato sets out consistently. First, belief is never self-evidently knowledge; if it ever coincides it must be because it meets certain criteria with respect to truth and supporting evidence. Second, belief belongs to the world of human experience where sense-perception tells us things come into being, change, and pass from existence. These two points together mean that for belief to become knowledge it must somehow transcend the limitations of sense-perception and its reports of a changing world. Belief as the taking up of a position (*doxa*) includes belief as confidence (*pistis*) in the persuasive power of perception when the things seen are clearly visible (i.e., 'testable'). But, as Plato's Socrates puts it in the *Republic*, "belief (*doxan*), widely construed, concerns things *becoming*. . . ."[436] It thus stands in contrast to what thinking, with reason, is capable of recognizing: *being*. Plato makes the point that belief and knowledge stand in relation to each other like being and becoming do. If so, then belief is like becoming—subject to change.

Isocrates's view of philosophy is an educational philosophy that aims at teaching practical wisdom—how to live in the world—with the conviction, as he puts it, that "the one who is wise is the person who by *belief* (*doxais*) in actual practice aims for and typically hits the best target in most matters."[437] He captures the adaptive nature of belief in remarks we cited earlier:

> It seems to me that while everyone sets their heart on their own advantage and wants to have more than others, they do not *know* (*eidenai*) the manner of practice that brings such results, but they take up different *beliefs* (*doxais*)—with some having suitable beliefs capable of hitting the mark, and others completely missing their target.[438]

Now we must grant that like an archer becoming more proficient in hitting a target, a person forms, tests, and adjusts beliefs in the adaptive effort to become more accomplished in meeting her or his needs. Isocrates himself likens living to crafting a fine speech. He says we need first to have an objective we want to accomplish and, "After you have marked off the general shape of your life, then

---

[434] Parmenides, *On Nature*, fragment 6, line 5.
[435] Parmenides, *On Nature*, fragment 8, lines 53-54.
[436] Plato, *Republic*, VII.534a.
[437] Isocrates, *Antidosis*, 271.
[438] Isocrates, *On the Peace*, 28.

you should reflect upon each day-by-day part with its actions to see how they will contribute to your original plan."[439]

Aristotle holds an optimistic view of belief, though he also qualifies it by his recognition of its malleability. But rather than despair that such malleability presents an insurmountable difficulty, he thinks the rational mind can work through belief's variability to discern that part which is adequately dependable. This means he also regards belief's malleability as adaptive, because there is some measure of trustworthiness in it. In his *Topics* he argues that in sound reasoning the particulars of an argument are to be accepted if they are "true and *endoxa*."[440] His notion of *endoxa* is especially important with respect to belief's malleability. Aristotle frames much of his discussion of belief (*doxa*) in terms of the persuasion aimed at in public (and private) discourse, and in such discourse the power of *endoxa* ("the strongly endorsed beliefs held by all, or by most people, or by the wisest, or simply put, those beliefs endorsed by all, or by most, or by the most notable of people")[441] is especially influential. In his *Nicomachean Ethics* he distinguishes between these groups—the belief of the many from the belief of a distinguished minority—but argues that, "It is reasonable to think neither of these groups will entirely miss the mark on everything."[442] The likelihood that both sides have some grasp on the truth offers hope in the face of an uncomfortable reality: beliefs on any given matter can and often do vary.

Epicurus distrusts reason based on his judgment that it is prone to wander astray from its governor, the senses, and thus the variability of belief poses an obstacle to knowledge. He writes to Herodotus:

> Therefore, Herodotus, first among the things that must be grasped is the meaning of words so that we may be well-positioned to judge things believed (*ta doxazomena*), or things investigated, or difficult matters, and thereby neither leave anything uncertain, running on in endless demonstrations, nor use empty words. For it is necessary that the first thing held in one's thoughts about each word be clearly visible and not needing any proving (*apodeixeōs*), if indeed we are to have a way forward on things being investigated, or difficult problems, or concerning what is being believed (*doxazomenon*).[443]

He immediately afterwards urges staying close to sense-perceptions (*aisthēseis*) and one's immediate feelings (*pathē*), "in order that we may have a way to mark for ourselves which are the things being waited upon for confirmation and

---

[439] Isocrates, *To the Children of Jason*, 8-10.
[440] Aristotle, *Topics*, 160b [VIII.8].
[441] Aristotle, *Topics*, 100a [I.1]. Greek (lines 22-23).
[442] Aristotle, *Nichomachean Ethics*, 1098b [I.8.7]. The distinguished minority are "men held in high repute" (ἔνδοξοι ἄνδρες, *endoxoi andres*); the other are the "common people and the ancients" (πολλοὶ καὶ παλαιοὶ, *polloi kaï palaioi*), i.e., popular opinion and that long held.
[443] Epicurus, *Letter to Herodotus*, in Diogenes Laertius, *Lives of Eminent Philosophers: Epicurus*, X.37-38 [*Epicurus*, 24].

which are those remaining obscure."[444] As Lucretius argues, beliefs may seem adaptive and yet rather than decrease anxiety actually increase it. Thus, he contends, unable to discern the cause of many things people attribute them to deity but their belief ultimately drives them to greater anxiety and despair in fear of the gods they imagine.[445] Those beliefs that are true are both supported by evidence and lack any disconfirming evidence—they are *unambiguously* clear, or "self-evident" (*enargeias*).[446] The Epicurean willingness to "wait" for confirming evidence is another indication of a desire to overcome the uncertainty and variability of belief.[447]

The Stoics also do not look favorably on the variability of belief. They contrast belief and knowledge so that the former is a kind of ignorance because of its lack of foundation in self-evident comprehension—or to put it simply, belief is the taking up of a position (*doxa*) absent comprehension (*katalēpsis*) as its criterion. *Doxa* is inherently unstable and variable because it lacks the anchor of *katalēpsis*. Anyone can believe anything based on any appearance—or nothing at all! Even though belief belongs to the reasoning faculty, all that ultimately means is that it *can* be governed, not that it *must* be. The consistent governance of reason is what separates the wise from the foolish.

The Skeptics are disturbed by the variability of belief, which they view as keeping insecure any claim to knowledge. Because belief can vary, it shifts the foundation of knowledge, making such a foundation nothing more than sand.[448] Arcesilaus, founder of the Middle Academy, prefers to dispense with talk of belief at all. Instead he wants to speak about the "movements" the *psyche* experiences, some of which are in accord with Nature and so to be cooperated with fully and easily, and the contrasting unnatural movement of belief, which is to be resisted. Belief introduces volition so that one may choose to go against the natural, adaptive response. Carneades and Clitomachus of the New Academy emphasize the persuasive character of some appearances leading to belief; obviously, persuasiveness is quite variable. Carneades sets certain criteria to help ensure that the persuasiveness anyone is swayed by is conducive to truth. But while belief's variability is accepted, the best one can hope to achieve is what is *probably* true, so one can and must impose structure to limit the negative effects of variability.

---

[444] Epicurus, *Letter to Herodotus*, in Diogenes Laertius, *Lives of Eminent Philosophers: Epicurus*, X.38 [*Epicurus*, 24].

[445] Lucretius, *On the Nature of the Universe*, VI.48-71.

[446] Sextus Empiricus, *Against the Dogmatists: Against the Logicians*, I.211. This passage is translated in the chapter on Epicurus.

[447] See Diogenes Laertius, *Lives of Eminent Philosophers: Epicurus*, X.34 [*Epicurus*, 22]. This passage is translated in the chapter on Epicurus.

[448] However, a Pyrrhonist is undisturbed by variability when the belief in question is immediate and circumstantial. To believe that one feels warm or feels cold at a given moment becomes incentive to do something about it—put on a cloak, for instance. Such beliefs are adaptive.

15
Reaching toward Knowledge

I still believe, like Aristotle, "All people by nature stretch themselves toward knowledge." But I also think that many stretch only as far as belief, mistakenly calling it knowledge, and reach no further. In the marketplace of ideas there is no shortage of hucksters plying their wares. The sheer diversity of voices claiming "*Here* is the true belief!" or "*Here* is knowledge!" contributes to a certain weariness, and often a settling for whatever is convenient and presently appealing. Aristotle observes in his *Rhetoric* that those who spout general maxims that seem to reinforce what people already believe are especially effective.[449]

Some people retreat to burrows of comfortable beliefs and affirm them with credulity.[450] As Cicero remarks, a surprisingly large number of people don't search out alternative viewpoints, but instead "after a single hearing they decide to unite themselves under one authority."[451] Cicero says that, content to rest in error, these people "belligerently defend that which they have fallen head-over-heels for, without any persistency in inquiring into those things said with much greater reliability."[452] Sometimes there is a superficial embrace of a variety of beliefs in the hope that by spreading one's bets at least one of them will pay off in the end. Others engage in another common intellectual retreat—an explicit, though shallow skepticism. They live with doubt, having abandoned any real search for truth. A fair number of people respond to differences by defensive skepticism—a rejection of everything to form an empty intellectual nihilism.

Our philosophers point us toward a better way. They teach us the basic but challenging questions we need in order to choose wisely as we filter out sense from all the nonsense. Unlike the superficial hucksterism preying on the credulous, serious epistemology offers us a way forward. In being taught how better to think we are given tools for credible judgments and genuine hope for knowledge.

---

[449] Aristotle, *Rhetoric*, 1395b [II.21.15]: "For they are glad if any general saying hits the mark of the belief they have about that matter at the time."

[450] Seneca, *On Anger*, II.24.1 writes, "Much evil is made by credulity." (*Plurimum mali credulitas facit*).

[451] Cicero, *Academics*, II.9 [ch. III]. This reminds one of Erich Fromm's (*Man for Himself*) notion of the herd mentality that seeks solace, like sheep, in circling about an authoritative figure to whom is granted power to decide for them their beliefs.

[452] Cicero, *Academics*, II.9 [ch. III]. I have rendered *constantissime* (a superlative) as "much greater reliability" since the term captures a sense of firmness, steadiness, and constancy.

It remains to us to now attempt a preliminary, but focused comparison of knowledge and belief by drawing on what we have learned to ask further questions, such as those that follow (but please remember that each question posed here is simply *one* possibility). This is a next step in continuing our stretching.

Knowledge	Belief	A Question about Relationship
Information (source)	Trust	Trust is the source of belief, but does it depend on information?
Reality (object)	Assertion	Assertion is subjective, reality objective; are they complements or rivals?
Judgment (method)	Judgment	The object of judgment is different for each, but do they share the same criterion?
Certainty	Confidence	If confidence can be considered a kind of certainty, is it partial or complete?
Clarity	Persuasion	Does the persuasion of belief rely on clarity, or does it arise where clarity is absent?
Recognition	Reliance	Does recognition require reliance, or reliance require recognition?
Sufficiency	Malleability	Both are a matter of degree but do they serve similar functions?

My pairings invite other possible ones but it seems to me these are natural enough and serve initially for comparing and contrasting knowledge and belief.

Core Element 1 (The Source): Information vs. Trust

The source of knowledge is *information*; that of belief is *trust*. Our question—Does trust depend on information?—has no unambiguous answer. We hope our trust rests on information, and trustworthy information at that. But we recognize the existence of so-called 'blind trust.' Sometimes information is lacking and people trust anyway. To claim that trust depends on information does not erase the difference between belief and knowledge as to how information is used. But it does suggest *both knowledge and belief ultimately share a common source that makes it possible for belief to be knowledge if everything aligns in a particular way*. We can call information, before selection for use, the source-behind-the-source for belief. In other words, though belief's immediate source is trust, that trust itself relies on information. On the other hand, for knowledge information is both the proximate (near) and distal (far) source; there is no mediator.

Let us contrast knowledge and belief in the use of information. In belief, everything takes place within the relational field of trust, which is why it is proper to term it the source of belief. It draws from the ultimate source of all information only that which it finds suited to its trust as determined by its own criteria. Belief's relational character necessitates personal involvement around trust. Belief seeks a criterion of trust to achieve enough confidence for assertion. Personal standards are set up to judge whether something or someone is trustworthy. These filter information. We can envision this as follows:

1. An objective source is . . .

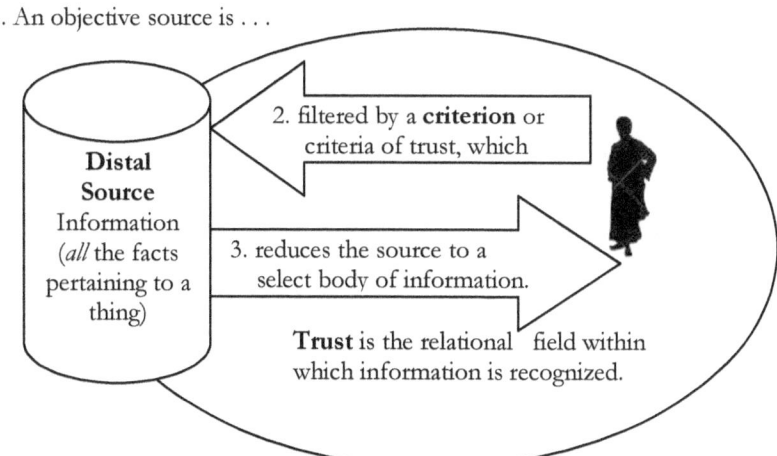

Distal Source Information (*all* the facts pertaining to a thing)

2. filtered by a **criterion** or criteria of trust, which

3. reduces the source to a select body of information.

Trust is the relational field within which information is recognized.

On the other hand, knowledge, at least *epistēmē* as a body of objectively se-cure, complete and unchanging information, is independent of what people wish or want it to be. To know something is to be compelled by the facts—the total available information—whether those facts are subjectively convenient or not. Belief seems to find it difficult to accept inconvenient facts. As we often discover with a little probing, belief tends to be more selective in the facts it trusts. Of course, some may argue that deciding what is relevant is itself subjec-tive and so 'knowledge' never escapes 'belief.' Even if one grants that point it seems believing typically finds idiosyncratic criteria by which to determine rele-vance, thus discarding some of what knowledge accepts as inconvenient but relevant, while also accepting as relevant other things knowledge rejects as irrel-evant. Subjectivism prevails in belief while knowledge aims at objectivity.

The above presumes belief's trust relies on information, or that it *should*. If we answer negatively, we are left wondering what trust is based upon if not in-formation. The most plausible response would be that *trust is based on itself*. An-other sense of 'source' is as that which informs, and trust does this. Perhaps trust is the source of belief in the primary sense of being that which informs based on itself: a relational investment, regardless of how subsequently justified to self and others as formed by intuition, feeling, or information. Perhaps trust is the purest subjectivity, an existential subjectivity in which all that one is holis-tically is brought into relation with some thing or person. Then trust is the source as the *ground* of belief, independent of information whether used or not.

This perspective comes at a cost. If trust is a pure, existential commitment of self, independent of objective causation and a matter of personal will only, then it can be shared by testimony, perhaps in unique ways replicated in others, but never judged in terms of any objective body of information. Truth as a cri-terion is either removed from consideration or made into Protagoras' 'what is true for me.' This more radical position has not been favored by most thought-ful people as it is so easily ripe for self-serving abuse.

The object of knowledge is *reality*; that of belief is *assertion*. Are they complements, or rivals? Reality, for our ancient thinkers—and still for most of us today—has to do with what *is* and not merely what *seems to be*. I recognize this formulation in itself is debatable, but most people when they use a word like "reality" have in mind something objective and external in existence, just as did our ancient thinkers. Belief is not disinterested in reality by any means. But because belief is about relationship, and trust necessitates personal involvement and commitment in the act of living, it cannot afford to wait to establish what *is* beyond doubt and so it constantly engages with what *seems to be* and, case by case, thing by thing, either affirms or denies that the latter (*seems to be*) is the same as the former (*is*). This is assertion, and it means declaring decisions in such a way as to express the commitment of trust in one fashion or another, whether by thought, feeling, will, or deed.

The objects of knowledge and belief are thus different, but the question remains: are they rivals or complements? Our figures at least implicitly wrestle with this query in their thinking. None of them imagine that assertion for its own sake is anything more than the kind of sophistry they objected to—mere prattling to persuade based on nothing more than eloquence. They prefer to envision assertion as acts of belief by which claims are made about reality that can be tested. Of course, they know some assertions are claims about temporary and personal experiences that need not be tested, such as "I am hot," or "I am cold." These immediate beliefs, which even radical Skeptics allow, come and go without much challenge because they are not claims about reality as such but merely one's experience of reality at the moment. In essence, then, they see assertions as ranged along a continuum, and only some of these merit serious attention. We must modify our earlier continuum on assertion as follows:

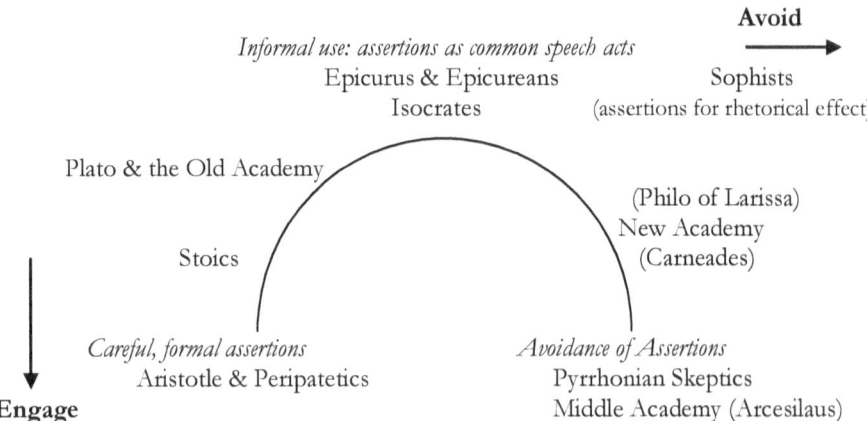

Thoughtful folk concern themselves with claims aiming to affirm what reality *is* and to what extent, if any, what s*eems to be* (appearances) coincides with what *is*. They do not worry themselves over ordinary assertions about moment-to-moment sense experiences of the individual, except when these are raised to assertions that what *seems to be* now and to me, is the same as what *is* at all times, either for me or for all people. As for mere playing with words like the Sophists' game of persuading first one way, and then its opposite, with no personal investment either way, thoughtful people disdain such as empty of value for either belief or knowledge. True Skeptics still care about and seek actual knowledge.

That assertion rather than reality is the object of belief is *utilitarian*, which fits the character of belief as something relational in nature that must act based on trust because knowledge is so often lacking. Uncertainty of information is answered by confidence of assertion—a decision is made because a decision *has* to be made to go on about the business of living. Belief aims at being adaptive.

But just because the objects of belief and knowledge easily complement each other does not mean they cannot at times become rivals. *The notion of complementarity requires belief and knowledge to continue the same shared interest in ultimately discovering what is real.* That means that the assertions that are the object of belief must bend toward affirming that what s*eems to be* has some true relation to what *is* if they are to be faithful to their nature. There is, then, a difference between 'belief,' a trivial assertion that my experience says such is what is the case right now, and 'Belief,'' a serious assertion about the nature of reality.

The objects of belief and knowledge become rivals when the object of belief—assertion—becomes more or less unhinged from its interest in truth. All assertions are to some extent claims about truth. But when truth itself—the criterion of knowledge—becomes of less interest than, say, persuasion, the assertion becomes more suspect. For belief to ever be knowledge its assertions must remain focused on truth. They have to be claims about truth more interested in truth than in persuasion. When the need to be right, or to feel trust, outweighs the need to find truth, then assertions weaken their own nature.

Our thinkers, to the extent they give formal attention to assertions, focus on it as utterances expressing assent; they affirm (or deny) things. Beliefs, by nature, are either-or. A thing is said to be *this* way, or it is *that* way; it either *is* or it *is not*. It may not be impossible to form beliefs that express 'both-and,' but basically beliefs are assertions on particular things that say they are this or that, or that they are not this or that. Obviously this is why beliefs so easily generate conflict. Assertions—beliefs—take up a position and take a stand. This creates disquiet among minds, which is a primary reason Skeptics avoid beliefs in the interest of psychic tranquility (*ataraxia*).

So long as the object of belief—assertion—remains faithful to seeking after truth, belief's object will remain complementary to the object of knowledge, which is reality. That is because, as our thinkers agree, truth is about reality. Truth expresses what *is*, the way things *are*, and so peels back whatever curtain may exist between appearances (the way things *seem to be*) and reality—or shows there is no curtain and appearances and reality are the same. Of course, it is on this very matter that our thinkers most often and profoundly disagree with one another's epistemologies.

The method of knowledge and of belief alike is *judgment*. Of course, that does not mean the judgments are of a like nature. The question is: Do they share the same criterion? A similar process with different criteria, applied to different sources and objects means a difference in judgment. The answer, we have argued, is that knowledge and belief do *not* have the same criterion (or criteria). Our thinkers posited for knowledge a criterion (or criteria) by which to establish *truth* and thus secure knowledge. For belief the method depends instead on some criterion (or criteria) for establishing *trust*. These are fundamentally different though the method remains a process of taking up a position.

One can still argue that even if the criteria differ they function similarly. Since judgment ultimately is the taking up of a position the fundamental nature of judgment in both knowledge and belief is the same. If there were not such fundamental and significant similarities we could not entertain the possibility that belief might ever be knowledge. *For belief to become knowledge the criterion (or criteria) for trust must produce the same results that the criterion (or criteria) for truth do.* Note the wording: it is not that the *criteria* must be the same, but that the *results* must be. When the results of trust mirror the results of truth, then one can argue that belief and knowledge are the same. Let us try to picture the situation.

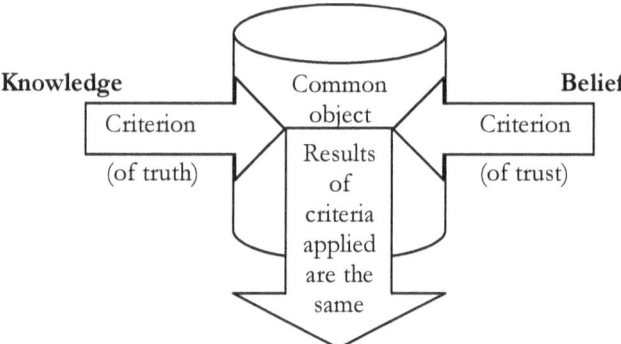

Though their criteria vary, if the results are the same there exists grounds for saying that belief has become knowledge.

This establishes the *possibility* of belief becoming knowledge. It does not say that such actually happens, or if it does how often. The bottom line is that in judgment, as in the matters of source and object, if there is not some way to conceptualize a point of contact between belief and knowledge such that the former can be the latter, then our basic question of whether they can ever be the same must be answered in the negative. To answer that they can ever be the same requires that in all three matters—source, object, and method—belief and knowledge must be capable of being linked. Thus, belief must depend on information, its assertions must be statements about truth concerning what is real, and the results of its application of trust criterion (or criteria) must be the same as the results attained by knowledge's criterion for truth.

A plausible argument can be made that confidence is to belief what certainty is to knowledge in being an element so closely associated with it in the popular conception that it might even be considered a core characteristic. The ties between confidence and certainty are recognized by epistemologists who reckon confidence a subjective certainty. Epistemic certainty, on the other hand, is objective; it requires that the source and method accurately reflect the object of knowledge. As we examined certainty earlier we noted that, *ideally, certainty means that the person's subjective certitude has objective warrant.* But our specific question—just one among many that might be asked—is: If confidence can be considered a kind of certainty, is it partial or complete?

We saw in considering the notion of certainty that our thinkers present a variety of views. Those like the Stoics, who argue that certainty must be complete, might make the case that certainty is truly an 'either-or' quality; one has it or one does not. If epistemic certainty requires an accurate reflection of reality, how can one argue that so-called "knowledge" only *might* be accurate or only capture *some* of the reality of a thing? Yet the actual practice of establishing certainty seems always a debatable matter. The Epicurean philosopher Philodemus complains about the Stoics that they "construct belief" through implausible arguments based on picking and choosing among the beliefs of others, and that they do so in order "to make more certain their own belief."[453] However fair one judges Philodemus' criticism, it does point to a subjective element involved. People make decisions—take up positions—as to whether an assertion faithfully represents reality. When constructing a body of dogma, even when ostensibly using only self-evident comprehension (*katalēpsis*) as the Stoics claim to do, a degree of self-serving selection can enter in so that epistemic certainty ends up being swapped out in favor of subjective confidence. How is one to know that alleged epistemic certainty isn't just a felt subjective certainty—confidence replacing actual accuracy?[454]

Not surprisingly, many thinkers and schools find a need to modify such an unqualified stand. Plato, for example, distinguishes between the certainty one can have about eternal Forms and the uncertainty that is inherent for the impermanent, changing things of the Sensible world. Aristotle avoids any strict division, but suggests a continuum where certainty is an ideal always being sought. Isocrates might concur, but his focus is on the practical unlikelihood that certainty will be achieved and so he argues one must do what one can with what one has, however partial it might be. The Epicureans offer their own distinction: all appearances are certain, but only some statements about them are.

---

[453] Philodemus, *On Methods of Inference*, XXXVIII.8-17.
[454] On this problem, see chapter 4 of Bolich, *Chasing the Ghost*, where the psychological research on confidence is presented that shows how frequently people exchange the certainty of accuracy for the certainty of confidence.

The Skeptics have an aversion to assertions of certainty as being one of the hallmarks of Dogmatism.

What those who modify the notion of certainty share in common is a realization of the difficulty in establishing it. An accurate representation of reality is certain only if it is *stable*, and such stability requires the information be consistent, the method be reliable and firm, and both not only correspond to the way things actually are, but lead to assertions that faithfully mirror it and continue to do so. This is a daunting goal and it is easy to see why so many offer caveats about it. But once partial certainty is allowed, the question shifts to sufficiency: What degree of certainty suffices to say a matter is certain enough? Or, how much certainty of a part of something suffices to say the entire thing is adequately known?

Such questions are hard, perhaps impossible, to resolve. A different approach has become popular, but it shifts the ground significantly. Instead of talking about partial *certainty* we may talk about partial *knowledge*. Now the question becomes, Can we know some aspect with fullness and such stability that we can declare certainty, even if other parts of the whole remain uncertain? If so, then we have epistemic certainty, but only partial knowledge. It looks like this:

Uncertainty about some parts +
Certainty about some part(s) =
Partial knowledge

This is what science seems to accept, and it seems much in line with Aristotle. It has become commonplace to talk about various physical "laws" that are presented as certain even though many of the things of reality to which they connect remain hypothetical (i.e., uncertain).

Defining Element 2: Clarity vs. Persuasion

We saw how important clarity (*enargeia*) is to our thinkers, especially to the Hellenistic philosophers. Such clarity is epistemologically relevant because it is a vividness and/or distinctness that says to one that something can only be *this* and not *that*—the very sort of thing one associates with knowledge, where its object, reality, is assumed to be either *this* or *that*, but not flip-flopping back and forth between *this* and *that*. We saw, too, the same could be said about persuasion's (*peithous*) importance to belief, that it inherently is a quality of it (though in this latter case it was an idea attached to belief long before the Epicureans, Stoics, and Skeptics). The connection between clarity and persuasion, each so important to their respective matters of knowledge and belief, thus seems an agreeable possible link between the larger wholes of which they are a part. If what is persuasive enough to generate belief proves also clear enough to undergird knowledge, then some belief—clear and persuasive belief—might be knowledge.

So our proposed question is a logical one. Does the persuasion of belief rely on clarity, or does it arise where clarity is absent? If the former, then perhaps an epistemological claim can be made that such belief is also knowledge, because the clarity being spoken about is so self-evident, so certain, that it cannot help but also be persuasive. It is a clarity that convinces one that the appearance of a thing must truly represent the reality, and perhaps even *be* the reality (i.e., that the way a thing *seems to be* is actually the way it *is*).

One way to approach this question might be to ask, How probable is it that anyone would believe something that is *not* clear? We might conclude that persuasion is unlikely in the absence of clarity, but it seems easy enough to call that idea into doubt. Purposeful obfuscation has been used by many people to effectively persuade others. Modern insurance language and most legal language, for example, is written in such torturous English it is hard to resist concluding it is written to be intentionally obscure. What gain is there in such a process? First, it provides plausible grounds for multiple interpretations so that the presenter can argue for whatever construal best suits his or her side at the time. But second, and more pertinent here, the audience often judges that the problem is not in a lack of clarity by the presenter, but a lack of understanding by the hearer. This effectively persuades the hearer to accept whatever interpretation is offered when questions arise.[455]

If clarity is meant to also include plausibility, as in any assertion needing to be logically sensible, that kind of clarity can also be absent and people still be persuaded. The Nazi propaganda machine understood that the bigger and more implausible a lie, the more likely many would be persuaded by it, under the idea that no authority would venture such an incredible assertion unless it were true. Aristotle understands this well. In his *Rhetoric* he writes:

> Another line of thought concerns things supposed to have happened but that are unbelievable (*apistōn*), because they could not have been believed (*edoxan*) if they had not been so, or nearly so. Indeed, this makes them even more likely: for we can take the position (*hupolambanousin*) that such things happened or likely occurred, because if truly unbelievable (*apiston*) or unlikely, they would not be conceded as true (*alēthes*); it is not because they are likely and plausible (*pithanon*) that people think as they do.[456]

The word *pithanon* addresses persuasiveness; Aristotle argues it is not because an unbelievable matter seems "persuasive"—as in credible, believable, or plausible—but because it seems so unlikely and unbelievable on the face of it that anyone believing it must have done so because it really happened, or at least

---

[455] Cf. Cicero, *On Rhetorical Invention*, II.54 [§165]. This was cited earlier in this volume, with Cicero's point being that people persuade themselves that someone speaking confidently to them must have a reason for their confidence.

[456] Aristotle, *Rhetoric*, 1400a [II.23.22]. The word ἄπιστων (*apistōn*) is often translated "incredible," which literally means "not credible," or "unbelievable." I have simply chosen to make this quality as obvious as possible.

could have happened. As naïve as this may seem to us, it fits Aristotle's general conviction that all people stretch toward knowledge and truth. He recognizes that an effective argument can persuade people even if the 'facts' it appeals to appear completely without credit, and manages to do so precisely because people tend to give others the benefit of the doubt, thinking that others, like themselves, seek truth and would only believe the unbelievable if it were really so.[457]

If we can imagine that the intrinsically unpersuasive can be persuasive, then the whole notion of belief's persuasion always or necessarily relying on clarity is thrown out the window. But *it might be that belief sometimes is a matter of persuasion resting at least in part on clarity and therefore sometimes might be knowledge* (assuming any other qualifications required for knowledge are also met). Perhaps the most reasonable answer to our question is to reject an 'either-or' perspective and suggest a 'both-and' one: belief's persuasion is a matter of both clarity sometimes and despite its lack sometimes. This conclusion aligns with the general tendency among our thinkers to say that belief is highly malleable. Moreover, our thinkers generally agree that belief is variably persuasive. Any given belief is more persuasive to some people than to others, and some beliefs are more persuasive to all people than are other beliefs. The role that clarity plays may be just one factor among many in determining what is persuasive.

The whole matter seems to spread along a continuum.

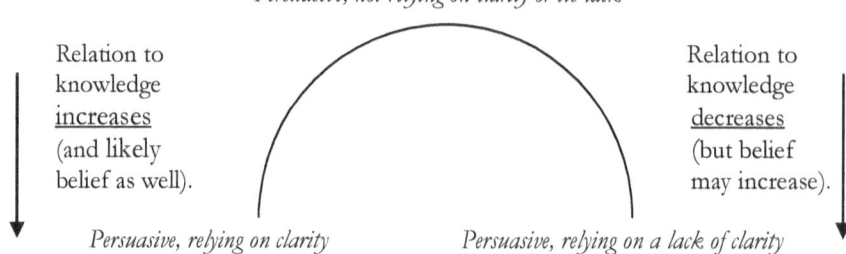

Persuasive, not relying on clarity or its lack

Relation to knowledge <u>increases</u> (and likely belief as well).

Relation to knowledge <u>decreases</u> (but belief may increase).

Persuasive, relying on clarity   *Persuasive, relying on a lack of clarity*

In sum, belief can increase independent of clarity; it depends on persuasion, not clarity. Yet, when persuasion is based on clarity it seems likely belief is thereby strengthened.

Defining Element 3: Recognition vs. Reliance

Reliance is a relational quality expressing dependence, a need to trust based on the trustworthiness of some person, idea, or thing. We saw that the concept embraces different elements, roughly arranged along a continuum ranging from the most minimal to the most intimate and profound: awareness, acknowledgment, recollection, and identification. We also saw that the concept remains relatively underdeveloped among our thinkers. In rough fashion they vary from

---

[457] This seems the rationale behind Tertullian's *Prosus credibile est, quia ineptum est* ("It is immediately credible—because it is silly"), followed by *et sepultus resurrexit: certum est, quia impossibile* ("He was buried and rose again: it is certain—because it is impossible") in his *De carne Christi* [*On the Incarnation of Christ*], 5.

viewing recognition as separate and perhaps prior to knowledge (Plato), to more complexly related to knowledge (Aristotle), to some dependence on the concept (if still undeveloped) in discussions of the 'signs' used in knowing debated between the Epicureans and Stoics. This situation makes our proposed question a rather vague one in that too much ambiguity remains in the term "recognition."

But perhaps we can still find it useful to probe the relation of knowledge to belief with our query: Does recognition require reliance, or reliance require recognition? Focusing on the first part, we are asking if recognition needs reliance—a personal relating dependent on evidence of trustworthiness. To answer that, we can take recognition in each of its four possibilities. Simple awareness would seem to need minimal evidence to establish. One 'relates' to something as soon as one becomes aware of it, but most of what we become aware of passes into and out of consciousness rather rapidly. Acknowledgment requires more persistence; awareness continues and draws forth a cognitive response. This suggests greater dependence on evidence and evidence deemed reliable to trust. But acknowledgement of something does not quite necessitate judging it trustworthy and so establishing a relationship of reliance on it. For that matter, neither does recollection or identification—the other two possibilities for recognition. We can remember something, and judge our recollection as trustworthy or unreliable. Identifying something classifies it, but hardly mandates placing trust in it. In fact, often our identifications themselves are judged of low reliability. So, it seems as though recognition does not require reliance.

Does reliance require recognition? If we go through the same process, comparing reliance to each possible sense of recognition, we end up with a very different picture. Reliance without awareness hardly seems possible, and even if so would constitute an exceptionally risky dependence. Reliance typically includes awareness, acknowledgment, recollection, and identification. A person, idea, or thing is judged trustworthy enough to depend upon when one is aware of it, cognitively acknowledges its existence and value, recollects its stability and persistence as an existing object of value, and in identification differentiates it from other persons, ideas, or things that may be trustworthy or not. Reliance needs recognition to avoid blind trust.

There seems to be an inverse relationship between recognition and reliance:

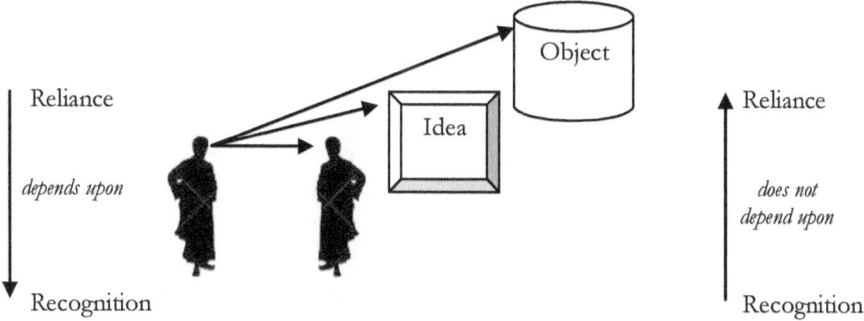

Although reliance requires recognition, recognition does not necessitate reliance. The relationship, if any, between belief and knowledge based on a relationship between reliance and recognition is unclear. Perhaps at best we can say that because reliance depends on some recognition it may reflect belief's own desire for knowledge. The closer one comes to knowledge (*epistēmē*)—the more knowing one achieves—the more reliable belief is. Whatever one relies upon, whether a person, idea, or thing, it is best relied upon with as much recognition of it as possible, and if things like recollection and identification are seen as aspects of knowing, then reliance incorporates elements of knowing and thus strengthens the possibility that at least sometimes belief can be knowledge.

Defining Element 4: Sufficiency vs. Malleability

Both malleability and sufficiency are elements capable of being measured quantitatively and/or qualitatively. Both are thereby a matter of degree, but do they serve similar functions? Although we could attempt to explore the complicated issue of how each can be measured, a more basic issue is the function of each. So our inquiry is about the similarity or dissimilarity of how each functions within its respective whole. Within that issue we can at least touch also on their variability.

Knowledge (*epistēmē*) as conceived by most of our thinkers is an objective body true in nature and perfect in completion. It can neither be added to nor subtracted from. When people speak of 'adding' to knowledge it is not adding to what is objectively true and complete, but adding to a person's or community's store of available information that increases understanding. Learning is a process of seeing more of what is there to be seen, not adding anything to what can be seen.

We might picture it like this:

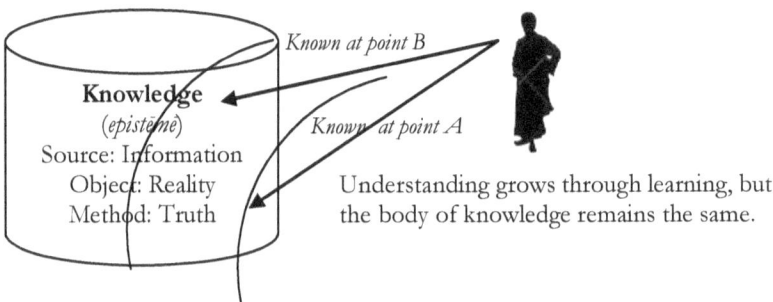

Understanding grows through learning, but the body of knowledge remains the same.

Thus the idea that sufficiency, as a property of knowledge, might be considered in terms of degrees of quality and/or quantity seems counterintuitive. But precisely because the concept allows for degrees of quality and/or quantity it is one that can be used by a thinker in a manner that fits the conception of knowledge that thinker holds. *The function of sufficiency is to provide some warrant for saying knowledge has been achieved.* For example, one can insist on *absolute* sufficiency such that nothing is lacking. Thus what one needs for sufficient *epistēmē* is

194

completeness, whether considered qualitatively or quantitatively. However, while that serves a theoretical purpose, the practical realities as shown above mean it is generally deemed desirable to speak of sufficiency in a *relative* sense—the degree needed to say one "knows" something even if not possessing *epistēmē*.

Most people think there exists some middle ground between knowledge and ignorance. In that middle ground sufficiency operates. One can retain a picture of knowledge as *epistēmē* (in the sense of a complete body of perfect and unchanging information fully comprehended), yet allow for degrees of "knowing" as increased understanding, increased accumulation of information, and so forth. If belief names that which exists between ignorance and knowledge, then sufficiency becomes a key characteristic for determining when belief might become knowledge. We can picture it as follows:

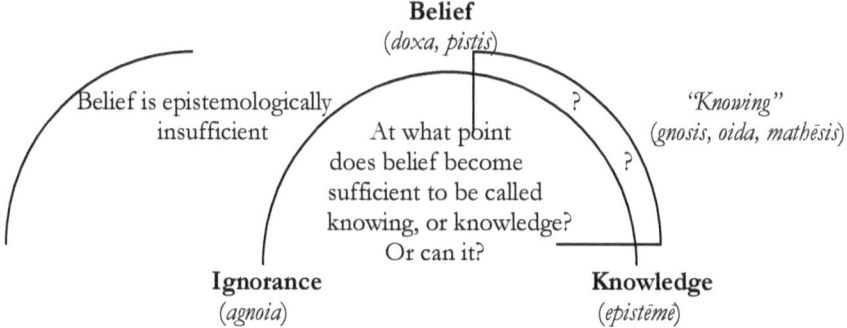

In such a scheme the question of sufficiency is pivotal. When is sufficiency of belief "enough" or "adequate" to qualify as "knowing" or "knowledge"?

Now we can turn our attention to malleability. *The function of malleability is to shape belief adaptively as a substitute for knowledge.* In other words, its adaptive nature explains why it is variable. Belief takes whatever shape it needs to—takes up whatever position seems required or desirable in order to substitute for knowledge where it is absent or uncertain. But this means that malleability's function might coincide with sufficiency's function. Since sufficiency exists to provide a warrant for when knowledge is at hand, if malleability shapes belief to meet the sufficiency required for knowledge, then the claim that belief is knowledge may be sustainable. So can and does belief, through its malleability, ever meet knowledge's requirement of sufficiency?

Let's admit two ideas: first, because belief sets a lower bar for sufficiency it is thus, second, more malleable in possibilities than knowledge. If sufficiency is a matter of being relevant (qualitative sufficiency) and enough (quantitative sufficiency), belief tolerates looser relevance and less adequacy because to insist on the same as knowledge does would keep belief from serving its function as a substitute for knowledge when it is absent or uncertain. Belief *has* to be willing to settle for less to call itself sufficient. But that does not exclude the possibility

195

that after reaching its lower bar it also manages to achieve knowledge's higher bar. So the possibility of belief in some cases also being knowledge remains real.

Our various thinkers do not agree on the degree of sufficiency required to say knowledge has been achieved. This means the possibility of whether belief can meet the bar of sufficiency for knowledge varies with how high or low the bar for knowledge is set. For instance, the Pyrrhonian Skeptics set what all others see as a ridiculously high bar for sufficiency, arguing that unless full and certain information is at hand—and its counterbalancing opposite lacking—knowledge cannot be said to have been achieved. Whatever theoretical possibility they might have allowed for achieving knowledge, in practice the Skeptics simply make it impossible. The Roman Epicurean poet Lucretius undoubtedly speaks the sentiment common against the extreme demands of the Skeptics.

> In fact, if anyone considers it impossible to know (*sciri*) anything, then such a person does not know (*nescit*) if it is possible to know (*sciri*) that, because this person confesses he knows (*scire*) nothing! Consequently, here I find no cause to contest against such a one, who stands stubbornly stationary on his head.[458]

Epicurus himself puts the matter more succinctly: "Nothing is sufficient for the one to whom what is sufficient is too little."[459] Some people can never be satisfied.

But most, perhaps all, of the so-called Dogmatists—including, according to Pyrrhonian Skeptics, the New Academy Skeptics—conceive of sufficiency in such a manner that it can be attained so that knowledge can be claimed to have been achieved. The malleability of belief then means that it *might* reach that bar. This is where the idea floated by Plato's Socrates of "justified true belief" being knowledge enters in. The New Academy's Carneades and Clitomachus may prefer to hedge things by speaking of probability, but for them a persuasive belief that meets their epistemological criteria can at least be called probably true and knowledge. The Epicureans similarly put the bar for sufficiency within reach, and do so for the sake of the practicality of everyday living. Even the Stoics, for whom there is such distaste for belief as to theoretically equate it with ignorance, acknowledge the role belief plays in life. They have a high bar for knowledge, and a low one for belief, thus constantly encouraging people not to settle for belief as a substitute for knowledge.

Through questions like those we have just asked, and many more, we can come ever closer to understanding knowledge and belief, and the relation between them. Our work has been preliminary and partial, but represents a start and all who stretch toward knowledge must start somewhere.

---

[458] Lucretius, *On the Nature of Things*, IV.469-472. The Skeptic's refusal to budge is depicted vividly as being like a person who rather than standing solidly on two feet instead tries to stand on his feet.

[459] Epicurus, *Fragments*, 68 (Bailey, *Epicurus*, 116, for the Greek text).

Appendix I:
Decision Tree on Epistemological Position

This appendix is devoted to a short series of steps to assist in better stretching toward knowledge through a guided sequence of decisions on very basic matters. This process is intended to help clarify the reader's present understanding. This material is best used if, having established what one currently thinks, it then spurs on further, closer reflection.

This section utilizes what is called a decision tree. The idea is that through forced choices one traces a path of ideas reflected by answers to questions aimed to progressively sort through the positions of our various thinkers. This tree is limited in that it confines itself to what we have been examining and asks the reader to translate her or his thinking back into ancient ideas and positions. Nevertheless, by doing this exercise one may better identify the influence of these important thinkers on one's present understanding of matters.

At each step select the answer that best fits your present understanding; then follow the arrow. With multiple arrows from a choice, choose only one.

To begin, let us return to a basic conviction shared by these various Greek thinkers: *knowledge is about what is real.* In terms of the metaphysical positions of our ancient thinkers, we can identify the following basic positions. Choose one.

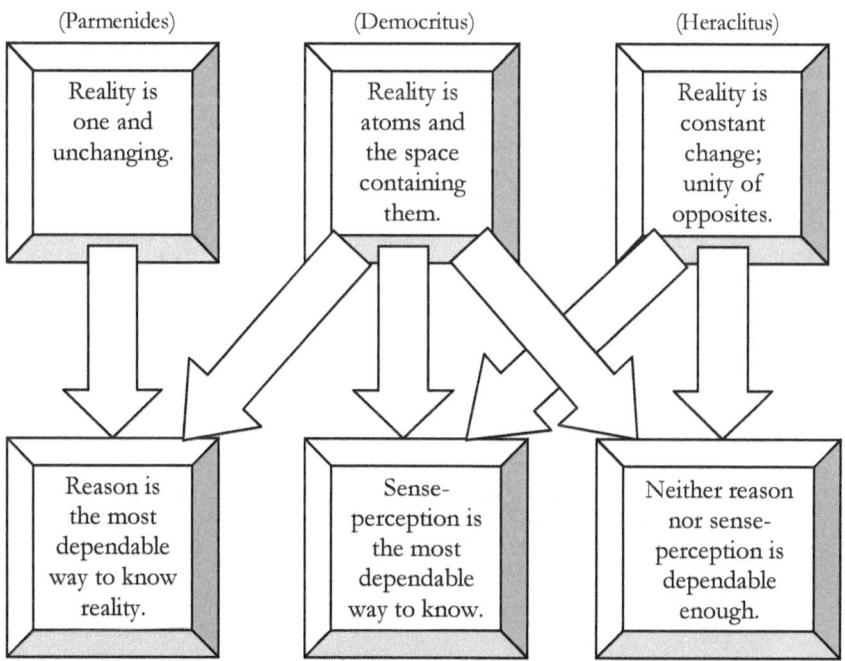

(Continue on the next page by starting with where you ended here.)

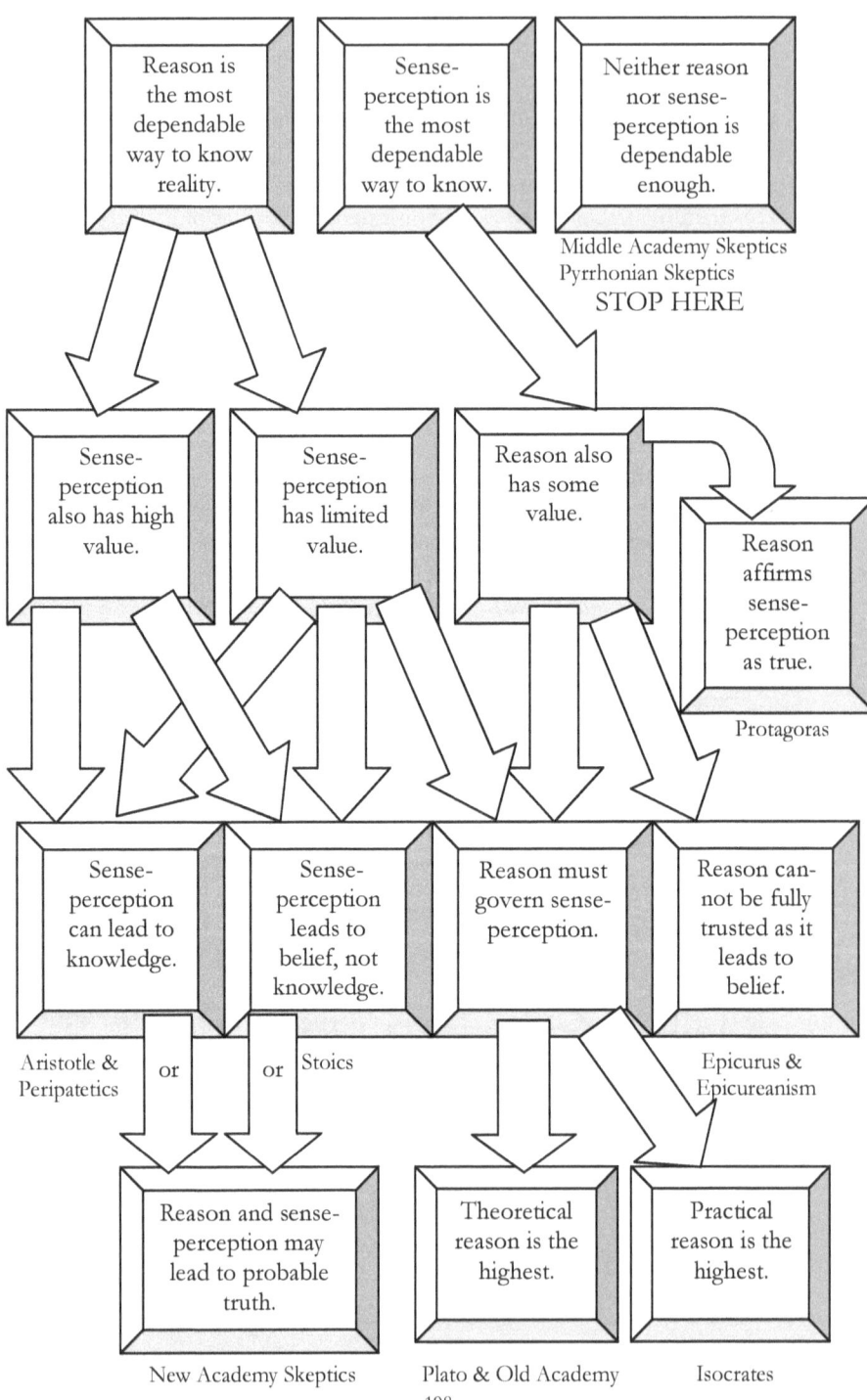

Reason is the most dependable way to know reality.

Sense-perception is the most dependable way to know.

Neither reason nor sense-perception is dependable enough.

Middle Academy Skeptics
Pyrrhonian Skeptics
STOP HERE

Sense-perception also has high value.

Sense-perception has limited value.

Reason also has some value.

Reason affirms sense-perception as true.

Protagoras

Sense-perception can lead to knowledge.

Sense-perception leads to belief, not knowledge.

Reason must govern sense-perception.

Reason cannot be fully trusted as it leads to belief.

Aristotle & Peripatetics   or   or   Stoics

Epicurus & Epicureanism

Reason and sense-perception may lead to probable truth.

Theoretical reason is the highest.

Practical reason is the highest.

New Academy Skeptics

Plato & Old Academy

Isocrates

Appendix II:
Short Summaries of Views on Belief

The Presocratics: Protagoras

We began our journey with Protagoras' provocative proposal that human beings are the measure of all things. By 'all' he meant both things that *are*, and things that *are not*, or to put it more simply, *reality*. People decide what reality is. As noted in chapter 3, Protagoras' position allows one to sidestep the metaphysical problem posed to epistemology about what really *is* by reducing epistemology to a psychology of belief about how things *appear to be*. It looks like this:

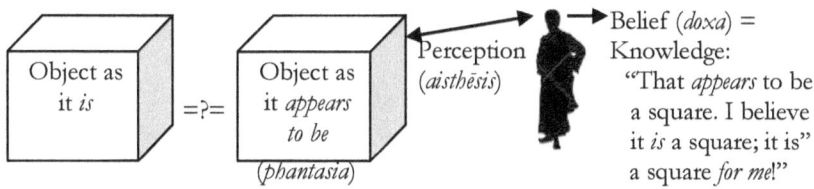

We may not know what an object is 'in itself,' but that pales in importance next to knowing an object as 'it appears to be.' That is because we can *always* know what something appears to be for us in this moment. As Socrates' friend Theaetetus first put it when trying to define knowledge, it is all about perception. For Protagoras, perception of what appears to be produces belief and such belief is what knowledge is *for me*. There is no difference between knowledge and belief because everything is relative to the individual.

The element highlighted by Protagoras' position is judgment. Belief is the taking up of a position that demonstrates how a person is the 'measure' of reality. A person judges her or his perceptions, and asserts them to be true. One is persuaded by what appears to be. This permits an individual to exercise trust in his or her own person. It yields confidence, as well as a reliance on one's own perceptual abilities and interpretation of them. Of course, there is variability in all of this; some perceptions are more persuasive than others and sometimes what we perceive changes. But, says Protagoras, change does not mean our first belief was incorrect. It simply means we exchanged one correct perception for another—and, hopefully, the latter one is better in terms of being healthier.

This last thought is especially important with respect to shared or communal beliefs. Individuals live in groups and groups also have beliefs. Each group, like each individual, has its own perception of things, makes judgments, asserts beliefs, and considers it knowledge. The goal of group belief is to present a standard of excellence and health that aids each individual member. Because belief is relative, it can be changed, and it can be changed in the direction of health and well-being. No individual, or group, has the right to judge the belief of another person or community as false, though judgments about its healthiness may and should be made.

Given the difficulties inherent in differentiating the position of Socrates from that of Plato we shall consider the two of them together. We examined their thinking about knowledge and belief in chapters 4-5. In the first of these two chapters we saw Socrates discuss with Theaetetus what the nature of knowledge is and, along the way, what belief is about. Most particularly, Socrates wrestled with the idea of whether, as Protagoras thinks, *all* beliefs are true. Can any belief be false?

Eventually Plato decides beliefs *can* be false. But some can be true. In fact, the idea that some can be both true and warranted leads to perhaps the most famous of all ideas about the relation of belief and knowledge, that knowledge is justified true belief. But that does not tell us what belief is. To probe this matter Plato uses both the words *doxa* and *pistis*.

In the *Republic* Plato subsumes *pistis* under *doxa*. His first use of *pistis* juxtaposes it with *doxa* and reveals for each what is central to him: judgment in the case of *doxa* and confident trust in the case of *pistis*. However, both *doxa* and *pistis* belong to the Sensible world—this realm of perceptions. In this world our human perceptions lead people to taking up positions (*doxa*), usually with confidence and trust in their accuracy (*pistis*), and this is what "belief" is. In direct comparison to one another, *pistis* is narrower in meaning. When Plato does his famous 'divided line' it seems *pistis* is the highest kind of belief—belief when it rises above mere imagining and takes a position in the Sensible world that represents the best a person can do apart from knowledge.

If we try to picture the matter we might be okay with this illustration:

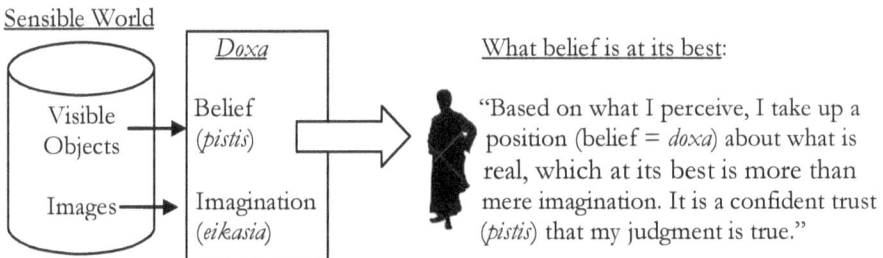

Sensible World

Plato does not wish to sidestep the metaphysical challenge like Protagoras does. He thinks belief is better than ignorance, that it has a real place in human affairs, but that not all beliefs are true. At its best belief is true, and confident trust in one's judgments may be warranted. But always belief entails some assertion about the way things are. Because belief is by nature malleable, some beliefs are stronger, some weaker; some are true, some false. Stronger beliefs (*pistis*) are based on evidence (e.g., what can be seen), which makes them more reliable. Also, the nature of stronger belief is that it is more persuasive.

Isocrates

As we saw in chapter 6, Plato's colleague Isocrates has a more positive appreciation of belief. He disdains the kind of theoretical musing and sophistical hair-splitting he finds in 'philosophers' around him—including Plato. Isocrates thinks belief is the very practical exercise of taking up a position (*doxa*) in such a way that it most of the time hits the target of the practical matter it is aimed at. Belief is practical because it is what is at hand and it *works*. In a world where a great number of matters are ambiguous and knowledge seems clearly unattainable, one must still *act*. Life goes on whether one has knowledge of something or not, and so it is prudent to focus on doing the best one can. That is what both belief and life are about for Isocrates: *doing the best one can*.

Belief is the art of taking up a workable position on imprecise matters. He likens it to archery, and as we did before, we can illustrate his position using such an image:

> Belief is the taking up of a position relative to a target, then taking careful aim by considering as many relevant factors as possible. It is also assertive action because it lets loose its arrow and so long as it hits the target reasonably enough to get by, that is quite sufficient. Belief need not be perfect; it only has to be *good enough* to reach one's intended target (or further progress toward it).

Isocrates sees belief as something belonging to an individual but not as solely an individualistic matter. He thinks a thoughtful person in taking aim uses the wisest counsel he or she can access, and like sailors at sea, relies on some fixed criterion to be guided by. That criterion is a purposeful goal. In life as a whole, Isocrates favors having a guiding purpose that helps directs one's aim toward goals.

The elements of belief most visibly prominent in Isocrates' position are judgment and malleability. He emphasizes the importance of taking a position—a purposeful aiming at a goal-directed target. But he recognizes that the complexity and uncertainty of much of life mean that beliefs will be highly malleable, both in their use of relevant information and in their adaptive effectiveness. Strong beliefs are marked both by being well-suited to meaningful goals and by being generally successful in meeting them. Isocrates also highlights the roles of trust and reliance, especially in seeking out sound advice from others. He understands every belief is an assertion of some kind, whether spoken or acted. He frames the whole process within a context where being educated, mastering one's culture, speaking well (i.e., persuasively), and contributing to society are all relevant to the formation of individual beliefs and the construction of a global belief system.

Plato's most famous student, Aristotle, loved words and often gave to them specialized meanings for technical philosophical use. As we saw in chapter 7, four words that can be rendered by our English word "belief" are important for us to consider. Two of these terms are our basic and familiar words *doxa* and *pistis*. In addition ὑπόληπψις (*hupolēpsis*), a word used occasionally by other philosophers, and ἔνδοξα (*endoxa*) are important—especially the latter. Of these four words, *endoxa* is the one most associated with Aristotle's conception of belief.

Because Aristotle draws on four terms, and because the incomplete nature of his work raises problems with finding as much consistency and exactness in usage as one might desire, summarizing Aristotle's conception of belief is especially challenging. Fortunately, one remark he makes seems to offer a key: "Every belief position (*doxē*) implicates a belief conviction (*pistis*), belief conviction likewise with persuasion, and persuasion with reason (*logos*)."[460] Here is a chain that says when we look at *doxa* it is reasonable to presume *pistis* is also present, and that *pistis* has come about from persuasion and persuasion as a result of *logos*. If I may say it in another way: we can reasonably assume that *in belief we have the taking up of a position that is based in personal conviction following being persuaded for specific reasons.*

Aristotle's use of *hupolēpsis* is a challenge. On the one hand, it can refer to a cognition employing reason to render judgments. On the other hand, it can refer to judgments that are weak, such as mere opinion. What it adds to our overall sense of Aristotle's conception of belief is another underscoring of his sense that belief is rooted in cognition. It is a matter first and foremost of thinking, where one makes judgments (i.e., takes up a position), for reasons.

Among the reasons one might take up a position is the influence of others. That is where the most significant term—*endoxa*—comes into play. Once again Aristotle's own words are especially important. He explains that *endoxa* refers to "the strongly endorsed beliefs held by all, or by most people, or by the wisest (i.e., philosophers), or simply put, those beliefs endorsed by all, or by most, or by the most notable of people."[461] What appeals to Aristotle about *endoxa* is that it is more stable than individual *doxa*. This means he envisions the best belief as *shared and enduring.* In such belief, communities—whether social or professional—are united by a common frame of reference and judgment.

For Aristotle, as it had been for his teacher Plato, belief belongs to the world of phenomena, to things as they *appear to be.* The role of *endoxa* is important in more than one way. First, the existence of strongly endorsed beliefs in a community means the individual in that community need not wrestle with

---

[460] Aristotle, *On the Soul,* 428a [III.3]. Rather than render both the forms of *doxa* and *pistis* as 'belief,' I have used phrases: "belief position" for δόξη (*doxē*), and "belief conviction: for πίστις (*pistis*). Obviously, there are other ways to render the text. Many use "opinion" for *doxē,* and a choice like "conviction" (used alone) for *pistis* in order to tease out the same senses I aim at with my phrases.
[461] Aristotle, *Topics,* 100a [I.1]. Cf. 105a [I.14].

forming individual belief in a vacuum. Many individual beliefs (*doxa*) are shaped in conformity with community beliefs or expert positions (*endoxa*), and that saves time, mental wear and tear, and stress. Moreover, when individual belief aligns with widely endorsed belief—*doxa* with *endoxa*—increased confidence, persuasion, and reliance occur. In short, such a match strengthens belief.

Although Aristotle emphasizes the connection to reason (*logos*), it is not hard to see how the intimately personal dimension of trust enters in. As Aristotle envisions it, belief is ultimately rooted in solid arguments that persuade a person to express a judgment of trust—in a thing, person, idea, or widely endorsed position. Implicit in *doxa* is *pistis* and both are most reliably enduring when they also part of *endoxa*. Though Aristotle aims at being a realist who soberly observes and reports the world, and who recognizes great variability in belief, one can catch a vision of belief not only as it is in its many degrees, but as it can be at its best.

If we try to picture such 'best belief' it might look like this:

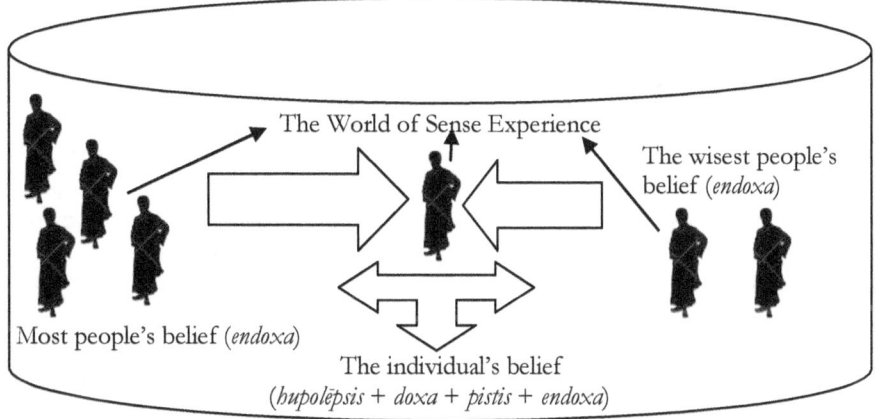

Each person interpreting the world of sense experience uses cognitive judgments (*hupolēpsis*) to take up belief positions (*doxa*) showing belief conviction (*pistis*) persuaded by *logos*. As this is happening, the influence of other peoples' strongly endorsed beliefs (*endoxa*) exerts itself. The individual, to belong to the community, typically endorses what is already strongly endorsed by others. This is not only what usually happens but is thought by Aristotle to be what is usually best to happen, since the result is more stable and enduring.

But Aristotle is aware of the existence of minority beliefs—*paradoxa*—the beliefs that run counter to the majority. These beliefs cannot be summarily rejected, he thinks, because *they might be right*. And individual beliefs can alter community beliefs. Thus variability always persists and maximizes adaptiveness precisely because any given individual at any given time might be right, might persuade others, and might aid a stretching toward knowledge and truth.

We began our discussion of Hellenistic figures and schools by noting that the situation in the world encountered by our thinkers led to important changes in the focus of epistemology. There was a shift in emphasis away from theoretical knowledge to practical knowledge and ethics. There was a reframing of the basic epistemological query from 'What is knowledge?' to 'Is knowledge possible?' New schools and movements came into existence, spread, and prospered. We examined the Epicureans, Stoics, and branches of Skepticism (Middle Academy, New Academy, and Pyrrhonism).

Epicurus & the Epicureans

Like Aristotle, Epicurus (chapter 8) thinks belief belongs to the rational part of the *psyche*. As such, belief is a cognitive judgment—a supposition (*hupolēpsis*)—about things. In Epicurus' view belief results from sense-perception and is thereby strongly tied to any general conception (*prolēpsis*) derived from repeated sense-perceptions. In fact, a *prolēpsis* may be considered not only a kind of belief itself, but always a true one. That is because according to Epicurus all sense-perceptions are true, these are reliably stored in memory, and the resulting general conception can be trusted and relied upon.

But that does not make *prolēpsis* the whole of belief or even its most prominent aspect. Indeed, like philosophers before him, Epicurus uses *doxa* as his basic word for belief and it is not the same as *prolēpsis*. Any given individual belief (*doxa*) can be a misapplication of a correct general belief (*prolēpsis*); all belief is fundamentally supposition (*hupolēpsis*) and so prone to the errors that enter when reason is at play. As mentioned in the chapter, this happens when, for example, the correct general belief of a dog is misapplied to the individual judgment that an animal in the distance is a dog when it is really a cat. In short, correct general beliefs do not infallibly lead to correct individual beliefs.

Belief, for Epicurus, is primarily an individual taking up of a position—making a judgment—that either is confirmed by the evidence as true in affirming a general conception and specific sense-experience, or lacks such evidence and is false. So *beliefs can be either true or false and the distinction between them lies in whether they are adequately supported by evidence.* We can illustrate his position thusly:

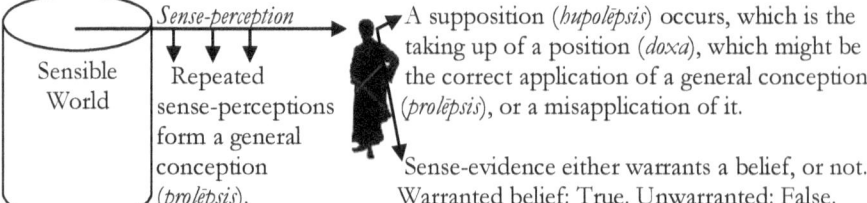

Fundamentally, belief is either a correct or incorrect judgment about some sense-perception. To be true they must be supported by evidence.

Stoics

Stoicism has been divided into three periods—Early, Middle, and Late—and we examined figures from each (chapter 9). One conviction the Stoics share in common is the preeminence of reason and the possibility of achieving knowledge. But unlike philosophers such as Socrates, Plato, and Aristotle, the Stoics set such a strong contrast between knowledge and belief that the latter can actually be equated with ignorance.

In Stoicism belief is the taking up of a position (*doxa*) absent comprehension (*katalēpsis*) as its criterion. This is why *belief is like ignorance: it freely offers assent to matters without relying on direct comprehension of them*. This means people may get things right—have true beliefs—but it is by accident rather than by design. Even though belief is under the jurisdiction of reason, an aspect of the rational *psyche*, it is what happens when reason is allowed to go amuck, without the guidance of a sound criterion for distinguishing true from false.

Let us see if this picture can be caught in an illustration.

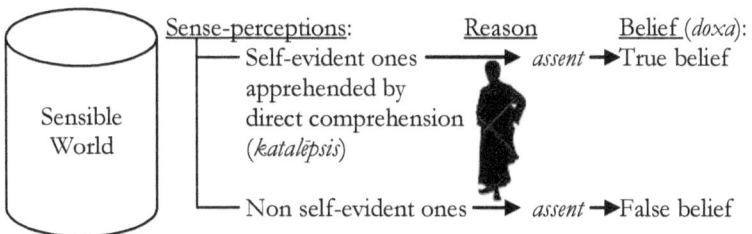

This general sensibility about belief is why Stoics also can speak about emotions (*pathē*) as belonging to belief. They also are a part of the rational *psyche*, expressing judgment by taking up a position. Feelings are, in short, a particular species of *doxa*—belief judgment that something is good or bad, a present fact or a future expectation. As we saw in the chapter on Stoicism, such belief is characterized by five qualities: "rationality"; judgment as making a supposition (*hupolēpsis*); erraticism, or exceeding motion; immediacy (i.e., "freshness"); and impermanence. So we can adjust the above illustration as follows:

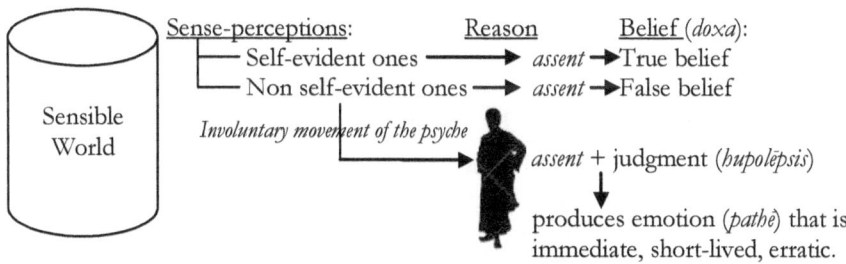

In this adjusted picture, strong feelings originate in an involuntary movement of the *psyche* in response to something experienced, which then is voluntarily given assent, with judgment, leading to belief as strong feeling.

205

The Skeptics never forged a common school from out of their various approaches. Instead, they took divergent paths that ended up in opposition to one another. We examined (chapter 10) the Middle Academy position represented by Arcesilaus; the New Academy position represented by Carneades, Clitomachus, and Philo; and Pyrrhonism as represented by Pyrrho, Timon, Aenesidemus, and especially by Sextus Empiricus.

Pyrrhonism, as set out by Sextus Empiricus, distinguishes between an acceptable kind of 'belief' (*dogma*) and unacceptable 'Belief' (*Dogma*). The acceptable kind is the sort of *doxa* that arises in the immediacy of being moved by something one experiences. For example, the belief "I am cold" is one occasioned in the present by some sensation and the assertion merely observes and reports what one is feeling; it is an assent to the fact of one's present experience. For a Skeptic this is a harmless, common "belief." What is not harmless, in the Pyrrhonist view, is the kind of *Dogma* that is an entrenched, stable, enduring and passionate belief that passes itself off as actual knowledge.

The Pyrrhonist says, then, that there are two kinds of belief, though both are rooted in persuasion. In either case, *all belief is a judgment—a taking up of a position (doxa)—following persuasion.* However, in the kind of belief someone who is a Dogmatist experiences, the persuasion leads to a strong sense of conviction. The person trusts and relies on the belief, asserts it strongly and with great confidence. In contrast, the Skeptic is persuaded in a more casual, less committed fashion. The Skeptic simply follows along with something to see where it might lead. There is a suspension of any final judgment; the matter simply seems to be the case *right now.* We can picture the Pyrrhonist position like this:

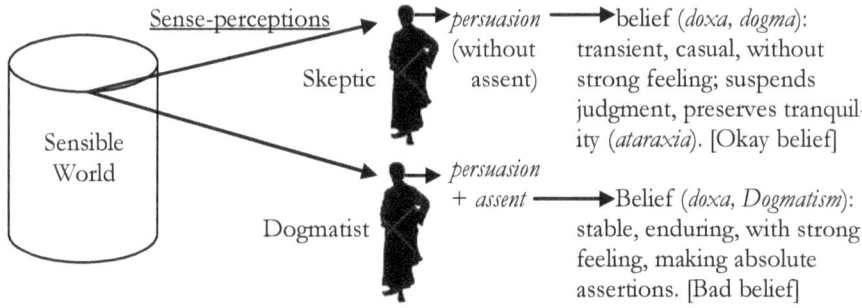

Sense-perceptions

Sensible World

Skeptic — *persuasion* (without assent) — belief (*doxa, dogma*): transient, casual, without strong feeling; suspends judgment, preserves tranquility (*ataraxia*). [Okay belief]

Dogmatist — *persuasion + assent* — Belief (*doxa, Dogmatism*): stable, enduring, with strong feeling, making absolute assertions. [Bad belief]

Though the Skeptic may be said to have 'belief' he or she does not have 'Belief.' In fact, Pyrrhonian Skeptics like to say they are "without belief" (*adoxastōs*). But what they seem to mean is they do not have a conflictual and unsettling dogmatic belief, with all its absolute assertions about things, like others do. The key difference is a simple one: the Pyrrhonian Skeptic refrains from giving assent to persuasive perceptions as being true (even 'probably' true), or as constituting knowledge.

Skepticism: The Middle Academy (Arcesilaus)

Under the leadership of Arcesilaus, the Academy turned toward Skepticism. Like Pyrrhonists, the Academicians of the Middle Academy like to say they are without belief. But Arcesilaus' conception of how this is possible appears to be distinctive as his own contribution though the final presentation is one that a Pyrrhonist like Sextus Empiricus finds congenial.

Arcesilaus seems to envision belief as one possible movement of the *psyche*, but not a necessary one. However, the world of sensations does occasion inevitable and necessary movements of the *psyche* as it impacts us. The first and primary movement Arcesilaus recognizes is the involuntary movement occasioned by sense-perception. A second, responsive movement—also quite natural in origin—is an internal impulse aroused by this sense-perception that generates goal-directed behavior. These first two movements are quite acceptable, being in accord with Nature. A third possible movement, though, is the formation of belief—and it is *un*natural. It is neither inevitable, nor necessary. In fact, the taking up of a position (*doxa*) is avoidable and should be avoided.

In chapter 10 this simple illustration was used to show his thinking:

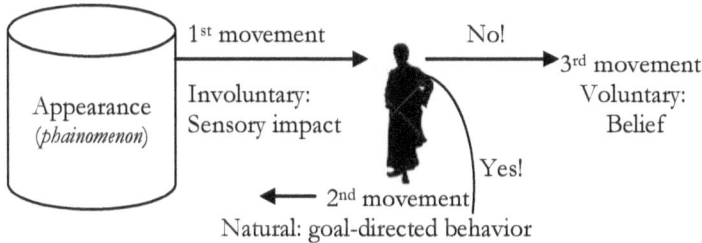

Now, however, we might modify our picture to perhaps better explain *why* it is desirable to avoid the movement of belief.

The second movement is a *natural* and appropriate response to environmental stimuli, one that is goal-directed toward ethical action. The third movement—belief—is *unnatural* because it is the voluntary intervention by the human will to choose its own position and direction. This leads to conflict and the absence of tranquility. Accordingly, in suspending judgment the Skeptic simply follows along the natural path suggested by Nature through environmental stimuli and avoids the artificially induced chaos of a mind filled with belief.

The New Academy Skepticism developed by Carneades and his followers is regarded by Pyrrhonists as just one more kind of Dogmatism, like that of the Stoics, Epicureans, or Peripatetics. But that is a one-sided view; the New Academy sees its position as substantially different from, and at odds with, Stoics and others. In their view, they avoid unreasonable claims to *know* something but find reasonable grounds for beliefs that are more-likely-than-not true.

The New Academy position is that *belief is a strong persuasion that something is true that continues to persuade us of its truthfulness and repeated testing of it confirms this persuasion.* In essence, Carneades sets three criteria for establishing a belief as more-likely-than-not true. (These all presuppose that whatever the object of belief is, it has generated a true appearance and this is what the individual is responding to when these criteria are applied.) First, a person must be strongly persuaded that what *appears to be* is true. Second, everything about the appearance must be congruent so that no factor strikes one as false but instead everything appears correct, and this continues to be the case. Third, upon close and repeated examination this process of testing continues to strongly persuade the person that the matter is true. None of this guarantees the belief to be correct; it is never knowledge and it is never a certain belief either. It is at best *probable*, but that is sufficient for effective action needed in daily life.

As we saw in chapter 10, Carneades' position has been styled as seeking "probable belief." Unlike Stoics and Epicureans, New Academy Skeptics resist claims to know something and instead modestly seek what seems to be true because it persuades us in the manner just described. We might picture his position in this manner:

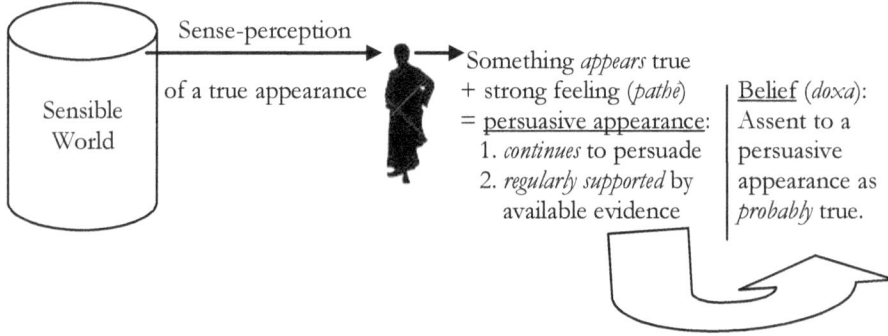

Belief is not where one starts, but where one ends—*after* strong persuasion that has been thoroughly vetted. In this manner, one might refer to Carneades' probable belief as much like the conception of true, warranted belief. But if one does so, then the criticism of the Pyrrhonists that this view is essentially a dogmatic claim to knowledge may have merit. Exactly where Carneades stood on such matters has been a subject of debate since his own time and we shall not resolve it here.

Appendix III: Key Figures & Schools

A very rough separation chronologically is shown by the staggered columns, but this is chiefly meant to show the order of appearance of the schools. Within each column the order of the thinkers within that school is also roughly indicated (e.g., Cleanthes follows Zeno). Vertical arrows show lines of influence; horizontal arrows show the movement of a person from one school to another.

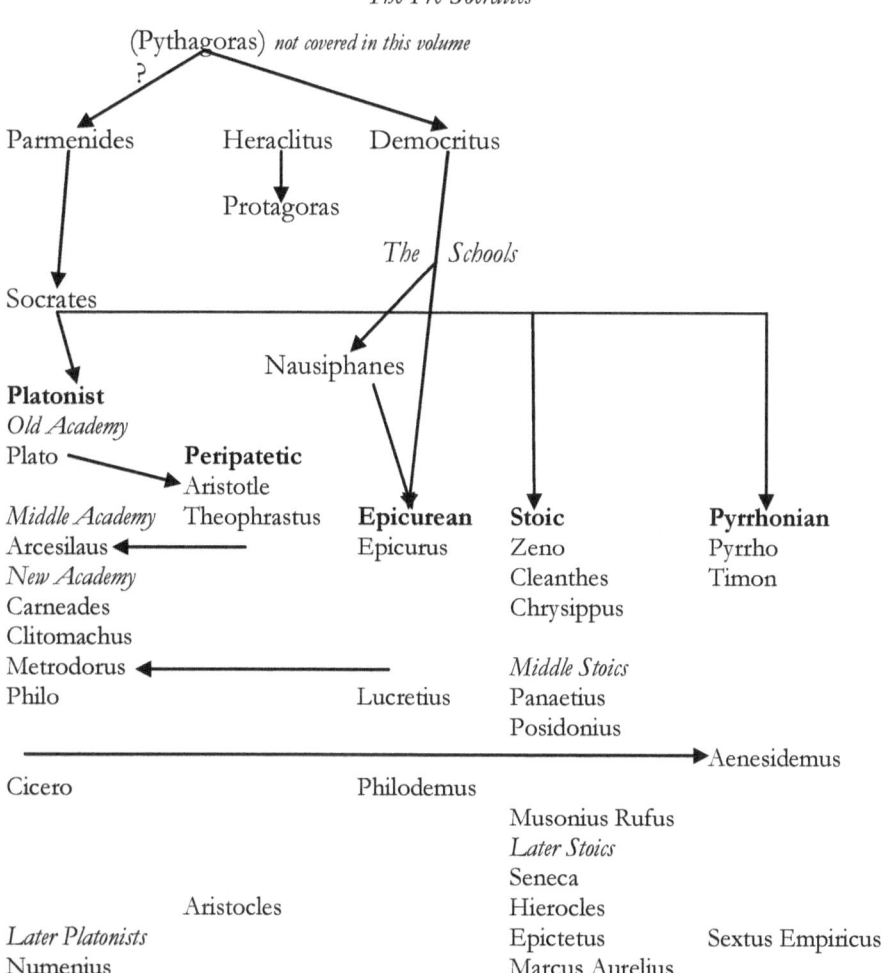

The Pre-Socratics

(Pythagoras) *not covered in this volume*

Parmenides   Heraclitus   Democritus

Protagoras

The Schools

Socrates

Nausiphanes

Platonist
Old Academy
Plato — **Peripatetic**
Aristotle
Middle Academy   Theophrastus   **Epicurean**   **Stoic**   **Pyrrhonian**
Arcesilaus   Epicurus   Zeno   Pyrrho
New Academy   Cleanthes   Timon
Carneades   Chrysippus
Clitomachus
Metrodorus   *Middle Stoics*
Philo   Lucretius   Panaetius
Posidonius

Aenesidemus

Cicero   Philodemus

Musonius Rufus
Later Stoics
Seneca
Aristocles   Hierocles
Later Platonists   Epictetus   Sextus Empiricus
Numenius   Marcus Aurelius

Isocrates was a colleague of both Plato and Aristotle, but not a member of either's school. He headed his own, but in terms of philosophy as it developed his school cannot be listed among those shown above.

Lucian, who takes a Skeptic's perspective in the *Hermotimus*, cannot be identified with any particular Skeptic perspective and so is not included above.

Appendix IV: Greek Key Words

The translations here are not the only possible ones but the chief ones used in this volume.

Greek	Transliteration	Translation	Notes
ἄγνοια	agnoia	ignorance	A lack of knowledge.
ἀδόξαστος	adoxastōs	without belief	A Skeptic claim.
αἴσθησις	aisthēsis	sense-perception	Perception by the senses (or by the intellect).
ἀλήθεια	alētheia	truth	What philosophers seek; related
ἀληθές	alēthēs	true	to the criterion for knowledge.
ἄλογος	alogos	irrational, or without reason	A basic contrast to the sense of *logos* as "reason."
ἀταραξία	ataraxia	tranquility	A psychological state of equanimity characterized by peace of mind; a key term in Skepticism.
γνῶσις	gnosis	knowledge	A common word for knowledge.
δόγμα	dogma	official teachings, judgments	Received assertions, beliefs, or principles accepted as true.
δόξα	doxa	belief	Principal words used in philoso-
δοξάζω	doxazō	believe	phy for "belief/believing."
ἔνδοξα	endoxa	widely-credited belief	A key term for Aristotle. What most or the best people believe.
ἐπιστήμη	epistēmē	knowledge	Full and certain information sufficient to understand a thing.
ἐποχή	epochē	suspension (of judgment)	Key term in Skepticism.
κατάληψις	katalēpsis	direct comprehension	Key Stoic term; often translated as "apprehension."
λόγος	logos	reason	An important and robust word in Greek, with different meanings.
πείθω	peithō	to persuade	Verb closely related to the noun *pistis* (belief, trust, faith).
πιστεύω	pisteuō	believe	Verb partner to noun *pistis*.
πίστις	pistis	belief, trust, confidence	Famous as the word "faith" in the New Testament.
πρόληψις	prolēpsis	anticipation, preconception	Epicurean term for "a general conception" built up in memory from repeated sense-perceptions.
ὑπόληψις	hupolēpsis	supposition	Used occasionally for a "weak belief" or "opinion."
φαινόμενα	phainomena	appearance	Objects of sense-perception, used as a synonym for *phantasia*.
φαντασία	phantasia	appearance	What the senses perceive.
συγκατάθεσις	sunkatathesis	assent	Key term in Stoicism.

Bibliography

Aristocles. *Aristocles of Messene. Testimonies and Fragments*, edited by Maria L. Chiesara. Oxford Classical Monographs. Oxford: Oxford Univ. Press, 2001.

Aristotle. *Aristotelis Ars Rhetorica*, edited by W. D. Ross. Scriptorum Classicorum Bibliotheca Oxoniensis. Oxford: Oxford Univ. Press, 1959.

———. *Aristotelis Politica*, edited by W. D. Ross. Scriptorum Classicorum Bibliotheca Oxoniensis. Oxford: Oxford Univ. Press, 1957.

———. *Aristotle. De anima*. Translated by R. D. Hicks. London: Cambridge Univ. Press, 1907.

———. *Aristotle. The Metaphysics. Books I–IX*. Translated by Hugh Tredennick. New York: Putnam, 1933.

———. *Aristotle. Minor Works: On Colors–On Things Heard–Physiognomics–On Plants–On Marvelous Things Heard–Mechanical Problems–On Indivisible Lines–Situations and Names of Winds–On Melissus, Xenophanes, and Gorgias*. Translated by W. S. Hett. Loeb Classical Library. Cambridge: Harvard Univ. Press, 1955.

———. *Aristotle. The Nicomachean Ethics*. Translated by H. Rackham. Loeb Classical Library. Cambridge: Harvard Univ. Press, 1956.

———. *Aristotle. Physics, Books 1–4*. Rev. ed. Translated by P. H. Wicksteed and F. M. Cornford. Loeb Classical Library. Cambridge: Harvard Univ. Press, 1957.

———. *Aristotle. Posterior Analytics, Topica*. Translated by Hugh Tredennick (*Posterior Analytics*) and E. S. Forster (*Topica*). Loeb Classical Library. Cambridge: Harvard Univ. Press, 1960.

———. *Aristotle. Problems: Books 1–19. Rhetoric to Alexander*, edited and translated by Robert Mayhew. Loeb Classical Library. Cambridge: Harvard Univ. Press, 2011.

———. *Aristotle. Problems: Books 20–38. Rhetoric to Alexander*, edited and translated by Robert Mayhew and David C. Mirhady. Loeb Classical Library. Cambridge: Harvard Univ. Press, 2011.

Aurelius, Marcus. *The Communings with Himself of Marcus Aurelius Antoninus*. Translated by C. R. Haines. Loeb Classical Library. New York: Putnam, 1916.

———. *M. Antonius Imperator Ad Se Ipsum*, edited by Jan Hendrik Leopold. Leipzig: Teubneri, 1908.

Bolich, G. G. *Chasing the Ghost. Adventures Finding and Knowing God*. Spokane: EVS, 2017.

———. *Honest Belief, Credible Faith. The History and Nature of Belief, Believing, and Faith*. Spokane: EVS, 2018.

Brittain, Charles. *Philo of Larissa: Last of the Academic Skeptics.* Oxford Classical Monographs. New York: Oxford Univ. Press, 2001.

Cicero, M. Tullius. *The Academica of Cicero. The Text Revised and Explained,* edited by James S. Reid. London: Macmillan, 1874.

———. *Brutus. Orator.* Translated by G. L. Hendrickson (*Brutus*) and H. M. Hubbell (*Orator*). Loeb Classical Library. Cambridge: Harvard Univ. Press, 1939.

———. *Cicero, XIX: De Natura Deorum, Academica.* Translated by H. Rackham. Cambridge: Harvard Univ. Press, 1967.

———. *Cicero. Tusculan Disputations.* Translated by J. E. King. Loeb Classical Library. Cambridge: Harvard Univ. Press, 1927.

———. *De Finibus Bonorum et Malorum.* Translated by H. Rackham. New York: Macmillan, 1914.

———. *De Finibus Bonorum et Malorum librae quinque,* edited by Theodor Schiche. M. Tulli Ciceronis scripta quae manserunt omnia, 43. Leipzig. Teubner. 1915.

———. *De Inventione, De Optimo Genere Oratorum, Topica.* Translated by H. M. Hubbell. Cambridge: Harvard Univ. Press, 1949.

———. *M. Tulli Ciceronis Rhetorica,* edited by A. S. Wilkins. Scriptorum Classicorum Bibliotheca Oxoniensis. Oxford: Oxford Univ. Press, 1902.

———. *Rhetorici Libri Duo Qui Vocantur de Invention,* edited by Eduard Stroebel. Leipzig: Teubneri, 1915.

———. *Tusculanae Disputationes. M. Tullius Cicero,* edited by M. Pohlenz. Leipzig: Teubner, 1918.

Cleanthes. *Cleanthes' Hymn to Zeus: Text, Translation, and Commentary,* edited and translated by Johan C. Thom. Studies and Texts in Antiquity and Christianity, 33. Tübingen: Mohr Siebeck, 2005.

Clement of Alexandria. *Clemens Alexandrinus, Zweiter Band: Stromata Buch I–VI,* edited by Otto Stählin. Leipzig: Hinrichs, 1906.

Diels, Hermann, ed. *Die Fragmente der Vorsokratiker.* Berlin: Weidmannsche, 1906.

———. *Doxographi Graeci.* Berlin, Germany: Walter de Gryuter et socios, 1929.

Diogenes Laertius. *Lives of Eminent Philosophers, Vols. I–II.* Translated by R. D. Hicks. New York: G. P. Putnam's Sons, 1925.

Epictetus. *Epictetus. The Discourses as Reported by Arrian, The Manual, and Fragments. Vols. I–II.* Translated by W. A. Oldfather. Loeb Classical Library. Cambridge: Harvard Univ. Press, 1925.

Epicurus. *Epicurea,* edited by Hermann Usener. Leipzig, Germany: B. G. Teubner, 1887.

———. *Epicurus: The Extant Remains with Short Critical Apparatus, Translation and Notes,* edited and translated by Cyril Bailey. Oxford: Clarendon Press, 1926.

Eusebius. *Eusebii Caesariensis Opera, Volume II. Praeparationes Evangelicae, Libri XI–XV*, edited by Wilhelm Dindorf. Leipzig: Teubner, 1868.

Evans, Ernest, ed. and trans. *Tertullian's Treatise on the Incarnation: The Text Edited with an Introduction, Translation, and Commentary*. London: SPCK, 1956.

Freidenberg, Olga. *Image and Concept: Mythopoetic Roots of Literature*, edited by Nina Braginskaia and Kevin Moss. Translated by Kevin Moss. Sign/Text/Culture: Studies in Slavic and Comparative Semiotics 2. London: Routledge, 2014.

Galen. *Galeni. De Placitis Hippocratis et Platonis. (Galen. On the Doctrines of Hippocrates and Plato. First Part: Books I–V)* 3rd ed. Corpus Medicorum Graecorum, V 4, 1, 2, edited and translated by Phillip De Lacy. Berlin: Akademie Verlag, 2005.

Geldard, Richard G. *Parmenides and the Way of Truth*. Rhinebeck: Monkfish, 2007.

Gellius, Aulus. *The Attic Nights of Aulus Gellius, Volume II*. Translated by John C. Rolfe. New York: Putnam, 1927.

Gutas, Dimitri, ed. and trans. *Theophrastus. On First Principles (Known as His Metaphysics)*. Philosophia Antiqua, 119. Boston: Brill, 2010.

Hierocles. *Hierocles the Stoic: Elements of Ethics, Fragments, and Excerpts*, edited by Ilaria Ramelli. Translated by David Konstan. Atlanta: Society of Biblical Literature, 2009.

Isocrates. *Isocrates, Vols. I-II*. Translated by George Norlin. Loeb Classical Library. New York: Putnam, 1928-1929.

———. *Isocrates, Vol. III*. Translated by Larue Van Hook. Loeb Classical Library. Cambridge: Harvard Univ. Press, 1945.

Laks, André, and Glenn W. Most, eds. and translators. *Early Greek Philosophy, V: Western Greek Thinkers, Part 2*. Loeb Classical Library. Cambridge: Harvard Univ. Press, 2016.

Liddell, Henry G., and Robert Scott. *Greek-English Lexicon*. 9th ed. Oxford: Clarendon Press, 1996.

Long, A. A., and D. N. Sedley. *The Hellenistic Philosophers, volume 1: Translations of the Principal Sources with Philosophical Commentary*. New York: Cambridge Univ. Press, 1987.

Lucian. *Lucian, vol. VI*. Translated by K. Kilburn. Loeb Classical Library. Cambridge: Harvard Univ. Press, 1959.

Lucretius. *Lucretius. On the Nature of Things*. Translated by W. H. D. Rouse. Loeb Classical Library. Cambridge: Harvard Univ. Press, 1924.

Lutz, Cora E. "Musonius Rufus: 'The Roman Socrates.'" *Yale Classical Studies*, 10 (1947) 3–147.

Mekler, Siegfried, ed. *Academicorum Philosophorum Index Herculanensis*. Berlin: Weidmannos, 1902.

Numenius. *Numenius. Fragments*, edited by Edouard des Places. Paris: Belles Lettres, 1973.

Parmenides. *Parmenides of Elea. Fragments: A Text and Translation with an Introduction.* Translated by David Gallop. Toronto: Univ. of Toronto Press, 1984.

Pearson, A. C. *The Fragments of Zeno and Cleanthes.* London: C. J. Clay and Sons, 1891.

Philodemus. *Philodemi. Rhetorica,* edited by E. Gros. Paris: Instituti Regii Franciae, 1840.

———. *Philodemus: On Methods of Inference. A Study in Ancient Empiricism.* American Philological Association, X, edited by Phillip H. De Lacy & Estelle A. De Lacy. Lancaster: Lancaster Press, 1941.

———. *Philodemus: On Frank Criticism.* Translated by David Konstan et al. Atlanta: Scholars Press, 1998.

———. *The Rhetorica of Philodemus.* Translated by Harry M. Hubbell. Transactions of the Connecticut Academy of Arts and Sciences, vol. 23, 243–82. New Haven: Yale Univ. Press, 1920.

Plato. *Plato. Euthyphro. Apology. Crito. Phaedo,* edited and translated by Chris Emlyn-Jones and William Preddy. Loeb Classical Library. Cambridge: Harvard Univ. Press, 2017.

———. *Plato. Laches. Protagoras. Meno. Euthydemus.* Translated by W. R. M. Lamb. Loeb Classical Library. Cambridge: Harvard Univ. Press, 1924.

———. *Plato, I. Euthyphro, Apology, Crito, Phaedo, Phaedrus.* Translated by Harold N. Fowler. Loeb Classical Library. Cambridge: Harvard Univ. Press, 1914.

———. *Plato, II. Theaetetus. Sophist.* Translated by Harold N. Fowler. Loeb Classical Library. Cambridge: Harvard Univ. Press, 1921.

———. *Plato, IX. Timaeus. Critias, Cleitophon. Menexenus. Epistles.* Translated by R. G. Bury. Loeb Classical Library. Cambridge: Harvard Univ. Press, 1929.

———. *Platonis Opera, Vols. I–V,* edited by John Burnet. Oxford: Oxford University Press. 1903.

———. *Platonis Protagoras. The Protagoras of Plato: The Greek Text Revised, with an Analysis and English Notes,* edited by William Wayte. London: George Bell, 1854.

———. *The Republic of Plato, II (Bks. VI–X and Indexes).* Edited and translated by James Adam. Cambridge: Cambridge Univ. Press, 1907.

Plutarch. *Moralia, Volume XIV: That Epicurus Actually Makes a Pleasant Life Impossible. Reply to Colotes in Defence of Other Philosophers. Is "Live Unknown" a Wise Precept? On Music.* Translated by Benedict Einarson. Loeb Classical Library. Cambridge: Harvard Univ. Press, 1967.

———. *Plutarch. Lives, Volume III: Pericles and Fabius Maximus. Nicias and Crassus.* Translated by Bernadotte Perrin. Loeb Classical Library. Cambridge: Harvard Univ. Press, 1916.

Politis, Vasilis. *Routledge Philosophy Guidebook to Aristotle and the Metaphysics.* New York: Routledge, 2004.

Polito, Roberto. *Aenesidemus of Cnossus: Testimonia*. Cambridge Classical Texts and Commentaries, 52. Cambridge: Cambridge Univ. Press, 2014.

Posidonius. *Posidonius, I. The Fragments*. Cambridge Classical Texts and Commentaries, 13, edited by L. Edelstein and I. G. Kidd. New York: Cambridge Univ. Press, 1972.

———. *Posidonius, II. The Commentary: (i) Testimonia and Fragments 1–149*. Cambridge Classical Texts and Commentaries, 14a, edited by I. G. Kidd. New York: Cambridge Univ. Press, 1988.

———. *Posidonius, III: The Translation of the Fragments*, Cambridge Classical Texts and Commentaries, 36, edited and translated by I. G. Kidd. New York: Cambridge Univ. Press, 2004.

Seneca, Lucius Annaeus. *Seneca. Ad Lucilium Epistulae Morales, Vols. I–III*. Translated by Richard M. Gummere. Loeb Classical Library. Cambridge: Harvard Univ. Press, 1917–1925.

———. *Seneca. Moral Essays, Volume I: De Provedentia. De Constantia. De Ira. De Clementia*. Translated by John W. Basore. Loeb Classical Library. New York: Putnam, 1928.

———. *Seneca. Moral Essays, Volume II: De Consalitione de Marciam. De Vita Beata. De Otio. De Tranquillitate Animi. De Brevitate Vitae. De Consolatione ad Polybium. De Consolatione ad Helviam*. Translated by John W. Basore. Loeb Classical Library. Cambridge: Harvard Univ. Press, 1932.

Sextus Empiricus. *Sextus Empiricus, I: Outlines of Pyrrhonism*. Translated by R. G. Bury. New York: G. P. Putnam's Sons, 1933.

———. *Sextus Empiricus, II: Against the Logicians*. Translated by R. G. Bury. Cambridge: Harvard Univ. Press, 1935.

Stobaeus, *Eclogues*. In *Stoicorum Veterum Fragmenta, vols. I–IV*, edited by Hans von Arnim. Stuttgart: Teubner, 1964.

Tieleman, Teun. *Chrysippus' On Affections. Reconstruction and Interpretation*. Philosophica Antiqua. Boston: Brill, 2003.

Traversa, Antonio, ed. *Index Stoicorum Herculanensis*. Pubblicazioni dell'Istituto di filologia classica dell'Università di Genova, 1. Geneva: stituto di filologia classica, 1952.

Usener, Hermann, ed. *Epicurea*. Cambridge Library Collection. Leipzig: Teubner, 1887.

———, ed. *Theophrasti de Prima Philosophia Libellus*. Index Scholarum Bonnensium. Bonn: Typis Caroli Georgi Universitatis, 1890.

Von Arnim, Hans, ed. *XIV. Bemerkungen zum Index Stoicorum Herculanensis*. Sitzungs-berichte der Kais. Akademie der Wissenschaften in Wien Philosophisch –Historische Classe, Band CXLIII. Vienna: Carl Gerold's Sohn, 1901.

———. *Stoicorum Veterum Fragmenta, vols. I–IV*. Stuttgart: Teubner, 1964.

White, Harvey. *What Is What-Is? A Study of Parmenides' Poem*. New York: Peter Lang, 2005.

Wright, M. R. *Introducing Greek Philosophy*. New York: Routledge, 2014.

www.ingramcontent.com/pod-product-compliance
Lightning Source LLC
Chambersburg PA
CBHW061400280526
45784CB00001B/320